Prince Eugene of Savoy

Prince Eugene of Savoy

The Life of a Great Military Commander of the
17th & 18th Centuries

ILLUSTRATED

G. B. Malleson

LEONAUR

Prince Eugene of Savoy
The Life of a Great Military Commander of the 17th & 18th Centuries
by G. B. Malleson

ILLUSTRATED

First published under the title
Prince Eugene of Savoy

Leonaur is an imprint of Oakpast Ltd

Copyright in this form © 2019 Oakpast Ltd

ISBN: 978-1-78282-796-2 (hardcover)
ISBN: 978-1-78282-797-9 (softcover)

http://www.leonaur.com

Contents

CHAPTER 1

Early Days

In the first half of the seventeenth century Thomas Francis, youngest son of Charles Emanuel I, Duke of Savoy, founded the branch-line of the House of Savoy-Carignan. Thomas Francis was one of the most restless politicians of a very restless age, and, being absolutely devoid of principle, he gave his sword and his talents to the cause which promised to advance his own interests, and fought alternately for and against the countries warring against each other, even for and against his own. He married Mary of Bourbon, sister and heiress of the last Count of Soissons. From this marriage he had two sons.

The elder of these, Emanuel Philibert, though deaf and dumb from his birth, possessed talents so great as to enable him to overcome even this great natural disadvantage. He had a very quick comprehension, wrote gracefully and with force, easily made himself understood, and in all the circumstances of life displayed a very remarkable shrewdness and power. At a rather advanced period of life he married, to continue his line, the Princess Maria Katherina of Este. The younger son, Eugene Maurice, took the title descending to him from his mother, of Count of Soissons.

Naturalised in France, he spent his youth at the Court of Versailles, where, regarded and treated as a Prince of the Blood, he occupied a considerable position. Brave as his father, he did not possess his unsteady and ever-changing temperament. On the contrary, his genial amiability and his sympathy with the courtly customs of the period, though unaccompanied by great abilities, made him many friends and caused him to be a very acceptable person at Versailles.

Whilst the Count of Soissons was still a young man, Cardinal Mazarin brought his nieces to France to finish their education. The advent of five sisters of the Mancini family and two of the Martinozzi, all closely related to the great statesman who governed France, all well educated—some of them even beautiful—caused no small excitement. They became at once queens of all the *fêtes*. What wonder that the heart of Louis XIV, then in his early youth, should be touched by their charms? She who first attracted him was the second of the Mancini sisters, the favourite of the Cardinal, the beautiful and gifted Olympia.

The Count of Soissons married Olympia Mancini. She bore him five sons and three daughters. The sons were Thomas Louis—who succeeded his father as Count of Soissons—Philip, Louis Julius, Emanuel Philibert, and Eugene Francis. The daughters were Johanna, Louisa Philiberta, and Franziska. None of them married. It is to a record of the deeds of the youngest son, Eugene Francis, born the 18th October, 1663, that the following pages will be devoted.

The admiration which the young King of France had felt for Olympia Mancini had survived her marriage. Interrupted for a moment by the still warmer feeling which caused the fickle monarch to dream of bestowing the crown of France upon her sister, Maria, it returned with double force when, to prevent the possibility of such an event Anne of Austria and the Cardinal caused Maria to quit France. The king's marriage with Maria Theresa, eldest daughter of Philip IV of Spain, seemed even to heighten his consideration for Olympia. She became superintendent of the household of the queen, and by her office as first lady of the Court, her influence and her connections, wielded enormous power. The king, but little attracted by his wife, used to seek in the Hôtel Soissons distraction and amusement. Nothing equalled the magnificence, says Saint Simon, which the Countess of Soissons displayed. The king was constantly with her. She was the supreme ruler of the Court and of his *fêtes*, she was regarded as the one being upon whose word depended the dispensing of the most earnestly-desired favours.

With such a man as Louis XIV, then in the hot blood of youth and surrounded by all the beauties of France, the permanent sway of the Countess of Soissons was scarcely possible. Not so, however, thought Olympia. To maintain that sway, she had recourse to exertions and intrigues of a very questionable character. In carrying out one of these she forced her husband, who was entirely under her influence, to quarrel with the Duke of Navailles. A challenge was the consequence, and this coming to the ears of the king, he banished the count from his court.

The banishment did not last long, but it was the first symptom of the waning influence of Olympia. It is true that for a time the previous friendship was renewed on its former footing. Again, was the Countess of Soissons the organiser and the leader of the pleasures of the king and of the court. But the new reign was a comparatively short one. The rising star of the Duchess de la Vallière eclipsed the planet which had so long dominated Versailles. Vain were the struggles of Olympia to retain her position. The cardinal, who might have saved her, was long since dead. The courtiers, true to their nature, repeated the indiscretions of the lady at whose shrine they had worshipped. They even whispered that it was due to her malevolence that the queen had become acquainted with the love of the king for the new favourite. There could be but one ending to such a state of affairs. On the 30th March, 1665, the Count and Countess of Soissons quitted the Court, furnished with an order from the king to reside only on their estates.

This order changed the nature of Olympia. She, who had levelled in the brilliant role she had played at Court, felt bitterly the loss of all that had made life endurable. Hers was not the nature to bear such a reverse with equanimity. A complete revulsion of her feelings followed. Where before she had loved, now she hated. Revenge became her watchword. And to carry out that revenge she took pains to inspire her children, especially her two favourites, Julius and Eugene, with an utter abhorrence of the French Court, and especially of the central right which she had once guided, and round which the highest names in France were grouped in adoration.

In spite of these feelings, of this longing for vengeance, Olympia was well aware that to obtain positions for her sons such as their birth entitled them to hope for, it would be necessary for her to turn once again to Versailles. She felt this especially when in 1673 her husband, on his way to join the camp of Turenne, suddenly died. Olympia went to Paris. There, tossed between the desire to regain some of her former influence and the fear that she might not succeed, the unfortunate lady deviated into strange paths. She took to consulting astrologers and wise women. Led on step by step she made the acquaintance of and became associated with a woman named Voisin.

Soon after, Voisin was tried and condemned on a charge of poisoning. In the process the name of Olympia became somewhat implicated, and on the condemnation of Voisin an order was issued to convey the Countess of Soissons to the Bastille. This was the last blow. Certain of the hostility of two eminent personages all-powerful with

9

the king—of Louvois, to whose son she had refused her daughter's hand, and of Madame de Montespan, then the reigning star—she fled from Paris by night (January, 1680) and escaped to Flanders.

During her absence, a process for being associated in the crime of Voisin was brought against her. Not a tittle of proof inculpating her was brought forward. She even offered to return and submit to the judgment of the ordinary tribunals, provided that she were guaranteed against being lodged in the Bastille of Vincennes before judgment should be pronounced. The condition was refused. It was wished above all things, by those about the king, that she should remain in exile. The vindictive hatred of Louvois pursued her even beyond the French frontier. He carried it so far as to despatch agents to Brussels to excite the people of that city against her, and it was only by the personal exertions of the Spanish viceroy, the Marquis of Monterey, that he failed.

By degrees the utter groundlessness of the charges brought against the countess became manifest. Her talents, her wit, her beauty—for she was still beautiful—brought to her *salon* the leaders of society in Brussels. The men and women who formed that society strove by their attentions to cause her to forget her wrongs. Under ordinary circumstances they might have to a great extent succeeded. But there was even then brewing in France a storm which was to rouse all her dormant feelings of hatred and revenge.

When the countess had fled from Paris she had been forced to leave her children behind her. They had remained in France under the care of their grandmother, Mary of Bourbon, Princess of Carignan. This lady had taken a great fancy to the eldest son, Thomas Louis, become, by the death of his father, Count of Soissons, and he, by her interest, had been appointed Colonel of the Regiment of Soissons, and, a little later, Brigadier-General (*Maréchal-de-Camp*). The ambitious princess entertained for some time the hope that her grandson might be elected King of Poland, but this was not to be, and shortly afterwards the count frustrated all her plans for his advancement by his marriage with Urania de la Cropte, natural daughter of Francis of Beauvais, Master of Horse to the Prince of Condé.

This act, which barred to the count the succession to the Throne of Savoy, greatly enraged not only his grandmother and his mother, but the king himself. To Olympia the agreement between herself and Louis upon this one point seemed for a moment to afford some ground of hope for a reconciliation. But in this she was doomed to be grievously disappointed.

The beauty of the young Countess Urania was of a nature to offer, in the eyes of Louis XIV, some justification even for the rash act of the Count of Soissons. She was beautiful, says the Duke of St Simon, beautiful as the glorious morn, possessing those large features which one is wont to associate with *sultanas* and Roman ladies, tall, with black hair, and a noble yet easy presence. Louis himself, unwilling from the first, by any hardship on his part, to sever the ties which bound the family of Soissons to France, soon became the most passionate admirer of the new beauty. But Urania had none of the ambition of her stepmother Olympia. She repulsed the advances of the king. From the moment when Louis felt he could not triumph over her virtue, the meaner passion of revenge took possession of his soul. Casting aside the interest which France had in retaining a hold over a family of foreign extraction, he abandoned the House of Soissons to its enemies.

Those enemies were many and powerful. Prominent amongst them was the still implacable Louvois, and the Count of Soissons himself and his brothers were made to feel that at the Court of Versailles and in France the door to a successful career was permanently closed to them.

This conviction stole gradually over the minds of the brothers. Two of them, when they awoke to it, came to the resolve to seek in other countries the career denied to them in the land of their birth. The third brother, Louis Julius, known as the Chevalier of Savoy, and the fourth, Emanuel Philibert, called the Count of Dreux, took service under the head of their family, the Duke of Savoy. Emanuel Philibert died shortly afterwards. Then Louis Julius, yearning for a wider field of activity, transferred his services, shortly before the outbreak of the war of 1683 with Turkey, to the Emperor Leopold, by whom he was received with distinction.

The conviction which had driven two of his elder brothers from France dawned likewise, in due time, on the mind of the youngest, Eugene. As that prince is the hero of this book, it seems proper that, before proceeding further, I should describe his appearance and his early training.

Eugene Francis, born the 18th October, 1663, was small of stature but strongly built. He had the dark olive complexion of a son of Italy. His somewhat turned-up nose and his short upper lip gave him the appearance of a man whose mouth was never quite shut, whilst the

11

exposure of the front teeth thus caused was ill calculated to impress favourably one who saw him for the first time. But his eyes were large, well-shaped, full of fire and of expression, and, noting them, the more acute observer could scarcely fail to divine the great spirit which lay hid under the outer shell.

He had received a careful education. From his early youth he had displayed a great partiality for the profession of arms. With an energy which knew no rest he had applied himself to the mastery of the subjects necessary for the acquisition of military knowledge. In mathematics he took a special delight, and it is said that Joseph Sauveur, who in late years obtained the chair of mathematics at the Royal College of France (1686) and became a member of the Academy of Science (1696), was his preceptor in geometry. The perusal of the lives of the great warriors of ancient Greece and Rome filled up the time not devoted to more serious studies and to bodily exercise. To the latter he paid special attention. Like the illustrious Turenne, he endeavoured, by hard work and exposure, to inure a frame not naturally strong to support fatigue. Feeling that a military life was his vocation, he devoted all his energies to fit himself to excel in it.

To a boy so endowed by nature, possessing a predilection so marked and a will so resolved, the announcement made to him on behalf of the king, that he must prepare himself for a priestly life, sounded like a death warrant. Eugene was ten years old when the decision was made known to him. It was a decision from which there was apparently no escape. The order of Louis XIV was neither to be disputed or questioned. From that time Eugene was known at the Court of Versailles as the Abbé of Carignan, and jestingly spoken of by the king as "the little *abbé*." For the moment he was too young to resist. Not for an instant, however, did he abandon his intention or neglect his studies, his reading, or his exercises. Years passed by and the Abbé of Carignan still cherished the secret wish of his heart. The time at length arrived when it could no longer be concealed.

Towards the end of 1682 Eugene took the opportunity personally to thank the king for the favours he had designed for him in the Church, and to beg that, in place of those favours, of which he was not worthy, His Majesty would deign to grant him rank befitting his position in his army. Louis not only refused his request, but he refused it in a manner which roused to white heat the anger of the young aspirant. Suddenly there rushed to his brain the thought of the wrongs of years, the long-suppressed feeling of indignation at the indignities suffered by his family, the two banishments of his father, the bitter reproaches of his mother. He could not, indeed, give expression to these burning thoughts, but he inwardly, on the spot, it is said, registered an oath that he would at once quit France, and never return to her unless as an enemy with his good sword in his hand.

Whither should he turn his steps? Before he had made his decision, the news reached him of the reception accorded by the Emperor Leopold to his brother Louis Julius. Not only had that reception been gracious, but it had been followed by the bestowal on the *chevalier* of the command of a regiment. This news decided Eugene. He abruptly quitted France for Vienna.

The earnestness of character, the dislike of the hollow ceremonies of courtly life, and the want of susceptibility which, even in his youth, had rendered him callous to the influence of the ladies of Versailles, and had tended to lessen the consideration for him of the courtiers of Louis XIV, produced an opposite effect on the statesmen of Vienna. On the Emperor Leopold, himself described as "the most virtuous and pious monarch of his time, endowed especially with composure, gentleness, sincerity, and a love of truth and order," the result was striking. He felt at the very first interview a sympathy for the young stranger.

Doubtless with this feeling of sympathy was united the joy of welcoming, at a period when his relations with France were somewhat strained, when the question of war between the two countries had always to be considered, a near relative of the reigning Duke of Savoy. Eugene came to him, moreover, at a moment when all Hungary was in insurrection, and when the insurgent nobles of that country were imploring, with an almost certain prospect of success, the intervention of the Ottoman Porte. Alike, then, from sympathy and policy, Leopold received Eugene with the greatest cordiality, bestowed upon him the commission of Lieutenant-Colonel in a regiment of cavalry, and bade him join the army then posted on the Raab, under the orders of Duke Charles of Lorraine. Eugene obeyed with alacrity. He had now an object in life. The career for which he had prepared himself during long years had begun.

CHAPTER 2

Learning the Trade—Against the Turks

The acquisition of Hungary by the House of Habsburg in 1526, if it had given to that house increased power, had brought with it many dangers. Prominent amongst these was a constant danger of war with Turkey. Scarcely, indeed, had Ferdinand I. been crowned ruler of his new kingdom, than Vienna, the capital of the hereditary States, was subjected to a perilous siege of three weeks' duration (September-October, 1529). Three years later the invasion was renewed, and it was only the heroism of the garrison and citizens of Guns, a little town on the borders of Styria, which saved (1532) Vienna from a second assault.

★★★★★★

The garrison was but eight hundred strong, but it was commanded by a hero, a Croat named Nicholas Jurisic. For twenty-eight days it resisted, and finally repulsed, all the attacks made upon the place by the army of Sultan Sulaiman.

★★★★★★

For the century and a half which followed, the war with Turkey was intermittent. The important city of Ofen (Buda) was conquered by the Osmánli in 1541, had never since been lost, and was held by them at the time when Eugene took service under the Emperor. From 1566 to 1568, from 1591 to 1606, again, from 1661 to 1664, open war had reigned. But, during the whole of this period, it is not too much to say that Turkish influence had been predominant in Transylvania and preponderant even in Hungary. The great magnates of Hungary, in fact, kings on their own vast estates, had ever looked to the Porte for protection against any act which might be distasteful to them of their liege lord, the Habsburg King of Hungary.

The most Serene Prince Eugene of Savoy.

PRINCE EUGENE OF SAVOY

At the period at which we have arrived the disorder of Hungary was at its height. Amongst the magnates who had complied to overthrow the authority of the House of Austria were the *Palatin*, Vesselenyi, the young prince Frederic Rákóczy, and Peter Zriny, the inheritor of a great name and of vast influence. The death of Vesselenyi before the actual outbreak of the revolt did not alter the plans of the conspirators. The representatives of the great families of Nadasdy, Frangipani, of Tattenbach, of Tokoly, acceded to the league.

The revolt burst out in 1671. The same year it was quenched in blood, contributed by the heads of the leading conspirators. Of those I have mentioned, Tokoly alone escaped. After some time he returned, assumed the command of the insurgents, and, after negotiations with the Emperor, which long promised success, and failed only because that sovereign refused to guarantee in a clear and unmistakable manner the rights of the feudal landowners, applied, with the secret support of France, to Turkey for material aid.

Nineteen years before, the Turks, after sustaining a defeat at the hands of Montecuccolli, had signed, at St Gothard, on the Raab, a peace for twenty years with the Emperor (10th August, 1664). That peace, then, had only one year to run when the *Sultan*, Muhammad IV, received the urgent solicitations of Tokoly. Simultaneously with those solicitations came the information that never before had the opportunity been so tempting, that the Imperial Army was at its lowest ebb, and that France would use all her efforts to prevent any of the Powers outside the Empire from rendering assistance to the Emperor.

Muhammad IV could not resist the temptation. Nominating Tokoly to be Prince of Hungary, subject to an annual payment to the Porte of forty thousand *thalers*, he despatched an army of two hundred thousand, under his *Grand Vizier*, Kara Mustapha, with instructions to attract to him the Hungarian malcontents, and to march directly on Vienna.

Such was the situation when Eugene set out from that city to join the army commanded by the Emperor's brother-in-law, Duke Charles of Lorraine. Before he could reach that army, Lorraine, finding that were he to hold his position on the Raab the advance of the enemy towards the Leitha would sever his communications with Vienna, had despatched his infantry, by the left bank of the Danube, to the capital, whilst with his cavalry he took up a position on the right bank at Hamburg, just above and nearly opposite to Pressburg. Here Eugene joined him.

18

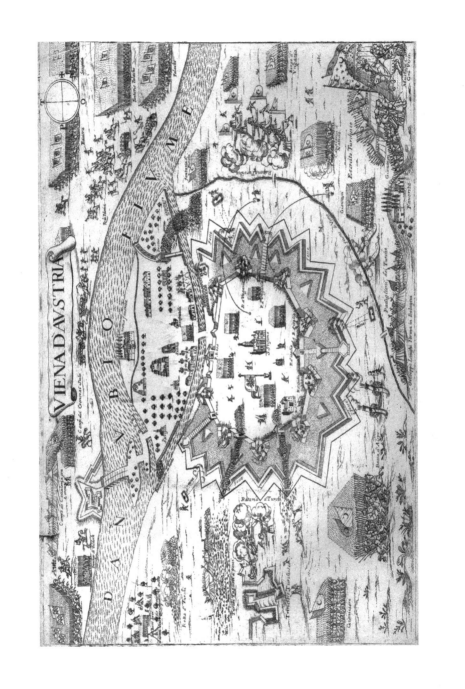

The advance of the Ottoman Army made Hamburg no resting-place for Lorraine. He accordingly commenced, in the first week of July, a further retreat towards Vienna. That retreat was covered by the Margrave Louis of Baden, with a regiment of dragoons of Savoy commanded by the brother of Eugene. On the 7th July, at Petronell, some few miles nearer Vienna, the Imperial Army was attacked with great fury by the van-guard of the Turkish Army. It was Eugene's first experience of actual warfare. In spite of the fury of the attack, Lorraine beat back the enemy. Eugene, however, had to lament the loss of his brother, who died six days later from injuries received in the fight.

That Eugene felt, and felt deeply, the loss of his brother can well be imagined. But the days were too short for lamentation, and the young warrior knew that every energy must be reserved for the defence of his adopted country. Attached to his brother's regiment, he followed the army in its continued retreat, until at length it halted in the Leopoldstadt, holding that suburb and the islands in the Danube contiguous to it. Still the Turks approached, and, after a bloody conflict, compelled Lorraine to evacuate the islands. The latter then took up a new position on Jedlesee, three miles from Vienna. Hence, he marched to Krems, from Krems, during the night of the 28th July, to Pressburg, and the following morning smote with great severity the rebel army besieging that place, commanded by Tokoly. Eugene served in that fight under the orders of his cousin, Louis of Baden.

From Pressburg, Lorraine turned sharply to the Marchfeld, fell upon and severely handled, near Stammersdorf, the rear-guard of a reinforcing army led by the Pasha of Grosswarden, then, on the 30th August, effected, at Hollabrunn, on the Tullnerfeld, a junction with the relieving army of John Sobieski, the hero-king of Poland. Meanwhile, the troops sent to support the common cause by Bavaria, Saxony, and the minor States of Southern Germany, had arrived at Krems, the appointed place of union. Sobieski and Lorraine waited on the Tullnerfeld till these should cover the distance which still separated them from the main army. This accomplished, the entire relieving army advanced from the Tullnerfeld on the 7th September, eighty-four thousand strong, attacked the Turks, who were most unskilfully disposed on the lower ground between the Kahlenberg and the city, on the 12th, and obtained over them a complete and decisive victory—a victory so decisive, indeed, that in that respect it may challenge comparison with any of which history makes mention.

In that battle, as in the fights which preceded it, Eugene took part,

PRINCE EUGENE'S DRAGOONS

serving throughout under the direct command of his cousin, Louis of Baden. Many opportunities were afforded him, alike after the junction of the allies on the Tullnerfeld and during their short stay in Vienna after the battle, of observing the different qualities of the several commanders, all men of renown, and three of them occupying or to occupy a very high rank in the estimation of their contemporaries. There was Sobieski, the type of the dashing cavalier, the living impersonification of Alexander the Great, as brilliant in conception, as daring in action, as successful in execution as was the immortal Macedonian.

Near him stood the Duke of Lorraine, modest and simple in his manners, silent in company, but in action resolute, prompt and inflexible. Beside him, again, Louis of Baden, regarded as the rising hope of the Imperial Army, gifted with considerable talents very shortly to be recognised. There, too, was Maximilian Emanuel of Bavaria, more impetuous even than Sobieski, but lacking the prudence which controlled the fiery instincts of that warrior. The contrast between the bearing of these four leaders, then meeting on a common ground, could not fail to make an impression on one who from his early youth had been forced to study the character of the men with whom he was brought in contact.

But the days of rest in Vienna were few. There was not one of the four commanders to whom I have referred who did not recognise the fact that a victory not followed up is a victory half won. Five days, then, after the victorious entry into the capital the allied army was on the track of the enemy, Eugene, as before, under the orders of Louis of Baden. Their advance-guard, composed of Polish horsemen, came up on the 7th October with the enemy, strongly entrenched at Párkány, on the left bank of the Danube, opposite Gran, and, dashing at them incautiously, was repulsed with great slaughter. Two days later the allied army—the cavalry of the right wing of which Louis of Baden commanded—avenged this repulse by storming the position. Twelve days later Gran surrendered, and with its conquest concluded the campaign for the year.

Eugene had indeed enjoyed the favours of Fortune. He had quitted France and tendered his services to the Emperor at the most opportune moment, on the eve of a war which was to change the face of Eastern Europe, and which was to afford the rarest opportunities to a man capable, by natural talents and by acquirements, of using them to advantage. In his first campaign Eugene had played naturally a subordinate part. But, attached to the person of one who had already proved himself a brilliant captain, serving, too, under two of the most renowned generals of the day, he had observed much, and had carefully stored up those observations. For himself, he had behaved as a gallant soldier, and when, on the conclusion of the campaign, he had an interview with the Emperor, Leopold, after complimenting him on his prowess, promised him the first regimental command which should fall vacant. A few weeks later, the 12th December, this promise was fulfilled, and Eugene was nominated Colonel of the regiment of Dragoons of Kufstein, then with the army at Gran. There Eugene joined it.

The campaign of 1684 opened late. The Imperial Army had wintered at Gran, the Turks at Ofen. On the 13th June the Duke of Lorraine, leaving a small force under General Hallwyl at Gran, marched on Visegrád. Visegrád fell five days later, but whilst engaged before that place, the Turkish cavalry had taken advantage of the bow made by the Danube to cross the half circle between Ofen and Gran, to fall upon Hallwyl and to nearly destroy his force. On the first intimation of this, Lorraine had despatched Louis of Baden to go to Hallwyl's assistance; but the order came too late, the Turks had time to make good their retreat to Ofen.

After Visegrád, the most important post on the Danube as it flows to Ofen, is Waitzen. Lorraine met the Turks on the flat ground near this town and completely defeated them. Waitzen at once surrendered. Crossing and following the stream, Lorraine then marched to and encamped at Szent Endre. Here he repulsed a resolute attack of the Turkish Army. In this engagement Eugene particularly distinguished himself. It was a charge made by him at the head of his regiment which first broke the enemy.

Still advancing, Lorraine appeared, the 14th July, before Ofen, and undertook the siege of that city, then occupied for more than a century and a half by the Muslims. The *Sultan*, foreseeing this event, had prepared a relieving force to succour the garrison. Lorraine attacked this force as it approached the place (22nd July) and completely defeated it. In this action Eugene distinguished himself in a manner to be mentioned by Lorraine in his report to the Emperor. The siege of Ofen was then resumed. But the courage and tenacity of the Turkish defenders prevailed against the skill and valour of the besiegers, and Lorraine was forced, on the approach of winter, to abandon the enterprise.

The defender of Vienna against the Turks, Count Rudiger Starhemberg, had from the first predicted the failure of an attack against Ofen unless the important town of Neuhausel should have been previously taken. Neuhausel lay on the direct road from Ofen to Vienna, seventy-six miles from the latter, and due north of Comoru. The fact of its being far removed from the disputed line of the Danube between Gran and Ofen, and the certainty that its fall would follow the fall of the latter, induced Lorraine to prefer attempting the more important place. Even now, though yielding to Starhemberg, he dreaded lest the Turks should take advantage of his divergence from the real line of operations to recover their losses of the previous year.

It happened as he had foreseen. When, in July, 1685, the march of the Imperial Army against Neuhausel was pronounced, the Turks, well informed, hastened their preparations to recover Gran. Lorraine had hoped, by pressing hard the garrison of Neuhausel, to return to the true line of operations before the enemy could work much damage But the Turks fought as well at Neuhausel as they had fought the preceding year at Ofen. The siege, which was commenced the 16th July, was prolonged without result to the 6th August. On that date the cries of the hard-pressed garrison of Gran forced Lorraine to march with the bulk of his army to relieve that place, whilst, with the remainder, Count Caprara should continue the operations against Neuhausel.

A double triumph followed. On the 16th August Lorraine attacked and completely defeated the Turkish Army besieging Gran, Eugene, whose regiment was in the second line, again so distinguishing himself as to be mentioned. Three days later Caprara took Neuhausel by storm. The campaign comprised these two occurrences only. But they were occurrences not only important in themselves, they cleared the way for operations of a more extended character in 1686.

Of Eugene's share in that campaign it may be said that though he had only commanded a regiment he had displayed a readiness, a coolness, an eye to seize opportunities which had greatly impressed his superiors. The Margrave Louis of Baden said to the Emperor:

This young man, will with time occupy the place of those whom the world regards as great leaders of armies.

For his conduct he was, during the winter, promoted to the rank of Major-General.

The campaign of 1686 began with the siege of Ofen. The besieging army—to a command in which Eugene was nominated—was under the orders of the Elector Max Emanuel of Bavaria, whilst Lor-

24

raine, with a second army, covered its operations. The siege began the 21st June. Three days later the besiegers forced their way through a breach in the outer wall and gained a lodgement in the lower part of the town. Max Emanuel, leaving Eugene with the cavalry to guard his camp, now directed an attack with his infantry along the low ground between the Blocksberg and the Spiessberg, through the suburb called the Raizenstadt, against the castle. Whilst so employed the garrison made a sortie and attacked the camp, but Eugene drove them back with so much vigour that some of his horsemen even entered the city with the *Janissaries* and the *spahis*, who fled before them.

Though Max Emanuel displayed great activity and resolution in the siege, the defenders were not one whit behind him. The defence, in fact, was magnificent. A first attempt to storm, made the 27th July, was repulsed. A second, made the 3rd August, was not more successful. On both these occasions Eugene was wounded.

Eleven days later a fresh Turkish Army, led by the *grand vizier* in person, made a fierce attack on the besiegers. It was beaten back with great loss, and Eugene, whose conduct had been especially brilliant, was selected by Max Emanuel to carry the news of the victory to the Emperor. It is characteristic of the young soldier that he quitted Vienna the very day after his arrival there, to return to his duties with the besieging army. He arrived to find the preparations for the great assault almost completed. That assault was delivered on the 2nd September. The resistance of the garrison was magnificent, nor was it till its commander and many of its leading officers had fallen that the assailants were able to make good their way. Towards evening, however, all resistance ceased, and Ofen, after having been held by the Porte, and regarded as the third city in the Ottoman Empire, for a hundred and forty-five years, was restored to the sway of the Habsburgs.

The next day Louis of Baden was despatched with twelve regiments of cavalry, of which that of Eugene was one, to follow up the victory. Proceeding nearly due south to the valley of the Diave, with great rapidity Louis recovered the towns of Simontornya, Funfkirchen, Sziklos, and Kaposvar. To hinder any attempt they might make during the winter to retake these places, he burned a great portion of the famous bridge over the Drave at Essegg. The campaign was terminated by the recapture of Szegedin by Veterani, after defeating a Turkish corps which had been despatched to effect its relief.

The successes of the campaign had been so marked and so important that the Emperor came to a determination not to lay down his

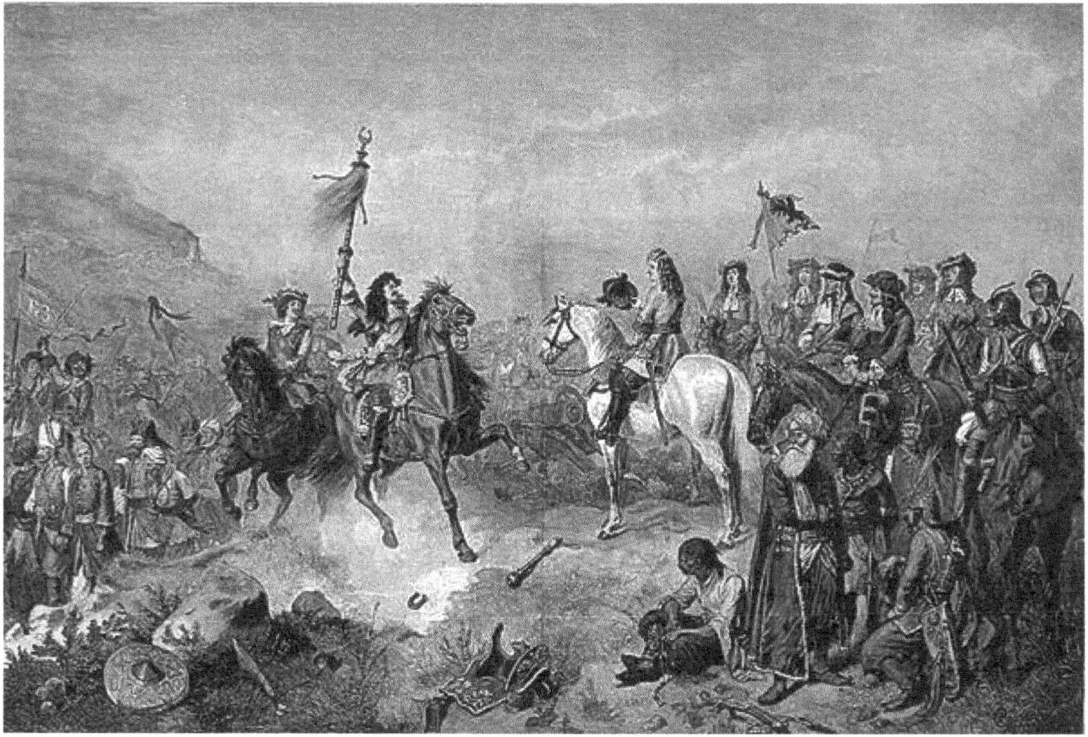

Battle of the Mohács

arms until he should have recovered all the provinces of which the Porte had robbed his ancestors. He caused an answer to this effect to be delivered to the envoys sent from Constantinople to treat for a suspension of arms. The better to enforce his resolve, he raised for the coming year two armies, the command of one of which he entrusted to the Duke of Lorraine, of the other to Max Emanuel of Bavaria. The choice of the latter was forced upon the Emperor, Max Emanuel having declared that unless he were nominated to an independent command he would withdraw his troops. (Max Emanuel had married the Emperor's daughter, the Archduchess Maria Antonia.)

It had been the earnest desire of Lorraine not to split up the army into detachments, but, by uniting its several component portions into one great whole, to march against the main Ottoman Army and defeat it. That once accomplished, the several corps might undertake the recovery of the strong places. By the exercise of great tact and reasoning he succeeded in imposing these views upon Max Emanuel, and in inducing him to place himself, for the moment, under his orders. The Turks, meanwhile, moving up the banks of the Danube, had taken, in the first week of August, a position at Mohács, the town near which, just a hundred and sixty-one years before (29th August, 1526), they had defeated the last of the Jagellons, and made Hungary virtually a fief of the Ottoman Empire.

After many marches and counter-marches, Lorraine, commanding the united armies of the Empire, reached the hill of Hassan, the summit of which commands a view of the surrounding country. From this point he beheld the Turkish Army drawn up in battle array, within easy striking distance, before him. Instantly his resolution was formed. He drew up his army in serried order, close to the enemy's lines, so as to provoke an attack. His knowledge of the Ottoman troops had taught him that, were an attack on their part once decisively repulsed, a rapid counter-advance would complete their defeat. He formed up his men, then, in close order, affording no opening, and but little opportunity for the use of the Turkish weapon, the sabre.

The Turks fell into the trap. They dashed furiously against the solid wall of infantry which Lorraine had drawn up before them, and were, after many desperate efforts, repulsed. Then Lorraine gave the order to charge, and cavalry from the flanks, infantry from the centre, charging with a purpose, completed the victory which had already been half gained. In vain did the fleeing infantry endeavour to make a stand behind the entrenchments of their own camp. Eugene, who com-

BATTLE OF THE MOHÁCS

manded the first cavalry brigade, charged them with a fury which overcame all resistance. Then he followed them up. The defeat became a rout as decisive against the Turks as the earlier battle on the same spot had proved to the Jagellons. For his brilliant conduct Eugene was once more selected to carry the news of the victory to the Emperor.

Whilst Eugene was journeying post-haste to Vienna a danger arose at headquarters which threatened to cause the loss of the fruits of the great victory which had been gained. The danger arose from the ambition of Max Emanuel to exercise a command independently of Lorraine. Unhappily, Louis of Baden, himself somewhat jealous of control, supported the views of Max Emanuel. When, then, after the victory, Lorraine decided to push on with the entire army and recover Transylvania, Max Emanuel and Louis of Baden insisted on a division of the forces, by which, leaving Lorraine to carry out his own plan, they should, with a separate and independent army, undertake the siege of Erlau. Had Lorraine been a weak man, the fruits of the victory would have very probably been lost, but when he insisted, and displayed his intention at all hazards to carry out his plan, the two malcontents quitted the army—Max Emanuel because his request had been refused, Louis of Baden avowedly because Lorraine had entrusted the command of a flying cavalry corps which he had sent into Slavonia to General Dunewald, and not to himself.

When Eugene rejoined the army it was on the march to Transylvania. Michael Apaffy, *ban* of that country, offered no opposition to the march of the Imperial armies. He even agreed to make submission to the Emperor, and to admit Imperial garrisons into his towns. Simultaneously Slavonia, though some of its great towns still held out, was occupied in a military manner by Dunewald, whilst, to crown the fruits of the year, Erlau surrendered to Count Caraffa in December, and Munkács, the last important town in Eastern Hungary held by the enemy, and which had been defended for three years by the famous Helena Zriny, wife of the not less famous Tokoly, the 6th January of the following year.

The work of the year had been a great work, and it was generally admitted that the part played by Eugene in it had been by no means inconsiderable. The departure of Max Emanuel and of Louis of Baden, much as he was bound to the latter by ties of blood, of admiration, and of affection, had proved, indirectly, of service to him by bringing him nearer to the commander-in-chief. His name and his exploits were already talked of in the courts of the continent. His cousin, Victor Amadeus II, Duke of Savoy, who had hitherto bestowed no attention upon him, now exerted himself to procure for him a provision worthy of his birth, and persuaded the Pope to bestow upon him the revenues of two rich abbeys in Piedmont. More valuable in the eyes of the young soldier was the promotion conferred upon him by the Emperor. Early in 1689 Leopold nominated Eugene to the command of a division, with the rank of Feldmarschall-Lieutenant. (There is no exactly corresponding rank in the British Army. It approaches most nearly to that of "Major-General commanding a division.")

During the winter the plans for the forthcoming campaign were fully discussed. The Emperor himself was bent on the recovery of Belgrade, the free road to which had been opened by the fall of Erlau. Belgrade, the key of the Lower Danube, and famous for the splendid and successful defence it had made against the *Sultan*, Muhammad II., had succumbed to Sulaiman the Great in 1522, and had remained since then in the possession of the Turks. The recovery of it now, when Christendom was beating back the tide of Turkish conquest, seemed to Leopold the logical sequence to the victories at Mohács. The siege of Belgrade then was resolved upon.

But who was to command the besieging army? Every consideration seemed to point to the illustrious commander the brilliancy of whose recent campaign was the theme of conversation in all the courts of Europe. But to such a nomination the ambition of Max Emanuel, supported by Louis of Baden, offered a serious obstacle. The Bavarian prince roundly declared that unless the command were entrusted to himself, he would march off with his numerous contingent, and leave the Emperor to the resources of the hereditary States. It soon became apparent that he would carry his threats into execution. At this crisis the Duke of Lorraine gave evidence of the truth of the opinion formed of him by Louis XIV, that he was "the greatest, the wisest, the most generous" of his enemies. He made a slight illness the pretext for begging the Emperor to relieve him of the care of conducting the coming campaign. Rather than imperil its success by a refusal which would have caused a serious diminution of his forces, Leopold complied, and conferred the command upon Max Emanuel.

The army intended for the siege had meanwhile been assembled under the orders of Count Caprara, at Essegg, on the Drave. Here Max Emanuel joined it the 28th July, and marching eastward to Semlin, began to cross the Save the 7th August. Comprehending the full significance of this movement, the *Seraskier* of Belgrade set fire to the suburbs of the fortress, and, throwing within it a strong garrison, withdrew to a point of observation in the vicinity. Max Emanuel, on hearing of this incident, despatched Eugene, with six battalions of infantry and one of cavalry, to prevent or repair the damage, but it had been accomplished before he could arrive.

The besieging army had completed the crossing of the Save, and had taken up its position against the fortress on the 10th August. On the night of the 11th it opened trenches, and on the 15th its batteries began to pour forth their missiles of destruction. Continuing this fire without intermission for three weeks, Max Emanuel, on the evening of the 5th September, pronounced two breaches to be practicable, and made arrangements for the storm the following morning. At 10 o'clock on the morning of the 6th September he gave the signal. A gallant and adventurous man, he himself, with Eugene at his side, directed the stormers. These men, gallantly led, dashed through the breaches with the full confidence of victory, when they suddenly found their further progress stopped by a broad and deep ditch, strongly fortified on the further side, of which they had had no cognisance.

Feeling instinctively that to halt in such a position would be fatal, their gallant leader, Henry Francis, Count of Stahremberg, dashed down into the ditch and attempted to scale the opposite face. Many of his men followed him, and Max Emanuel and Eugene, who had seen the greatness of the danger, dashed forward to the support, followed by their men. Whilst both sides were making superhuman efforts—the one to scale the wall, the other to repulse the assailants—three attacks directed successfully on other points came to weaken the defenders. Their resistance slackened, and, after a determined resistance, Belgrade surrendered without conditions.

Eugene as he descended into the ditch, had lost his helmet by a blow. Shortly afterwards a musket-ball struck him in the leg, just above the knee. This wound, which was very severe, necessitated his being carried to the rear. Thence, as soon as possible, he was conveyed to Vienna. There his condition caused his fiends the greatest anxiety, nor was it till January of the following year that his recovery was complete.

Meanwhile the tide of conquest had rolled on. Veterani had taken Karansebes (on the Temes) and Sikover; Louis, of Baden, several places in Bosnia, and beaten the *pasha* of that province in a pitched battle. Finally, Semendria, abandoned by the Turks, received an Imperial garrison. The success of the campaign had been complete.

Kayserslautern
Spire
Heydelberg
Engelfingen
Philipsbourg
Heilbron
Hall
Landau
Lowenstein
Lauffen
Gr. Sachsenheim
Weissenbourg
Winenden
Lauterburg
Waiblingen
Rastadt
Weil
Stuttgardt
Leonberg
Kuppenheim
Haguenau
Calw
Boblingen
Tubingen
Rottenburg
Urach
Offenburg
Gengenbach
Pfullingen
Hechingen
Gamertingen
Hohenzollern
Schomberg
Kappel
DANUBE
Rothweil
Fridingen
Burkheim
Dutlingen
Vieux Brisach
Stockach
Freyburg
Ratolfszell
Stuhlingen
Constance
LAC
Schopsheim
Waldshut
Mulhausen
Lorrach
Huningue
FRAUENFELD
ZURICH
Greiffen

SOUTH WEST

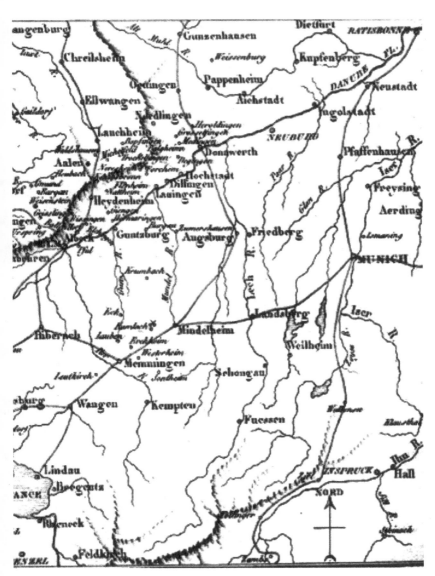

GERMANY

CHAPTER 3

Learning the Trade—Against the French

Alone of all the sovereigns of Europe, Louis XIV. had watched with jealous disquietude the success of the Imperial armies. Whilst not daring to declare himself the open supported of Islam against Christianity, he had, at the commencement of the war, used all his efforts to deter the independent princes of Europe from offering aid to the Emperor, and, after the defeat of the Turks before Vienna, he saw in each fresh victory of their enemy an increase of power to the hereditary rival of France, fraught with future danger to himself. When, then, the campaign of 1688 had restored to the House of Habsburg supremacy in Hungary and in Transylvania, he resolved to prevent the consolidation of their power by seizing an opportunity to declare war on the Rhine.

His mind once made up, the pretext was not difficult to find. A contention between the Prince Wilhelm Egon of Furstenberg and Prince Joseph Clement of Bavaria for the electoral hat of Cologne, and the decision of the Pope in favour of the latter, were eagerly seized upon by Louis to despatch, in the winter of 1688, an army under the *dauphin* to support the claims of Furstenberg and to attack the German frontier fortresses.

The armies of the Empire were for the most part in Hungary. The *dauphin* found little difficulty, then, in capturing Philipsburg and Mainz. Furstenberg, on his part, delivered to them without a combat, Bonn, Kaiserswerth, and the other strong places dependent on the Archbishopric of Cologne.

It happened that, just at the time when intelligence reached Vienna of the French invasion, the Emperor received from the Porte the most earnest solicitations, for peace. It was in the power of Leopold, by granting, even by imposing terms very favourable to the interests of his House, and then transferring his well-disciplined army to the Rhine, to administer to the King of France a very severe lesson. A strong party at the court, at the head of which was the Duke of Lorraine, and which was supported by the Spanish ambassador, the princes of the Empire, and by almost all the members of the Ministry, urged this course. But Leopold possessed a more than ordinary share of the hereditary obstinacy of his family. From reasons which to ordinary men were "hard to understand," he resolved to continue the war with the Porte whilst he repelled the invasion of the French. The more effectually to succeed, Leopold allied himself with England, Holland, Spain, Denmark and the Pope, against France. To sound Duke Victor, he despatched Eugene to Turin. On his representations of the pliability of his kinsman, the Emperor opened secret negotiations with him which ultimately (4th June, 1690) brought that prince into the alliance.

Meanwhile the French Army had taken advantage of the defenceless state of the German frontier to plunder and devastate the Palatinate. With a cruelty as disgraceful as it was needless, the French generals reduced to ashes the important cities of Heidelberg, Mannheim, Speyer, and Worms, and burned to the ground more than a thousand villages, nor was it till June, 1689, that the Emperor was able to despatch a sufficient force to put a stop to these atrocities.

Not, indeed, that he had been idle. Throwing his whole soul into the work, which was essentially his own, Leopold had caused four armies to be raised. That destined to act against the Turks he had entrusted to the command-in-chief of Louis of Baden. The others, to be directed against France, were disposed of as follows. The main army, fifty thousand strong, then in the course of concentration at Frankfort under the orders of General Count Souches, to be commanded by the Duke of Lorraine, was to recover Mainz.

A second, thirty thousand strong, commanded by Max Emanuel of Bavaria, was to operate on the Upper Rhine, maintaining touch with the main army whilst it covered Swabia and Franconia, whilst a third, under the orders of the Elector of Brandenberg, was to cover the Lower Rhine and drive the French from the Archbishopric of Cologne. Eugene was nominated to a command in the army commanded by Max Emanuel. It is with the movements of that army, therefore, that we are chiefly concerned.

In consequence, mainly, of the insistence of Max Emanuel, the orders prescribing the movements above stated to the army under his command were somewhat modified, in the last week of July, consequently, he, accompanied by Eugene, led about one-fourth of his men to join in the siege of Mainz, leaving the remainder, under Count Caprara, to cover the Upper Rhine.

The siege was now pushed on with vigour. Again did Eugene display the boldness and daring which had won him respect and honour in his former campaigns. He did not escape unhurt. On the 4th August he was struck by a musket-ball on the head, and, though the bullet did not penetrate the skull, the effect on the system caused for some time great alarm. He recovered, however, in sufficient time to take part in the storm, which was successfully delivered from three different points, against the covered way on the 6th September. Three days later Mainz surrendered. Bonn followed the example of Mainz. With the capture of this place the campaign ended, the troops went into winter quarters, and Eugene went to Frankfort to be present at the crowning of the Emperor's eldest son, Joseph, as King of the Romans.

Everywhere, in 1689, had success attended the Emperor's armies. Louis of Baden had beaten the Turks on the March (Morava), and on the Kriegsberg, close to Nisch (Nissa) (23rd September), and had conquered the country as far as the Balkans.

This victory seemed to justify the obstinacy of Leopold when he refused the terms offered by the Turks, and decided on carrying on simultaneously two great wars. But he had soon to repent it. During the winter, and in the very early spring, there occurred on the eastern frontier a series of events which justified all the forebodings of his councillors. The Turkish Army, led by the *grand vizier*, Surmeli Ali Pasha, surprised and cut up the outlying Imperial corps on the Lower Danube commanded by Colonel Strasser, defeated the main body, taking prisoner its *commandant*, General Heissler, then, pursuing its advantages, retook Fort Nissa, then Belgrade, garrisoned though that was by the best regiments in the Imperial Army.

These mishaps, followed as they were by the death (18th April) of the Duke of Lorraine, forced the Court of Vienna to make arrangements on a still more extended scale for the campaign of 1690. Fortunately, as it was deemed at the time, Victor Amadeus of Savoy agreed, the 4th June, to join the Grand Alliance. It was at once arranged that a contingent of five thousand Imperial and ten thousand Spanish troops should be despatched to operate with his forces in Northern Italy. The command of the Imperial contingent, which consisted of two full regiments of cavalry, two of infantry, and one of mounted infantry, or dragoons, was confided to Eugene

Leaving his troops to march with all possible speed through the Grisons, Eugene rode on as hard as he could, and joined the Duke of Savoy at Carpeneto, about five miles from Carignano. He found his kinsman in an entrenched camp endeavouring to protect a portion of his territories against a superior French force commanded by a general whose achievements added great glory to the reign of Louis XIV, the illustrious Marshal Catinat. He found him, moreover, eagerly bent on delivering a battle to the enemy, without waiting for the reinforcements of which he himself was the forerunner.

★★★★★★

Catinat was the eleventh of sixteen children of Pierre de Catinat de Vaugelay, President of the Parliament of Paris. His great talents were of such general application that it was said of him that, splendid though he was as a general, he would have shone equally as a minister or a chancellor.

★★★★★★

Eugene, then, examined the military position. Bold and daring as he was, willing ever to incur risk if results were within a reasonable distance of attainment, he shrank from an engagement which offered so few chances of success. He wrote to Vienna:

Without our troops, little can be accomplished. The Spaniards will not fight with any heart unless the army corps of the Emperor is on the spot to give them the impetus they require.

Meanwhile the advance of that army corps was much slower than his eager nature could tolerate. He sent despatch after despatch to urge increased speed. But Catinat was well aware how important it was that a battle should be fought before the enemy's army should be strengthened. To tempt the Duke of Savoy to leave his strong position, he broke up his camp (17th August) before Carpeneto, and marched towards Saluzzo—where the duke had considerable magazines—exposing, as he did so, his flank to the Piedmontese Army.

Victor Amadeus fell into the trap. He at once quitted his camp, followed Catinat, and took up (the 18th August) a position close to the French Army at Staffarda. This was exactly the movement Catinat had desired. When, however, he came to examine the new position occupied by the Piedmontese Army, he began to doubt whether, in reality, he had gained anything. He found their right covered by a

VELDTSLAG VAN STAFFARDE IN PIEMONT.

TASSCHEN DE FRANSCHEN EN DE GEALLIEERD MAGT VAN DE PRINS
EUGENIUS EEN GEDEELTE COMMANDEERDE AFTOGT HIER MET.
SO LEEL GROOT ALS D'OORLOGTUEGHEYT EN GLOIRE

BATAILLE DE STAFFARDE EN PIEMONT.

ENTRE LES FRANÇOIS A LES ALLIÉ DONT LE PRINCE EUGENE
COMMANDA UNE PARTIE & FIT LA RETRAITE AVEC AUTANT D'HEURE
QUE DE PRUDENCE & DE GLOIRE

marsh, apparently impenetrable, its outer rim was covered by three detached farmhouses, each separated from the other by a quickset hedge, with two deep ditches, one beyond the other, in front of it. The left seemed equally impracticable, the marsh which covered it extended to the banks of the Po. A front attack on an army so posted was not to be thought of. The longer Catinat reconnoitred, the more he recognised the strength of the position. But his resolution to attack was not shaken. Concentrating his infantry on the right flank, he passed the ditches, and the hedges behind them, in spite of the palisades which defended them, carried the farmyards, and then threw himself with all his force on the enemy.

The Piedmontese infantry, taken in flank, fell back before him. In vain did Eugene perform prodigies of valour to cover their retreat. The flight of the Piedmontese as far as Moncalieri, and the loss of four thousand men, of eleven pieces of cannon, of powder, field equipages, and standards in abundance, testified to the decisive character of the victory which Catinat had gained.

At Moncalieri Victor Amadeus stayed some weeks to recruit his army. Here he was joined by Eugene's corps, augmented to seven thousand men, and a little later by the Spaniards. It soon became apparent, however, that these latter had received instructions to avoid a general action.

Meanwhile Catinat had taken advantage of his victory to devastate the territories of Victor Amadeus, looting and burning in all directions. Victor Amadeus made no serious attempt to prevent him. The only feat which redounded to the credit of his arms was accomplished by Eugene when, with a portion of his cavalry and some Piedmontese infantry, he waylaid, attacked, and cut up a detachment of the enemy, rich with the booty of the two hours previously plundered village of Rivoli.

With the approach of winter both armies went into winter quarters. Leaving strong garrisons in the places he had conquered, Catinat withdrew his army behind the French frontier. On the side of the allies, the Spaniards were distributed in the Milanese, the Piedmontese in their own country, and Eugene and his corps in the country of Montferrat.

For Eugene these quarters offered anything but repose. The Duke of Montferrat had sold himself to the King of France, and he used all his efforts to incite his subjects against their guests. The consequence was that these were waylaid, poisoned, and insulted. On one occasion there was even a mass rising of the peasantry against them. Throughout the winter the contest against this persistent hostility required even more watchfulness than the presence of an enemy. At first Eugene had tried gentle methods. When he saw that these only encouraged the rioters he resolved to make an example.

At the head, then, of a detachment of four hundred chosen infantry, he marched on Vignale, the headquarters of the disturbers. On his way thither, he was jeered by the bands of peasantry who lined the road. Arrived before Vignale, he informed the populace that he had come with peaceful intentions and hoped that they would respond in a similar spirit. The occupants replied, however, with abuse and showers of stones Eugene could hold out no longer. He stormed the place and made the rioters pay in blood for their misconduct. Thenceforward, though the hostility of the duke continued, the soldiers remained free from molestation.

The safety of his troops provided for, Eugene hastened to Vienna (March, 1691) to take part in the consultations there taking place regarding the campaign of the coming spring. At the conferences which followed his arrival, he insisted upon the necessity of greatly strengthening the Imperial Army in Northern Italy, at its existing strength, he asserted, it was powerless for good, policy required either its entire withdrawal or its large increase. In these views he was supported by the Vice-Chancellor of the Empire, Count Leopold William of Konigsegg—a man whose opinion the Emperor ever held in respect— by the Court Chancellor (Hofkauzler), Count Strattman, perhaps the ablest and most influential man in Vienna, and by General Count Carafa. The only statesman at Court whose word would have weighed to some extent against theirs was Count Ulrich Kinsky, Chancellor of the Kingdom of Bohemia. But that word was not spoken, and Kinsky threw the weight of his opinion in support of the proposals of Eugene.

It was resolved, then, to increase the force in North Italy to twenty thousand men, but as it would be necessary to draw these troops from the contingents furnished by the *Diet*, it was considered advisable that they should be commanded by a prince of the empire. Eugene and Carafa were, therefore, empowered to proceed to Munich and offer the command to Max Emanuel of Bavaria. Max Emanuel having consented to take it, Eugene pursued his return journey (May, 1691) to Piedmont. There he found affairs not in a very promising condition. A new commander, indeed—a man who he had some reason to think would not hesitate to employ actively his troops, the Marquis of Leganez—had assumed the guidance of the Spanish contingent. This was encouraging. On the other hand, the Duke of Savoy was hard pressed by his enemy Catinat had taken Villafranca (21st March), Montalban (23rd), St Hospice (24th), Nice (4th April), and Avigliana (29th May). Immediately afterwards (10th June) he captured Carmagnola, and he was at the moment threatening Turin. The Court, in terror, had fled to Vercelli, whilst to Eugene, who still commanded the Imperial contingent, the defence of the city was entrusted.

Catinat, after some consideration, preferred, to the siege of a place which would cost him time and troops, the complete conquest of all Savoy. He turned, then, against Cuneo, a place which he regarded as the link which connected the country of Nice with Piedmont. The garrison, however, offered a resistance so stubborn as to give time to the vanguard of the reinforcements from Germany to reach Moncalieri. Eugene, thus strengthened, resolved to attempt to relieve the beleaguered town.

At daybreak on the 26th June Eugene set out at the head of two thousand five hundred cavalry on the road to Cuneo. On his way the armed levies which had been previously warned joined him. He escorted large supplies of gunpowder with the intention, should he fail to relieve the place, at least to furnish the defenders with a material of which they were in urgent need. Catinat, who, whilst entrusting the conduct of the siege operations to a subordinate, was prosecuting his schemes against Savoy, had timely intimation of Eugene's intention, and despatched a superior force to prevent his success.

Intimation of the approach of this force reached Eugene whilst he was yet on the way. On the instant he renounced the greater scheme in order the more certainly to carry the lesser. He left, then, the levies behind, and pressed on with his cavalry. On approaching Cuneo, he found, to his astonishment, that the news of his approach had reached the French commanding general—de Bulonde by name—in an exaggerated form, and that he had actually raised the siege. (Catinat placed him under arrest, but he was soon afterwards released.)

Eugene returned to Moncalieri. There he remained during the best season of the year in forced inactivity. The Spanish commander, from whom he had hoped so much, would attempt nothing. In vain did Eugene urge him to action. He would do nothing as long as the enemy forbore to threaten the Milanese. Eugene wrote to Vienna:

If everyone would do his duty the enemy would soon be beaten.

At last the full reinforcements arrived. With them came the young Duke of Schomberg, son of the friend of William III. recently killed at the Boyne, leading regiments formed of French and Swiss Protestants in the pay of England, Counts Carafa and Pálffy and Prince Commercy at the head of twelve thousand Imperial troops, and, last of all, Max Emanuel with five thousand chosen Bavarians.

Eugene had waited with impatience the arrival of Max Emanuel. In him he knew the conqueror of Belgrade, the man whose soul revelled in the clash of arms, who, fearless of death, had shown himself ever enterprising, daring, and self-reliant. He had now forty thousand good troops under his command, a number more than sufficient to deal with the French Army, even though that army was led by Catinat.

At first Max Emanuel acted as though he were about to prove himself worthy of his great reputation. The very day after his arrival he broke up the camp at Moncalieri, and, ascending the Po, marched to Carignano. Catinat, divining his intention to force him to a battle, left a good garrison in that place, and, recrossing the Po, fell back on Saluzzo. He could not ward off a very sharp attack which Eugene, who had penetrated his intentions, made with great success on his rear-guard, but he succeeded in reaching his entrenched camp near that place, a camp whence, well furnished with provisions, he could bid defiance to the enemy.

Max Emanuel, anxious for a battle, followed Catinat, and took post at Staffarda He hoped either to force him to fight or to starve him out. When he became satisfied that the one and the other were alike impossible, he called a council of war.

At that council Eugene, while expressing his opinion that a direct attack on Catinat's position was not to be thought of, urged that means should be employed to render it untenable. He advised, therefore, that the army should cross the Po and approach so close to the French position as to hem in the French Army and sever its communications with Saluzzo, Carmagnola, and Savigliano. The better to accomplish this he recommended the arming of the peasantry, and the withdrawal from the vicinity of their carts and cattle. Should the council not listen to these views, Eugene recommended, as an alternative plan, that Montmelian, the strongest place in Savoy, then hardly pressed by the enemy, should be at once relieved.

There were many heads in that council, but few of them were wise. The only decision arrived at was that the allies should undertake the siege of Carmagnola. To facilitate the project by preventing the garrison from receiving reinforcements, Eugene was despatched at once with two thousand cavalry. On the 28th of the same month he was joined by the main army. Ten days later Carmagnola surrendered.

Catinat, however, took advantage of the absence of the allies on this errand to fall back, at his ease, on Pignerol. Still, however, the allies might have advantageously attacked him, and Eugene, convinced that the French commander would make many sacrifices to avoid a battle, and would even recross the mountains into France if he were hardly pressed, urged that he should be vigorously pursued. But such action was too decided for the once resolute Max Emanuel. He listened, apparently with approval, to Eugene's counsel, but, far from following it, he allowed Catinat ample leisure to make his dispositions. The French general, then, sending his cavalry back to France, strengthened the garrisons of Pignerol and Susa, and took a strong position in close vicinity to the latter.

Meanwhile the allies had resolved to besiege that place. But the measures taken by Catinat showed them, when they reconnoitred it, that the task would be hopeless. Pignerol seemed equally beyond their means, and Montmelian was too far off to be succoured. They therefore decided to retreat into winter quarters. This operation Catinat allowed them to carry out without much molesting them. His mind was bent on Montmelian. No sooner, then, had he seen the allies in safe quarters for the winter, than he hastened to Montmelian, pressed the siege vigorously, and forced it to surrender the 29th December.

Of this campaign, it must be admitted that the glories of it belonged to the French commander. With an army smaller than that of his enemies he had baffled the latter at almost every point. He had lost, indeed, Carmagnola, but, in return, he had mastered the whole of Savoy, and he had seen his enemy's operations close with a failure. Never did a commander show himself more completely conscious of the true points to be striven for, never did one employ his means better to gain those points. His action was highly appreciated by his master, who created him Marshal of France, and named him a Chevalier of the Order of St Louis.

The operations of the allies, on the other hand, were conducted without decision, and were wanting alike in fixed purpose and in enterprise. Eugene, who had ample means of judging, attributed this combination of faults to the deterioration which had taken place in the character of Max Emanuel, and in the vacillations of Count Carafa. Regarding the latter, he wrote at this period to Count Tarim:

I know no one who is less of a soldier, and who understands war so little, as Carafa.

He informed the same official that rather than serve again under such a general he would quit the Imperial service.

The army having taken up winter quarters, Eugene obtained permission to proceed to the Netherlands to visit his mother, whom he had not seen for six years. Thence, after a short visit, he journeyed (January, 1692) to Vienna, where he at once began to make preparations for the next campaign.

Whether or not the Court of Vienna entirely shared Eugene's opinion regarding Count Carafa, the Emperor resolved to replace both him and Max Emanuel of Bavaria. The command-in-chief, then, of the allied army in Italy, for the campaign of 1692, was confided to the Duke of Savoy. To him was joined, as commander of the troops of the Empire, Count Æneas Sylvius Caprara.

Though Caprara was a nephew of the famous Piccolomini, and a relative of the still more illustrious Montecuccoli, he had not inherited their military talents. He was unenterprising, avaricious, envious and cruel, careless of the comforts of his soldiers, and never possessing their confidence. It was under such an inapt master that Eugene was to continue his military education.

It seemed, at the beginning of the campaign, that the allies would have an easy task before them, for Louis XIV, who was conducting the campaign in Flanders in person, had drawn several regiments from Catinat's army. Still he had not withdrawn Catinat, and Catinat was a host in himself.

Catinat still held a strong position, nearly identical with that which he had taken towards the close of the previous campaign, that is, holding Susa and Pignerol, he had occupied a strong position between the two, ready to carry himself upon either.

Now, as the allied armies outnumbered that of the French in the proportion of two to one, it seemed certain that they would be able to overwhelm Catinat. How best to do this the Duke of Savoy assembled at Pancalieri, the headquarters of his army, a council of war. At this council the question was posed whether the allies should attack Catinat in his entrenched position, or should penetrate into France by the valley of Barcelonnette. Eugene gave it as his opinion that the attack on the entrenched position, however hazardous an operation, would be preferable, if thereby the recovery of Pignerol could be assured.

Unless it could bring about such a result, it would entail a useless waste of life. He inclined to favour the second proposition, as easier and as likely to produce greater results. His opinion was adopted by all the generals present, and it was resolved to carry it into effect.

In consequence the allied army was divided into several corps, each with a specific object before it. One, fifteen thousand strong, commanded by Count Pálffy, was to remain in Piedmont as a corps of observation watching Catinat. A second, six thousand strong, under General Pianezza, was despatched to blockade Casale. Of the remaining troops, constituting the main army, twenty-nine thousand strong, destined to invade France, the first corps, with which were the Duke of Savoy, Caprara, and Leganez, was to march, by way of Cuneo, on Barcelonnette, the second, commanded by Marquis Parella, was to proceed, by way of Saluzzo, Castel Delfino, and the Col de Longet, to Guillestre, in the Val de Queyras; the third, led by Schomberg, through the valley of Luserna against the fort of Gueiras. To Eugene was committed the command of the vanguard of the second column.

These operations, carried out with dexterity, were crowned with success. Guillestre and Barcelonnette fell at once into the hands of the allies, Embrun, after a valiant resistance of fourteen days, during which Eugene received a contusion in the shoulder. But the injury was very slight, and on the 19th August, he was again leading the vanguard of the army against Gap. This mountain-town—the Vapingum of the Romans—furnished his tired soldiers plentifully with provisions and wine.

Hence Eugene desired to march deeper into France. "There is nothing to prevent us reaching Grenoble," he exclaimed. But success had made his colleagues timid. The majority of them dreaded a further advance from their base. Whilst the differences were yet undecided, the Duke of Savoy was struck down by fever, and was removed in consequence to Embrun. He had but just arrived there when the fever developed into smallpox, and for many days the life of the duke was in the greatest danger.

This illness stopped at a critical moment the continuance of the operations. The severity of the attack seemed to forebode a fatal result, and, in that event, there was every probability of a disputed succession. When at length the duke recovered and returned by easy stages to Turin, the allied army returned with him. The only practical result of the campaign had been the burning of the town of Gap, and the demolition of the fortifications of Guillestre and Embrun. Eugene, greatly disgusted, proceeded to Vienna, to lay before the Emperor Leopold

NEUHAUS.

R. GRAN

S. PRESSBURG

VIENNA

NEUHAUSEL

COMORN

RAAB

GRAN

WAITZEN

ST ENDRE

ERLAU

BUDA
(OFEN)

PESTH

GÜNS

R. RAAB

Csepel Is.

Platten See

KAPSOVAR

SZEGEDIN

R. DRAVE

FÜNFKIRCHEN

ZENTA

MOHACS

SEINLOS

BECSE

ESSEGG

BACS

R. SEGA

TITEL

R. TEMES

PETERWARDEIN

BROD

R. SAVE

BELGRADE

PANESOVA

DOBOI

MAGLAY

HUNGARY.

R. DRINA

ADRIATIC.
SEA

BOSNA SERAI
(SARAJEWO)

VISEGRÁD

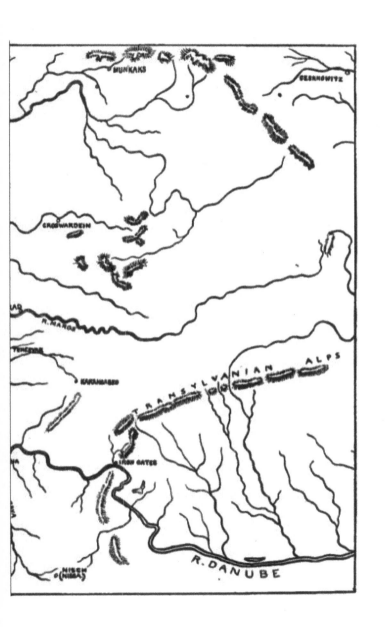

a plan for the campaign of the following year, which should not be absolutely barren of results.

In his opinion one main reason why all the plans had practically miscarried was that no serious operations had been commenced before July. He strongly urged, then, an earlier opening of the campaign, an attack on Pignerol, followed by a renewed invasion of France. But the voice of Eugene had not then in Vienna the influence which it afterwards commanded. The campaigns to be undertaken on the Rhine and in Hungary against the Turks attracted greater attention than the more distant campaign in Italy. No decision regarding the mode in which that campaign should be carried on was arrived at. The unenterprising Caprara was left in command, and Eugene, created Field-Marshal, was directed to serve under him.

In spite of his entreaties and expostulations, but little attempt was made to begin the campaign at an earlier period. The several divisions of the army assembled at Carignano only in June. Then the Duke of Savoy, having first despatched a corps under Leganez to besiege and take the castle of San Giorgio near Casale—a work successfully accomplished—marched against and laid siege to Pignerol, then occupied by a strong garrison under the Count de Tessé. It was a weary business. At the end of three months he captured the fort of Santa Brigida. It had been possible then, to attempt a storm, but the duke preferred to try the less hazardous method of a bombardment. If less hazardous it was also less effective, for the hearts of the defenders were stout, and they continued to wave defiance to their enemies.

Meanwhile the skilful and enterprising Catinat, confident in the valour of the Count de Tessé and his companions, lay in apparent inactivity at Fenestrelles. Inactive though he was, he had been engaged, whilst watching sharply the Duke of Savoy, in pressing on the reinforcements which should make him stronger than his enemy. When these, in the third week of September, had all reached him, he suddenly broke up his camp, and, marching rapidly, reached on the 28th, Bussoleno in the valley of Susa.

For the Duke of Savoy this movement was decisive. Believing Turin to be threatened, he hurriedly blew up Santa Brigida, raised the siege of Pignerol, and marched towards his capital. But he had not been quick enough for the French Marshal Catinat had hurried forward before him, and had taken up a strong position on the plain between the villages of Marsaglia and Orbassano, some eight miles to the south-west of Turin, barring to him the way to that city.

Duke Victor was never the man to avoid a battle. Still less inclined was he to do so on the present occasion on account of the personal grudge he had against Catinat, who had, wantonly he believed, destroyed several of the castles reserved for his private use. He therefore gave the order for attack. He confided the command of the left wing to Leganez, and of the centre to Eugene, whilst with Caprara he led the right.

The battle began 4th October with a combined attack by Catinat on the allied line. Whilst the assaults directed against the allied right, commanded by the duke and Caprara, and the centre, led by Eugene, met with a stubborn resistance, that made where Leganez commanded, and led by Catinat in person, was successful. The defeat of the left wing uncovered the left of the allied centre, and Catinat, not losing time in pursuit, at once caused a portion of his victorious troops to wheel to his left to assail Eugene on the side which till then had been protected, whilst with the cavalry he galloped to assist the assailants of the allied right. There, after an obstinate resistance, he succeeded. Eugene meanwhile had, with great difficulty, maintained himself. But now, with both flanks exposed, he could do so no longer. He abandoned, then, the field of battle, and, joined by broken parties from the beaten wings, fell back under the walls of Turin.

The loss of the allies in this battle, which, known as the Battle of Marsaglia, had lasted four hours, was considerable. Nor were the French unscathed. Indeed, so much had they suffered that Catinat was unable to follow the Duke of Savoy in his retreat upon Turin.

Not long did the allies remain there. Recovering boldness, they marched unmolested to Moncalieri, and there, in an entrenched camp, covered northern Piedmont. Catinat contented himself with levying contributions in the northern portion of the duchy. In December he took up his winter quarters on French soil, and the campaign, which had been signalised only by an abortive siege and a barren victory, came to an end.

During the winter Victor Amadeus entered into secret negotiations with France, and finally promised, whilst allowing his troops to appear to act with the allies, so to conduct himself as to thwart all their schemes.

It can easily be understood why, under these circumstances, the campaign of 1694 was not more fruitful of result than had been that of 1693.

★★★★★★

"We certainly received," wrote Catinat, on the 26th August, 1694, "apparently by virtue of our understanding with the duke or with one of his ministers, information, always accurate, regarding the contemplated movements of the enemy."

★★★★★★

In this new campaign Eugene had replaced Caprara in the command of the Imperial troops. He had caused Pálffy to place his army in the field at Orbassano towards the end of May, but, under a thousand protests, his cousin had delayed the sending of his quota, nor was it till the end of July that the Piedmontese troops joined the Imperial camp. As soon as he knew that the Piedmontese were in march Eugene came to Turin, encouraged by the further information that his cousin meditated an attack upon Casale. Great was his disappointment to find that Victor Amadeus threw a hundred obstacles in the way of such a scheme, especially insisting upon the fact that the allies were not strong enough at the same time to undertake a siege and resist Catinat in the field.

After many days, however, Eugene insisted upon making the attempt. In three days, he recovered San Giorgio, the fort captured the previous year, but which Catinat had retaken after Marsaglia. He then caused Casale to be blockaded. But that was all he could accomplish. Every other contemplated undertaking was ruined beforehand by the Duke of Savoy.

Before, on the conclusion of the campaign, Eugene proceeded to Vienna, he left the blockading force before Casale, and, very suspicious now of his cousin, he returned to Turin in March, resolved to force him to an explanation. At the conference which ensued there Eugene represented the Emperor, Marquis Leganez and Count Louvigny, Spain, and Lord Galway, England. The Englishman was completely taken in by the high tone assumed by the Duke of Savoy, and wrote to the ambassador in Vienna to the effect that no one was more embittered against France than Victor Amadeus. Eugene, however, was not deceived. Unable to prove his cousin's duplicity, he resolved nevertheless so to conduct himself as to counteract, as far as possible, his intrigues.

On the 19th March he had his army assembled, ready for movement at Frassinetto, on the Po. The day following, he rode to reconnoitre the still-blockaded Casale. On his return he conferred with Lord Galway and Count Louvigny, and, supported by the latter, resolved to undertake the formal siege of the place. Forcing from the duke an unwilling consent, he opened trenches as soon as the weather would permit. On the 9th July Casale capitulated.

Eugene then turned his arms against Pignerol. But his cousin, whilst openly expressing his assent, despatched secretly to Count Tessé, commanding the garrison of that fortress, a detailed account of the allied plans. In other ways he threw such obstacles in the movements of the troops that winter had set in before they could be overcome.

Convinced now that his cousin was playing the part of a traitor, Eugene proceeded to Vienna to lay his proofs before the Emperor. For a time, the professions of the Duke of Savoy lulled the suspicions which Eugene had roused in Vienna. Eugene then returned, June, 1696, to Turin. But he had not been there many days before he wrote to Vienna his conviction that a secret though unsigned alliance did actually exist between Savoy and France. So closely did he question Victor Amadeus that the latter was forced at last to admit that it was so. Shortly afterwards, the 29th August, the Duke of Savoy signed a treaty with the King of France, and on the 16th September joined the French camp with his troops and took command of the allied army.

The immediate result of this act of the Duke of Savoy was the evacuation of Italy by the Imperial troops. There can be no doubt, however, but that the defection of his ally contributed very much to dispose the Emperor to conclude the war. The fact that the same dispositions existed in England, in Holland, and in Spain, paved the way to a common concert, and on the 20th September and the 30th October of the following year, 1697, articles were signed, on the first date by the three last-named Power and France, and on the second by the Emperor, which constitute the general agreement known in history as the Peace of Ryswick.

HUNGARY.

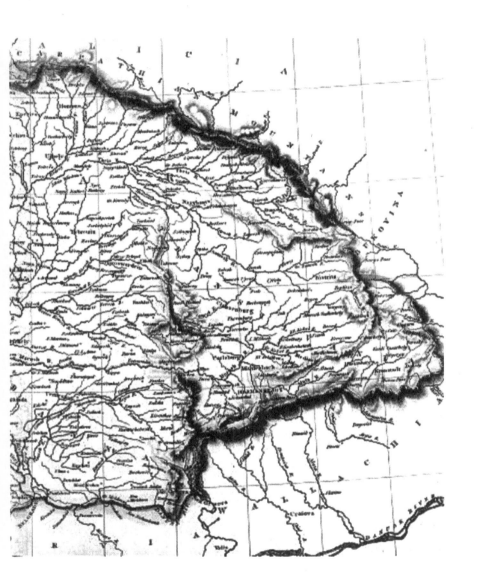

CHAPTER 4

Zenta—And Its Consequences

Whilst the Emperor had been warring against France in Italy and on the Rhine, he had likewise been contending in Hungary with varying fortunes against the Turks. How Belgrade had been taken by the Imperialists, led by Max Emanuel, the 6th September, 1688, I have told in the second chapter. But in 1690 the Turks had recovered Belgrade, and, encouraged by this success, had marched, a hundred thousand strong, against Essegg, a town and fortress on the Drave, the most important place in Slavonia. But Essegg was defended by Guido Starhemberg, and the valorous resistance of that commander had given time to the Margrave Louis of Baden to collect an army sufficiently strong to repel the invasion.

The Turks then raised the siege of Essegg, and met Margrave Louis on the field of Salankament. There, on the 19th August, 1691, they were totally defeated. Grosswardein fell, then, into the hands of the Imperialists. But there their good fortune ended. An attempt made to recover Belgrade miscarried, and in 1694 the Imperial Army, block-aded for many months in Peterwardein, was decimated by sickness. In the following year the Emperor committed the command of the army in Hungary to the Elector of Saxony, the famous Augustus the Strong. From this prince, as well as from the very eminent soldiers who served under his banner, great things were expected.

But those who cherished such expectations were disappointed. Augustus showed himself incapable as a commander, and, in the campaigns of 1695-6, not only did he gain no advantage over the Turks, but he was beaten at Olasch near Temesvar, 27th August, 1696. His election, shortly afterwards, to the dignity of King of Poland caused him to throw up his command. The danger to the Empire, towards the end of 1696, had become very threatening. Sultan Mustapha II was

THE GREAT TURKISH WAR

making stupendous efforts to reconquer Hungary. He had established a new cannon-foundry, replenished his finances, and placed his army in a state of great efficiency. It was known that he would command, in person, in the approaching campaign. In this emergency the Emperor recognised the necessity of selecting the most capable leader at his disposal. His choice, guided very much by the opinion of his best advisers, fell upon Prince Eugene of Savoy.

It was not until the end of June, 1697, that Eugene received his patent, and was able to join the army at Essegg. He found it in the most miserable condition the men in arrears of pay, their clothing in rags, ammunition and supplies wanting. The difficulties, too, looming in the future were neither few nor easy to overcome. The divisional commanders were at variance with one another. To this cause was it due that two of them, Count Auersperg and Prince Bathyany, had but just been repulsed before Bibacz. An outbreak in Upper Hungary, provoked mainly by the excesses committed by the starving garrisons stationed there, was being forcibly repressed by Prince Charles Thomas Vaudemont. Added to this, Mustapha II., with the finest army the Osmánli had raised since their defeat at Mohacs, was at Belgrade preparing to attack Peterwardein.

Eugene's first act was to despatch Count Solar to Vienna, to obtain, on the one hand, necessary provision for the re-equipment of his army, on the other, permission to act as he might judge best. When his demands had been partially met he sent instructions to Auersperg, who had been repulsed at Bibacz, to Vaudemont, who had just repressed the outbreak in Upper Hungary, and to Count Rabutin, who commanded in Transylvania, to join him with all haste on his march, and, breaking up from Essegg, set out, the 25th July, for Peterwardein. Auersperg and Vaudemont promptly set out to obey the summons, but Rabutin delayed, and it needed a special order direct from the Emperor to bring him to his senses. Until he should join, Eugene halted at Cobila. He learned there that the Turkish main army was concentrated at Belgrade, and had thrown bridges across the Danube and the Save.

The opinion prevailed generally in the Imperial camp that Peterwardein was the object at which the Osmánli aimed. Instead, however, of crossing the Save, as was anticipated, the *Sultan* moved his army eastward, crossed the Danube at Panesova, and despatched thence his ships up stream to the mouth of the Theiss. He thus obtained a position whence it was easy for him, by a rapid movement, to cut off

Count Rabutin, then on his march with eight regiments to join Eugene. Comprehending this on the instant, Eugene garrisoned Titel, on the Theiss, where the Bega flows into it, with eight battalions and eight, hundred horse under General Nehem, and detached two regiments up the stream to watch the movements of the enemy. He himself marched along the Theiss to meet Rabutin.

But the *Sultan*, neglecting Rabutin, marched direct on Titel, and forced Nehem to evacuate the place and fall back on Peterwardein. During this time Eugene had been joined by Vaudemont as well as by Rabutin. He then marched towards Peterwardein to cover that place against any possible attack.

He arrived within two marches of the town just in time to baffle an attempt made by the Turks to destroy the bridges across the morasses at St Thomas and Syreck. He pushed on the next day, the 5th September, towards the ground known as the Roman trenches—a plot of land between the Danube and the Theiss, protected by earthen ramparts—and on the 6th marched to, and encamped near, the marsh on the western side of Peterwardein, about two miles and a half from the Turkish camp. Whilst making this movement he was followed by countless swarms of Turkish cavalry, always making as though they would attack him, but ever prevented by his bold attitude.

Early the next morning, General Nehem, who had reached and assumed command at Peterwardein, sent a messenger to Eugene to tell him that clouds of dust were visible in the Turkish camp, but that he had been unable to ascertain whether or no they signified the enemy's departure. It soon transpired that this was actually the case. The *Sultan*, rightly concluding that the arrival of Eugene had spoiled his chance of gaining Peterwardein, had set off by the very route Eugene had just quitted, and had already taken his army across the first morass.

A deserter brought the news that this movement had been determined upon on the advice of Count Tokoly, and that the *Sultan* had further resolved to march up the Theiss as far as Szegedin, and, after capturing that place, to move rapidly into Transylvania. Instantly Eugene ordered his troops under arms, and, leading himself with the cavalry, followed the track of the enemy, restored the destroyed bridge over the morass at St. Thomas, and reached Becse, a town on the right bank of the Theiss, the 10th September.

Here the news reached him that the enemy were halted at Zenta, a town in the county of Bácska. Eugene at once summoned his generals to council, and, the first to speak, declared to them his opinion that it was advisable to attack the enemy there, or, should they have left, at their first halting-place before they could reach Szegedin. One and all agreed with him.

Before daybreak on the 11th September the prince formed his army into twelve divisions—six cavalry and six infantry—the artillery in the centre, the baggage under a strong cavalry guard in the rear, and set out in pursuit of the enemy. At 9 o'clock some scouts came to him with the information that they had seen the enemy's watch-fires at Zenta. Eugene promptly despatched some light cavalry to the front, and these had the good fortune to capture, after a slight skirmish, a *pasha* who had been despatched by the *Sultan* to reconnoitre.

Eugene turned to prompt use the capture of this prisoner. Threatening him with death should he refuse to speak, he forced from him the most important disclosures. He learned that the *Sultan*, finding Eugene on his track, had renounced the enterprise against Szegedin, and had halted at Zenta for the purpose of throwing a bridge over the Theiss, and marching straight into Transylvania. The bridge had been completed the previous day, and the *Sultan* himself, with a part of the cavalry, lay already on the opposite side of the river. The heavy artillery and the baggage were engaged at the moment in crossing, but the entire infantry and the remainder of the cavalry, with more than a hundred guns, lay still entrenched on the right bank, and parties were engaged in constructing a bridgehead within the entrenchment.

As Eugene, attended by a small escort, galloped in front of his army, he found many indications proving the truth of his prisoner's statements. He halted at a distance of about three miles from the enemy's position, and waited there impatiently the arrival of his men. When at last they came up, he formed them in order of battle. To Sigbert Heister, a general of great experience in Turkish warfare, and possessing to a remarkable degree coolness and resolution, he intrusted the command of his right wing, which rested on the steep bank of the Theiss, to the Prince of Commercy, under whom served Count Rabutin, Count Reuss, and the old, experienced commandant of artillery, General Borner the centre, to Guido Starhemberg, the left.

Eugene placed himself with the centre, ready to gallop where his presence might most be needed. He was about to fight the first battle in which he had supreme command. In his conduct before and in the course of it he displayed the same energy, the same self-reliance, coolness, and presence of mind, the same capacity to adopt and carry to a successful issue the resolution of the moment, which characterised him throughout his career as a commander. His dispositions on this day are peculiarly worthy of study. If we cannot admit to the full the correctness of the criticism of an eye-witness that "he left to the goddess Fortune no opportunity for the exercise of her influence against him," we shall be bound to admit that in the presence of such an enemy as the enemy whom he fought his daring violation of rules was amply justified.

As the Imperial Army, ranged in the order I have stated, advanced, swarms of cavalry issued from the Turkish camp to hinder its progress. The prince did not, on their account, check the advance of his main body, but, taking from the second line of each wing three segments of dragoons and some light guns, despatched them to the front to clear the way. These drove back the enemy, and then, as the army approached within cannon-shot of the entrenchment, re-took their place in the line. Just as they had done so a tremendous fire opened upon the advancing force from the Turkish batteries Eugene had his guns ready to hand, and these coming to the front, replied, the whole line still advancing.

The Turkish camp formed a kind of irregular half-moon, the base of which, about four thousand paces in length, rested on the Theiss and covered the bridge. It was covered throughout by earthworks, provided with a ditch, and with redoubts carrying heavy guns. Behind this outer defence, in the centre, was another wall, the only portion which still remained of an old Imperial store-house, and where this wall ceased there ran a newly-constructed strong palisading right up to the banks of the Theiss, on both sides of the bridge-head. Close to the bridge-head there was a long row of wagons, disposed in the most perfect order for crossing, each in its turn, the bridge, and capable, likewise, of being used as a means of defence.

Below the bridge the banks were steep and inaccessible; but above it, the water being extremely low, there was a narrow sand-bank, some forty paces in length, which the Turkish cavalry had utilised, but which, for the moment, was unoccupied. This sand-bank did not escape the penetrating glance of the Imperial leader. He extended his left so that its extreme infantry regiments touched the Theiss above the entrenchment. This movement gave the enemy an opportunity of which he made no attempt to avail himself.

Had he done so—had he, by a sudden assault, pierced the weakened line and rolled up the centre on to the right, the record of Zenta might have been different. But the attention of the Turkish leader was

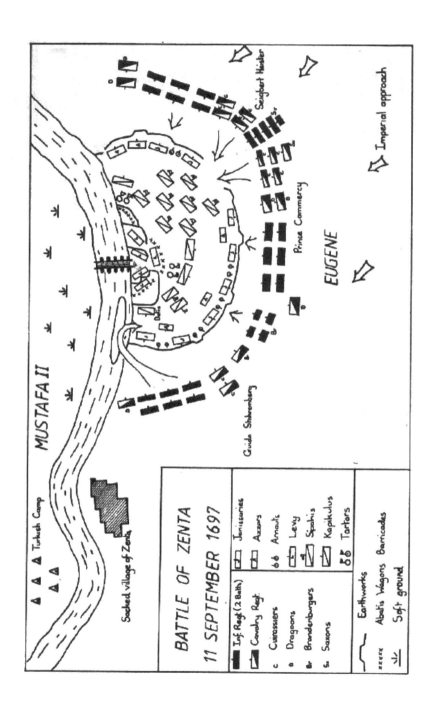

MUSTAFA II

Turkish Camp

Sacked village of Zenta

Seigbert Heister

Prince Commercy

EUGENE

Guido Stahremberg

Imperial approach

BATTLE OF ZENTA
11 SEPTEMBER 1697

Inf Regt (2 Batt)   Janissaries
Cavalry Regt.   Azzaps
c Cuirassiers   Arnauts
o Dragoons   Levy
Br Brandenburgers   Spahis
Sx Saxons   Kapikulus
                     Tartars

      Earthworks
xxxx Abatis Wagons Barricades
      Soft ground

apparently absorbed by his endeavour to despatch his wagons to the opposite bank. It wanted, then, little more than two hours of sunset, and should the enemy but defer his attack to the morning, the Turkish host was safe.

A conviction of this truth had been flashing in the mind of Eugene and urging him to superhuman efforts to complete his dispositions. At length, just two hours before sunset, the extremities of both his wings touched the Theiss, the left above, the right below, the Turkish entrenchment, his main army thus forming a half-moon round, and larger than, the Turkish half-moon. There was no time to be lost. From both extremities he at once opened an artillery fire on the bridge. Having seen that this fire was well in progress he directed a general assault along the whole length of the entrenchment. Whilst he super-intended this himself, he sent orders to Guido Starhemberg to push his foremost infantry regiments on to the sand-bank, and with them to force his way thence into the entrenchment from its rear.

Starhemberg executed these orders to the letter. He reached the sand-bank, and thence, in spite of the fierce opposition of the *Janissar-ies*, penetrated into the entrenchment. It is certain that this diversion greatly affected the defenders of the front, for the Imperial centre and right wing, after having been valiantly withstood there for some time, found suddenly that the defence was faltering. Then, led by the gallant Eugene, they, too, penetrated the entrenchment. Neither the second wall, nor that of the store-house, nor the palisading, offered to them an effective resistance. After a very brief interval, these succeeded in carrying the last line of defence, formed by the wagons.

The *Janissaries*, meanwhile, had been displaying that splendid dar-ing which had given them a reputation as soldiers second to none in the world. Very hardly pressed, they had cast aside their muskets, and, drawing their sabres, had rushed to a hand-to-hand encounter with their foe. But before long they were assailed on three sides. Then, rec-ognising further struggle to be unavailing, they made a rush for the bridge, their only way to safety. But before they could reach it, Guido Starhemberg had interposed between it and them. Despairingly they dashed into the Theiss, and, in the cold embrace of its waters, met the death they sought in vain from the foe. A few only reached the op-posite bank.

In other parts of the entrenchment the fierce Imperialists were continuing their work of slaughter. They gave no quarter. None was asked for. When the battle ceased about twenty thousand Osmánli

A View & Representation of ye Battle of ZENTA fought on ye 11th of Sept. 1696.—

lay on the ground; some ten thousand had been drowned, scarcely a thousand had reached the opposite bank. There were but few prisoners. Amongst the slain were the *grand vizier* and four other *viziers*, the Governors of Asia Minor and of Bosnia, the *aga-vizier* of the *Janissaries*, thirteen *beglerbegs*, and many *pashas*. Some of these, it is said, were slain by the *Janissaries* in the fury of defeat.

The *Sultan* had beheld from the opposite bank of the river the storm of the battle. When, one after another, his hopes of victory vanished, he bethought himself of his own safety. Fearful lest the victors should cross the bridge and attack him, he mounted his horse at nightfall, and, accompanied by his cavalry, rode, without drawing rein, to Temesvar. He reached that place at mid-day, but, not deeming himself safe there, he pursued his journey, two days later, to Belgrade.

By 10 o'clock at night not a single living Osmánli remained on the right bank of the Theiss. Eugene then withdrew his troops from the stormed entrenchment, and, forming them along the river, gave them the much-needed repose. Early next morning he crossed and took possession of the *Sultan's* camp.

Then, for the first time, he realised the greatness of the victory he had gained. The booty found in the camp surpassed all his expectations. Everything had been left by the terror-stricken *Sultan*. There was the treasury-chest, containing 3,000,000 *piastres*; a mass of weapons of every kind, the entire artillery and baggage, a countless number of horses, camels, and oxen, colours and trophies of every description. The most valuable of these trophies was the Great Seal, always worn round his neck by the *grand vizier*, and which had never before been taken, not even when a *grand vizier* had, as at Salankament, been slain. The cost of these spoils had been to the victors only three hundred killed and two hundred wounded. Eugene despatched them at once to Vienna, under an escort commanded by Count Dietrichstein. He had sent off Prince Charles Thomas Vaudemont from the battlefield the previous evening to announce his success.

The Battle of Zenta, the last great battle fought in the eighteenth century, yields in importance to few of its predecessors. Regarded as part of the warfare which had raged for two hundred years between the Osmánli and the Imperialists, it was the last, the most telling, the decisive blow. From the moment that it was gained the condition of warfare between the two peoples was inverted. Never again were the Osmánli to act the part of the aggressor on the realms of the Emperor. The novel task of defending what they had greatly gained was thence-

BATTLE OF ZENTA

forth to be theirs.

Of the manner in which Eugene fought the battle there never has been but one opinion. He displayed the power of taking in with a rapid glance the position of the enemy, its weaknesses as well as its strength, the not less valuable power of so determining his action on the moment as to reap the fullest advantage from the weaknesses. Take, for example, the manner in which his eye detected the purpose to which the neglected sand-bank might be employed, the effective and decisive manner in which he caused it to be utilised, whilst by a front attack he diverted from it the attention of the enemy. Nor must I omit to call attention to the earnest and rapid manner in which, before the battle, he pursued the enemy from the moment he first heard of their movements. It was this rapidity and this earnestness which enabled him to take them *in flagrante delicto*, their army cut into two portions by the waters of the Theiss.

The victory having been gained, the question then arose whether it should be utilised by a march on Temesvar. Eugene was of opinion that the season of the year was unfavourable for a campaign in the marshy county, of which that city is the capital, and that the difficulty of transporting provisions would be almost insurmountable. He deemed it would be wiser and more efficacious to send some light cavalry to follow up the defeated enemy, whilst he should march on Szegedin. His generals, whom he summoned to a council of war, unanimously agreed with him. Upon this, despatching a corps of 600 light cavalry, under Colonel Glockelsperg, to follow the Osmánli, he marched with the rest of his army to Szegedin.

There he divided it into five corps. The greater part of the infantry, and the Brandenburg soldiers, he sent across the Danube to Mohács and Ofen (Buda), the cavalry and the Saxon troops through the country to the left of that river, to Pesth, the artillery, with the exception of two batteries of six guns each, and two mortars, to Bohemia, there to take up winter quarters; Count Rabutin and his cavalry back to Transylvania, with orders to attract to himself the attention of the Turks. Under his own command he retained a corps of chosen troops of all arms, with which to make a raid into Bosnia. Eugene's corps consisted of the twelve guns and two mortars I have referred to, four thousand cavalry, two thousand five hundred chosen infantry, and a proportion of sappers and miners.

At the head of this body of troops he marched, 18th September, by way of Mohács, to Essegg, crossed the Drave the 6th October, then pushed on to the Save, crossed it at Brod, entered Bosnia, stormed the castle of Doboy on the 16th, Maglay on the 17th, and continued his way along the Bosna to Zeboche. This place was taken on the 18th. The following day Wranduck was occupied, and, as the roads from this point were extremely difficult, Eugene left there his guns and eight hundred men, to maintain communication with Brod. Thence he pushed on with the remainder of the force towards the capital, Sarajevo, called by the Germans Bosna-Serai, reached it on the 23rd, and—to punish the Turkish garrison for having attacked the party he had sent the day previous, under a flag of truce, to summon them to surrender—caused the city to be plundered and burnt, and then sent a party to overtake the fleeing garrison.

From Sarajevo, on the 25th, he fell back towards the Save, accompanied by an ever-increasing number of Christian families, eager to leave their homes to obtain, beyond the Save, Imperial protection. On the 5th November Eugene recrossed the Save, and leaving the infantry to escort the numbers who followed him, rode with his cavalry to Essegg. He was still there when he received information that Rabutin had made a successful raid into Turkish territory, had passed the Iron Gates on the 29th October, and had taken by storm Ujpalanka, on the 6th November. The campaign ended with the burning of Pancsowa.

Eugene then placed his troops into winter quarters, and returned to Vienna. There he was received with the highest consideration by the Emperor, who presented him, amongst many other gifts, with a sword richly set with precious stones.

★★★★★★

I mention, only emphatically to contradict, the fable invented by Rink (*Leopolds des grossen Leben*) and repeated, amongst others, by Major-General John Mitchell (*Biographies of Eminent Soldiers*, Blackwood, 1865), that, for fighting the Battle of Zenta in the face of the positive orders he had received to undertake no offensive movement against the enemy, Eugene "was placed under arrest, his sword was taken from him, and he was about to be brought before a court-martial when the Emperor himself interfered, put a stop to the proceedings, and replaced him at the head of the army." For a complete proof of the falsehood of this story I refer the reader to the contribution of Lieut.-Colonel Schels to the *Austrian Military Periodical Journal* for 1834 (*Öesterreichisehe Militärische Zeitschrift, Jahrgang*, 1834).

★★★★★★

RÉGIMENT D'ALSACE.

ALSACE REGIMENT 1696

The Viennese gave him a tumultuous welcome. Since the return of Louis of Baden from the campaign of 1691, no such multitudes had thronged to greet a conqueror. A medal was struck to commemorate the great day of Zenta.

The peace of Ryswick, concluded some seven weeks later (30th October, 1797), enabled the Emperor to turn his undivided attention to the Osmánli. But his treasury had been so completely exhausted by the strain of the double war, that, for the moment, he was powerless to take full advantage of the improved military position. The troops in Hungary suffered, then, during the winter that followed Zenta, alike from want of pay and often from want of proper food Many of them bore their sufferings bravely. Some could not conceal the bitterness of their indignation. The men of the dragoon regiments of Saxe-Gotha and Herbeville went so far as to plot to murder their officers and then to join the Turks. The plot, however, was discovered in time, and the mutiny was quelled.

Fortunately, the Porte was in no disposition to take advantage of this state of the Imperial Army. Possibly it was not aware of it. Sultan Mustapha II. had, indeed, done all in his power to repair the terrible loss, not less in prestige than in men and munitions of war, which he had suffered at Zenta. He had refilled the cadres of the regiments, and had bestowed the office of *Grand Vizier* upon Hussén Koprili Pasha, the representative of a family which had already furnished five great dignitaries to his empire, and himself a man of rare ability. Just at the moment, to console him, to a certain extent, for the slaughter of Zenta, there reached him the information that his coadjutor, Hussén Mezzomorto, Dey of Algiers, had gained a great victory over the Venetian fleet near Tenedos, and, a little later, that the important town of Basrah had been recovered from the Persians.

In other respects, he was in as bad a condition as the Emperor. The war of fifteen years' duration which the Porte had now carried on against the Empire, had emptied the Ottoman treasury, and Mustapha was not all indisposed to listen to the advice, which the English Ambassador at Constantinople pressed upon him, to conclude peace. He did not, however, slacken his efforts to raise a new army, and he so far succeeded, that the Grand Vizier Koprili had collected, in the spring of 1698, a force of considerable strength under the walls of Belgrade. He was resolved, however, to act solely on the defensive.

On the opposite side Eugene stood with his army, at the same time, at Peterwardein. Thence he marched towards Belgrade, and reconnoitred the enemy's position, but found it too strong to be attacked with any hope of success. In a thousand ways he endeavoured to entice Koprili from his cover. The *grand vizier* was immovable. He felt that upon him rested the hopes of the Ottoman Empire, and he was resolved, against an adversary such as Eugene, to risk nothing.

The spring, then, and the summer passed away, and nothing had been accomplished. The monarchs on both sides earnestly wished for peace: The Emperor, not only because his people were exhausted, but because the succession to the Spanish throne loomed in a very near future; the *Sultan*, because he had lost all hope of victory, and dreaded lest a defeat should force upon him conditions harder than those which, under the actual circumstances, he might hope for. When both the minds of the principals tended to the same end, it was certain that that end would be obtained. By the mediation of England and Holland, the two sovereigns, and the allies of the Emperor, Russia, Poland, and Venice, agreed to send representatives to treat for peace, to the little town of Carlowitz, on the right bank of the Danube, opposite to the fortress of Peterwardein.

Here, after much negotiation, lasting seventy-two days, was concluded, the 26th January, 1699, the famous Peace of Carlowitz. The condition that each party should possess the territories occupied by each at the moment of the meeting of the congress formed its basis. By the treaty, then, the frontier of Hungary, which, when the war broke out, extended only to within a short distance of the then Turkish towns of Gran and Neuhausel was pushed forward to within a short distance of Temesvar and Belgrade. Transylvania and the country of Bácska, between the Danube and the Theiss, were yielded to the Emperor. To Poland were restored Kaminietz, Podolia and the supremacy over the lands watered by the Ukraine, the Porte receiving from her in exchange, Soczava, Nemos, and Soroka, to Venice, who renounced the conquests she had made in the gulfs of Corinth and Ægina, part of the Morea, and almost all Dalmatia, including the towns of Castelnuovo, and Cattaro, to Russia, the fortress and sea of Azof.

The Peace of Carlowitz was the consequence of the great victory of Zenta. That peace constitutes a memorable point of departure alike in the history of Austro-Hungary and the history of Europe. By it the Ottoman Power lost nearly one-half of its European dominions, and ceased to be dangerous to Christendom. Never more would the discontented magnates of Hungary be able to find a solid supporter in the *Sultan*. The relations of the Osmánli towards Europe were absolutely reversed. From having been the spoilers, the children of Oth-mán were thenceforward to become the despoiled. Two great blows had caused this change. The first had been struck by John Sobieski, under the walls of Vienna, in 1683, the last, by Prince Eugene at Zenta, in 1697.

THE 9 YEAR'S WAR

CHAPTER 5

War of the Spanish Succession—
Campaigns in Italy of 1701-2

On the conclusion of the Peace of Carlowitz, Eugene returned to Vienna. At that time there was a rage amongst the higher nobility of Austria for building summer palaces on the ground occupied by the Turks during the memorable siege. Large and spacious houses were run up there with extraordinary celerity. Eugene himself had been bitten by the universal mania. He had purchased, in 1693, a spot on a rising ground to the south-east of the city, commanding an uninterrupted view of the same, and having on the other side of it the pleasant Kahlenberg. By degrees he acquired the gardens and meadows in its vicinity, and on the spot itself he had begun to build the palace which is well-known to visitors to Vienna as the Belvedere.

The Emperor, after the Battle of Zenta, had bestowed upon him a domain in Hungary, on the territory between the Drave and the Danube, at the point where those rivers unite. He had also purchased himself, in 1698, from the widow of Count von Heissler, the island Csepel, in the Danube, below Pesth, upwards of thirty miles in length, bringing with it also the right to the possession of Promontor, extending five square miles along the right bank of the Danube, below Pesth. The leisure which the Peace of Carlowitz gave him was employed on these properties.

The visit to Vienna of one of the most illustrious men of the age came pleasantly to interrupt him in his occupations. This was the founder of the Russian Empire, the famous Czar Peter. Peter had come to Vienna from England and Holland in the retinue of his own ambassador. He was received there with the highest honours. His stay was marked principally by the attention he paid to all that concerned the Imperial Army, then, in consequence of the campaign of Zenta, at the height of its reputation. He was thus brought necessarily much in contact with Eugene. It is, therefore, the more to be regretted that no record exists of the impression which these famous men made upon one another. After having satisfied himself upon all points, Peter was about to start for Venice, when the news of the insurrection of the Strelitz forced him to return to Moscow by way of Poland.

Peace still reigned in Europe when, on the 1st November, 1700, Charles II, King of Spain and the Indies, the last of the Spanish Habsburgs, died. It had been the natural wish of the Spanish statesmen to preserve under one head his vast dominions, comprising, besides Spain and the Indies, the Netherlands, Milan, Naples, Sicily, and Sardinia. Supported in this view by the King of France, they had persuaded Charles to disregard the claims of his Austrian kinsmen to make a will in which he recognised the Duke of Anjou, grandson of Louis XIV, as his sole heir.

This arrangement had not been so secretly conducted but that some inkling as to the contents of the will transpired. Already, some weeks before the death of Charles, Count Harrach, the Imperial ambassador at Madrid, had reported the rumours afloat regarding it. A little later he was able to transmit more certain information. It was hoped in Vienna that the dying king might yet be induced to change his mind. The news that he had died before such a change had been worked out caused, then, the greatest indignation.

The Imperial ambassador at Madrid was instructed to protest alike against the infraction of the rights of his master contained in the will and against the occupation of the throne by the Duke of Anjou, and to quit the capital. At the same time, the Emperor published a manifesto in which he presented proofs of the rights of the House of Habsburg, and disputed alike the validity of the will and the power of the king to disinherit his nearest kinsman.

Nor was he satisfied with wordy protestations. A few days after the receipt of the news he had summoned to a council the President of the War Department, Count Rudolph Starhemberg, and the three Marshals, Caprara, Eugene, and Commercy. To these he announced in energetic terms his determination to assert his claims by force of arms, and intimated to Eugene his intention to despatch him with an army to Italy, there to recover for the House of Habsburg the cities and places which had acknowledged the sovereign rule of the King of Spain.

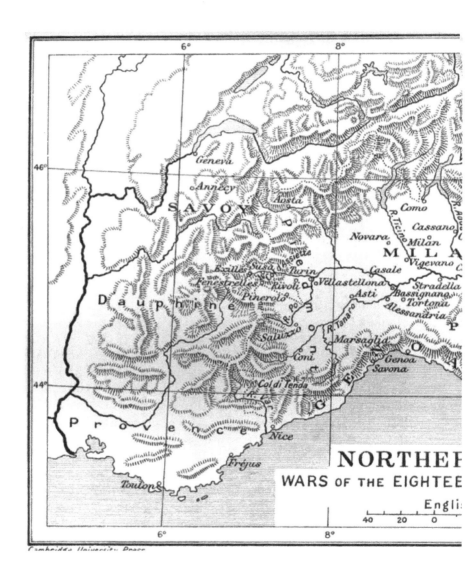

NORTHER

WARS OF THE EIGHTEE

Englis

40 20 0

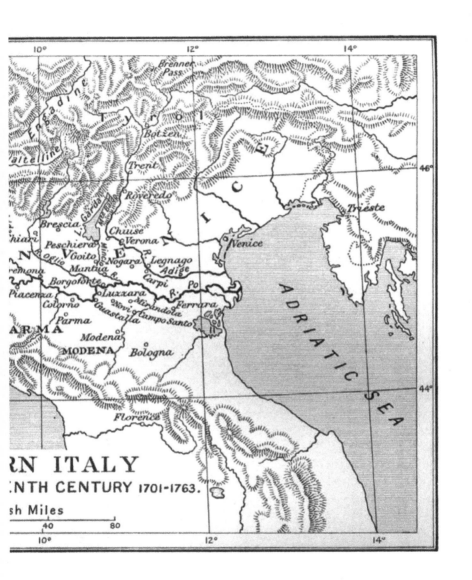

RN ITALY
NTH CENTURY 1701-1763.

sh Miles

40   80

It was a bold resolution, for, at the moment, the Emperor had not an ally in Europe. The two great Sea-Powers, England and Holland, had recognised the Duke of Anjou as King of Spain. The Duke of Savoy had been won over by the promises of France. The Princess of Mirandola, purchased by the same Power, had admitted French troops behind the strong walls of her capital. The Duke of Mantua had followed her example Pope Clement XI had at first declared himself neutral, but he, too, soon began to display a decided leaning for Philip.

Nor, in Germany itself, could the Emperor command complete unity of action. His son-in-law, Max-Emanuel of Bavaria, whom we have seen commanding the Imperial armies in Hungary and in Italy, had asserted claims in the female line to the Spanish possessions. These, on the promise made to him by Louis XIV that France would conquer for him the Grand Duchy of Baden, and on the assurance from the same sovereign that he might retain all that he could conquer in Germany from the House of Habsburg, he had renounced, and had given in his adhesion to France. His action was supported by his brother, Joseph Clement, alike Elector of Cologne and Bishop of Liege. Other princes of less importance, the most prominent of whom were the Dukes of Wolfenbüttel, followed the example of Bavaria.

The power of the Emperor seemed, indeed, so hemmed in that it would be difficult, if not impossible, for him to assert by arms, with any chance of success, the undoubted claims of his House. Before he had put a soldier in the field, not only had the Duke of Anjou been received at Madrid as King, under the title of Philip V, but all the dependencies of the Spanish Monarchy had recognised his authority. Within three months of the death of Charles II., in January, 1701, likewise, a French Army, under Count de Tessé, had entered Upper Italy, and, in complete understanding with the Spanish forces there, had occupied the strong places.

But the resolution of the Emperor was unshaken. He continued to make preparations for the war which, unless Europe were prepared to submit to the domination of France, was inevitable. From Hungary he withdrew all the troops that could be spared, and, forming them into a solid corps thirty thousand strong, despatched them under Guido Starhemberg, to Roveredo, on the Leno d'Aria, near the junction of that river with the Adige. There, on the 20th May, Eugene assumed command. He had under him, besides Starhemberg, who commanded the infantry, General Bonier, chief of the artillery, and, as such, possessing a reputation second to no other in Europe; Prince Charles

ThomasVaudemont, son of the Spanish Governor of Milan, who had declared for Philip, but himself a staunch adherent of the House of Habsburg, commanding the cavalry, and Prince Commercy

Whilst the Imperial force had been gradually collecting at Roveredo, the French, under Count de Tessé, had quitted their positions in the fortresses, and had occupied the passes which, from Lake Garda to the Adige, lead from Tirol into Italy. Whilst they were thus posted, Catinat arrived to assume command. This famous general at once detected the point, alike the weakest and the strongest of the defence. This was the pass of Chiusa di Verona, ten miles to the north-west of the city of that name, having on the right side the deep foaming Adige, on the left a steep wall of rock. The path, now wide and easy, was then narrow and difficult, and the end was dominated by a blockhouse. Catinat at once occupied alike this pass and the strong positions on the southern face of Monte Baldo He believed he had thus completely barred Italy to Eugene.

Such was not the opinion of his opponent. No sooner had Eugene assumed command of his army at Roveredo than, accompanied by his generals, he proceeded to examine the country. He soon recognised that, whilst he could advance by any one of the four roads which led to Vicenza, Verona, Brescia, and Bergamo, it was of the highest importance that he should deceive the enemy as to which he should select. Finally, he resolved to cross the mountains leading to Vicenza. Having spent four days in rendering the paths passable for his guns, he set out on the 26th May, despatching a portion of his army by way of Alá—a town ten miles south-south-west of Roveredo—through the Val Fredda, another by way of Peri across the mountains.

Both roads were extremely difficult. It was found necessary to dismount the field-guns from the carriages, and haul them by strong ropes to the summit of the heights the carriages were taken to pieces, and carried in portions. The heavy guns were left behind in Roveredo, to follow as soon as the roads had been made practicable for their passage. The cavalry, meanwhile, proceeded by way of the Val Duga, to the left of Roveredo, whilst four battalions of infantry, under General Guttenstein, were despatched to the summit of Monte Baldo, to observe thence the movements of the French. Care was taken, at the same time, by watching the entrance of the passes from the side of Tirol, that no information of these movements should be carried to the Italian side.

After three days of hard labour, not unlike that which had been

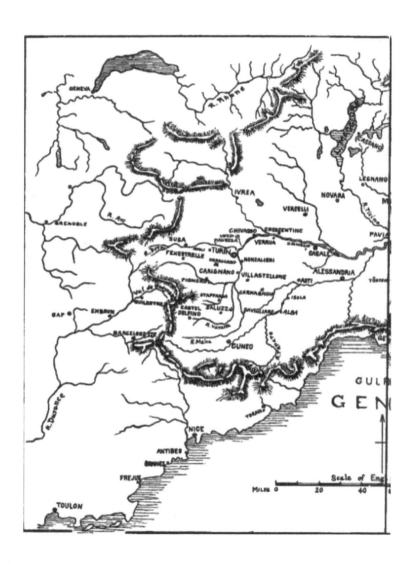

A
SKETCH MAP
ILLUSTRATING THE CAMPAIGNS
OF
PRINCE EUGENE
IN
NORTH ITALY
AND FRANCE

forced two thousand years before upon Hannibal—for, on many points of the Monte Baldo, Eugene had to cause the rocks to be blown up before he could make a practicable road—the infantry entered Venetian territory and encamped on the heights of Breonio. They waited there till all the force, including the heavy guns, should arrive. These were transported by a road made by the soldiers and peasants across the mountains, nine feet in width each of them was drawn by fifteen pairs of oxen, and by the side of each walked soldiers and peasants with ropes, to help them over difficult places. At length, on the 3rd June, the entire army was assembled on Breonio. The following day Eugene set it in march, and on the 5th reached St Antonio, twenty-four miles from Verona. He had made one of the boldest and most daring marches known till then to modern warfare.

Catinat was completely surprised. He had deemed the mountains behind Verona a sufficient defence, and had made all his preparations to meet Eugene, if Eugene should debouch at all, in Brescian territory. Recognising at once that if his enemy should cross the Adige the Milanese would be in imminent danger, he hastened to occupy the principle defensive posts on that river. But Eugene, masking his real intentions by movements the object of which was not apparent to his enemy, suddenly turned southwards to Castelbardo, where a detachment he had sent in advance under Count John Pálffy had thrown a bridge over the river. There he crossed, and, after having reconnoitred the island Villabuona, formed by the canal Bianco and the canal Malopera, proceeded to Arcole. At that place, destined in future years to be immortalised, he halted to obtain further information regarding the movements of the enemy. He hoped that, uncertain regarding his enemy's position, Catinat would divide his forces, when he would pounce upon them and destroy them in detail.

Catinat was, in fact, much perplexed. He could not divine the reason of that sudden march southward. The uncertainty of his mind upon this point made the man who was ordinarily so resolute, so prompt, so decided, as uncertain as a girl. Eugene had caused Rivoli to be occupied by four battalions under Guttenstein. To watch these, whose strength he did not know, Catinat employed his entire left wing. The remainder of his army he stretched out along the Adige, wearying the men with continued marches and counter-marches. When at length he discovered that Eugene had crossed the Adige at Castelbaldo and had reconnoitred the Canal Bianco, his fears redoubled, and he proceeded to mass his troops to prevent a movement which would have left Central and Southern Italy exposed to attack.

But before he could so mass them Eugene had thrown bridges across the canal, had transported eight regiments to the further bank of the Po, and had likewise cast a bridge over that river at Occhiobello, thirteen miles south-west of Rovigo. Convinced now that Eugene intended to invade the Modenese, Catinat, in his haste to be before-hand with him, left General St. Fremont with a weak corps at Carpi, and hastened with the remainder of his troops towards Ostiglia. This was just the movement to which Eugene had been trying to force him. He prepared instantly to take advantage of it. Crossing the Tar-taro the night of the 8th July, with 11,000 men he fell, with the early grey of the following morning, on the entrenchment of Castagnaro, on the right bank of the Adige, occupied by the French. After a fierce resistance on their part, he stormed it. He then attacked and carried a second entrenchment which the enemy had thrown up at the point where the canal separates from the Adige. Then, reassembling his force, he marched on Carpi.

The difficulties of the road, caused by morasses, canals, rice-fields and bushes, were great, but they were overcome. Suddenly, as the force approached Carpi, the enemy made a fierce attack upon the advance guard, composed of the *Cuirassier* regiment Neuburg. This attack brought on a general action. It was fiercely contested on both sides. At length, just as the French were being driven back, defeated, Count de Tessé arrived on the field with a strong reinforcement. A cool and ca-pable man, Tessé allowed the fleeing troops to pass through and round his formation to the rear, and, whilst their officers rallied them there, advanced to check the further progress of the Imperialists.

But an impetus had been already given to their fierce onslaught which could not be resisted. Eugene himself led them on, and where he led they followed. Neither the loss of his horse, shot dead, nor a wound from a spent ball in the knee, stopped his impetuous course. At length Tessé's troops gave way. The rallied soldiers followed their example. The battle was gained, and the town of Carpi and the French camp close to it fell into his hands.

But Eugene was one of those real generals who hold that a vic-tory not followed up is a victory thrown away. He pressed on early the next morning to San Pietro di Legnago, where had been posted another detachment of Catinat's army. Before he reached it informa-tion reached him that the enemy, terrified by the result of the Battle of Carpi, had evacuated it during the night. He marched on, however,

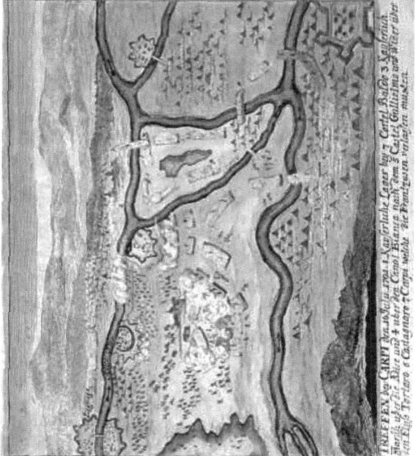

TREFFEN bey CARPI den 9. Julii 1701. 1. Kayserliche Lager bey 2. Castel Roller 3. Nazdrauek. 4. Flecke Carpi uber die Riue und 5. uber den Canal Bianca nach dem 6. Castel Guillieima wo 7. Herz uber ein Fluß Teriano 8. Cadagnore 9. Corps welche die Franzosen verlassen mussen

and occupied it. He now found himself master of the entire country between the Mincio and the Adige, for Catinat, as soon as he heard of the disaster which had befallen his troops at Castagnaro and Carpi, had ordered a general retreat behind the Mincio.

Not yet satisfied with his success, Eugene concentrated his army and marched in a north-westerly direction by way of Buttapietra, and Villa Franca to the Mincio, behind which Catinat had drawn up his army. Reconnoitring early on the morning of the 18th July, he beheld the French Army occupying a strong position, apparently unassailable, near Goito. He spent two days in examining it, to endeavour to discover its weak point, and then called a council of war. The question whether the army should cross the Mincio or the Po was at that council freely discussed. Of four generals who were present the opinions were divided. The casting vote was Eugene's, and he decided for the passage of the Mincio.

An hour before midnight on the 27th July Eugene put his army in motion. Ascending the Mincio he reached Salionze, and hastened the preparations for crossing which, by his orders, had already begun. At mid-day on the 28th those preparations were completed, Eugene then crossed, and before nightfall the Imperial Army stood on the right bank of the Mincio.

The enemy, of whom, meanwhile, Victor Amadeus, Duke of Savoy, had assumed the nominal command, had made no attempt to disturb Eugene in this operation. The troops which had occupied the heights near Salionze had fallen back on the main army, and the main army, letting go its touch on the Mincio, had fallen back on its entrenched camp at Volta. Eugene followed it, occupied Mozambano, Castel Goffiedo, and Castiglione, and was pushing forward further when information reached him that the enemy were in full retreat.

Catinat, in fact, who, notwithstanding the presence of Victor Amadeus, still really directed the movements of the French Army, feared least the continued advance of the Imperialists should provoke a rising of the population, already greatly embittered against the French, in his rear. Despatching, then, the Prince of Vaudemont, father of Prince Charles Thomas who was serving under Eugene, and Count Tessé, to hold Cremona and Mantua, he quitted his camp at Volta and marched with all speed to take a position behind the Oglio. He succeeded in crossing that river without opposition, and took post at Fontanella, seventeen miles nearly due south of Bergamo. There he received information that the King of France had removed him from his command in favour of Marshal Villeroi, and that the latter was on his way to join.

Villeroi was a far inferior general to Catinat. Saint Simon has described him as:

> A man formed expressly to preside at a ball, to act as judge at a carousal, and if he had had the voice, to sing at the opera the idles of kings and heroes, very well suited to lead the fashions— but for nothing else.

Voltaire, though not so scathing, is scarcely more flattering. That eminent writer says:

> He was a man with a pleasant, even an imposing face, very brave, very honest, a good friend, agreeable in society, magnificent in everything. But his enemies said of him that, as general of an army, he was more occupied with the honour and pleasure of commanding than with the plans of a great captain.

There can be no doubt but that he was a most incompetent commander.

Such was the man who on the 22nd August succeeded the skilful Catinat. Catinat, however, remained with the army. The day following, the 23rd, Eugene crossed the Oglio with a strong body of cavalry, and reconnoitred the French position at Fontanella. He then rode back to Chiari, and entrenched his army under the walls of that town.

Villeroi, confident that he had only to show himself to force Eugene to retreat behind the passes of Tirol, set his army, greatly strengthened by reinforcements, in motion and crossed, the 29th and 30th of August, to the left bank of the Oglio, Eugene offering no opposition. He halted the 31st, but on the 1st September, one hour after midnight, resumed his forward movement towards Chiari and attacked the entrenched camp of the Imperialists. Eugene, well acquainted with the fury of the first onslaught of French troops, and their rapid transition, when repulsed, from confidence to dismay, had ordered his men to remain kneeling behind the entrenchment and to deliver their fire only when the French should be within a few paces of them.

They carried out this order to the letter. The soldiers of France, however, gave an example that day of courage and discipline not to be surpassed, and it is possible that if they had been well led they might have gained the day. Neither discouraged nor even checked by the result of the fire of the Imperialists, they continued to press on. But their efforts were made on the point where the entrenchment offered the greatest difficulties. Villeroi attempted no diversion. He appeared, in fact, to have been so bewildered as to be incapable of giving any order. Seeing this, Catinat and the Duke of Savoy directed the troops to fall back. They had lost two thousand men, of whom two hundred were officers. The loss of the Imperialists amounted to thirty-six killed and eighty-one wounded. Villeroi retreated to the left bank of the Oglio, and formed an entrenched camp near Urago. There he remained inactive.

Eugene, though he had repulsed the attack on Chiari, did not feel himself strong enough to follow up the enemy. In fact, he was so certain that the attack would be renewed that he allowed three days to elapse before he despatched a courier to Vienna to announce his victory. Even then his inferiority in numbers was so marked—his whole force counting but one-half that of the enemy—that he did not consider himself justified in risking a general action. Remaining, then, in his camp at Chiari, he employed all the means at his disposal to harass the enemy. On the 15th September one of his parties surprised, and to a great extent destroyed, a French convoy at Orzinovi. This operation was again and again repeated at other places.

At the end of October two Spanish cavalry regiments were surprised and cut up by Prince Charles Thomas Vaudemont near Cassano, losing nine standards and all their baggage. As one consequence of these successful skirmishes, the Duke of Sesto, who commanded for the enemy on the Adda, fell back to within twenty miles of Milan. The sympathies of the population were entirely in favour of the Imperialists. Villeroi wrote to his master:

> Every night, heavily-laden wagons enter the Imperial camp without an escort. On the other hand, we have provisions for only two days remaining. The weather is bad, the rains are continuous, the roads are in a fearful condition. Nothing more can be undertaken. If we stay here longer we shall lose all our cavalry.

The circumstance which greatly affected the French commander at this crisis was, no doubt, the firm and solid position of his adversary as contrasted with his own. And when he saw that that position became every day more firm and more solid, that Eugene was laying in supplies and building huts with the evident intention of passing the winter at Chiari, he could hold out no longer. On the 9th November he despatched a courier to the king announcing the impossibility of remaining where he was. On the night of the 12th he recrossed the Oglio.

Eugene had expected this. On the first intimation, then, that the French were quitting their camp he hurried forward with his troops and arrived in time to disturb very considerably their passage of the river. His guns worked great execution on the retreating enemy. Catinat, who had ridden to the rear to observe the Imperialists, was wounded by a musket-ball in the right arm. This wound, by giving him an opportunity of proceeding to Versailles, afforded him a good excuse for releasing himself from the false position he had occupied under Villeroi.

But Eugene was not satisfied with the simple retreat of the enemy. Whilst Villeroi marched southwards towards Cremona, Eugene, bent on quartering his army for the winter in Mantuan territory, marched on the 19th south-eastward to Ostiano, on the Oglio, and occupied that town. Thence he marched to Canneto, in the same direction, on the same river, appeared before it the 1st December, and forced it to surrender, almost under the eyes of the French Army, on the 4th. Then, by a rapid march, he seized Macaria, and drove the French from their entrenched camp at Torre d'Oglio. As a reply to this, Count Tessé surprised and defeated an Imperial detachment under Lieutenant-Colonel Mercy, the 10th December Eugene's answer to this was the capture of Borgoforte, Governolo, Ostiglia, and Ponte Molino. Of the places in the Mantuan territory only Mantua and Goito remained in the possession of the enemy, and these he now proceeded to blockade.

Still, however, Eugene was not satisfied. On the night of the 13th December he despatched four regiments across the Po to attack Guastalla. On the 16th he himself occupied that place, and arranged there the following day for the disposal of his troops in winter quarters.

His success had not only been brilliant, it had encouraged the Italian princes, who sympathised with the Emperor, but who feared France, to declare themselves. The Princess of Mirandola was the first to lead in that direction. Calling to herself an Imperial regiment, she expelled the French garrison from Mirandola, then the Duke of Modena allowed Eugene to occupy Brescello, a place well furnished with ammunition, arms and provisions. Nor can there be any doubt but that it encouraged the newly-made King of Prussia, Frederic I., to promise to aid the Emperor with a corps of ten thousand men, and the King of Denmark to follow his example with one of six thousand.

Battle of Cremona

The death of the exiled King James II. of England (September 1701), and the unwise recognition of Louis XIV of his son as titular king of that country, so roused the people of England, that from that moment the active adhesion of the Sea-Powers to the enemies of the House of Bourbon became a mere question of time. They did not, however, declare war till May of the year following.

During the winter, Eugene blockaded Mantua and Goito. He had sent pressing letters to Vienna stating in moving terms the wants of his army; how the commissariat department was so badly managed that his soldiers were likely to starve in the midst of plenty; how his troopers were in want of horses; how there was even a scarcity of powder, lead, and of money; how, moreover, he required reinforcements in order to conduct efficiently the coming campaign. For long the Court answered his requests with promises. But when performance did not follow the promises Eugene despatched one of his most trusted officers to Vienna to represent the absolute necessity of prompt compliance with his requisitions.

During the absence of this officer the fertile mind of the prince conceived a scheme which, bold and daring as it was, further reflection commended more and more to him, and which, therefore, he proceeded with the least possible delay to execute. This plan was the surprise of Cremona—the headquarters of Marshal Villeroi!

Cremona is a fortified city on the Po, forty-eight miles south-east of Milan. It possessed a castle, broad, irregular streets, and, for its size, a scanty population. The summit of its bell-tower, Torrazzo, the highest in Italy, commands a view of the entire course of the Po through the broad plains of Lombardy. At the time of which I am writing, it was strongly garrisoned, and contained within it walls not only Marshal Villeroi, but some of his best officers.

Some three months before the idea took a practical shape in the mind of the Imperial leader, one of his generals, Prince Commercy, had entered into relations with a priest in Cremona. This man had informed Commercy that there existed a dry water canal, unguarded by, probably unknown to, the French, which extended from the cellar of his house to the country outside the walls. The idea which now occurred to Eugene was that by means of this canal he might surprise the place. The enterprise seemed the less difficult when he ascertained that the French garrison, entirely unsuspicious, supplied but a feeble guard to the gates, and that there were no sentinels on the walls.

Resolved to strike the blow, Eugene summoned, the 28th January, Guido Starhemberg and Prince Charles Thomas Vaudemont to his councils, confided to them his plan, and issued his orders. He directed Starhemberg to hasten, as quickly as possible, to Ostiano, to make there, with great secrecy, the still remaining preparations, to march then direct on Cremona, whilst Vaudemont, with about five thousand men, was to proceed by a circuitous route, so as to assault the south-western, or Po, gate of the city at the moment when Eugene and Starhemberg should carry that on its northern face. After giving these instructions Eugene proceeded to Montagnano to make further arrangements with Prince Commercy, and returned thence, to avoid observation, to Luzzara.

On the evening of the 31st January, Eugene, Commercy and Starhemberg met in a solitary house about five miles beyond Ostiano. Their troops, numbering about twenty-seven hundred infantry, and thirteen hundred cavalry, were marching silently in the same direction with orders not to halt until they should meet their commanders. Those commanders anxious but resolute, rode forward without waiting for them, from the solitary house to a hut within twelve hundred yards of Cremona. The night was stormy, and it rained heavily. At about 5 o'clock on the raw morning of the 1st February all the troops were assembled close to this hut. Thence two hundred men commanded by a very intelligent officer, Major Hofman, were conducted by a guide sent by the friendly priest to the outer entrance into the dry aqueduct. They then entered the aqueduct, marching, of necessity, in single file.

Hofman had orders to remain concealed in the priest's house until a detachment of two hundred men under Count Nasary and a similar number under Count Kufstein should have entered the city by the same path. Then, whilst Hofman should fall upon the guard at the Margherita, or northern, gate, and Nasary should master the main-guard and the Council house, Kufstein should assail the house occupied by the vice-governor, and support the two other parties. Whilst these three detachments were creeping along the aqueduct Eugene despatched Count Mercy with two hundred and fifty picked horsemen close to the Margherita gate, with orders to dash through it when it should be opened, then to traverse the city with all speed and secure the south-western or Po gate for the troops approaching under Vaudemont.

Hofman, Nasary, and Kufstein carried out their instructions to the letter. Their men collected in the priest's house, Hofman, then

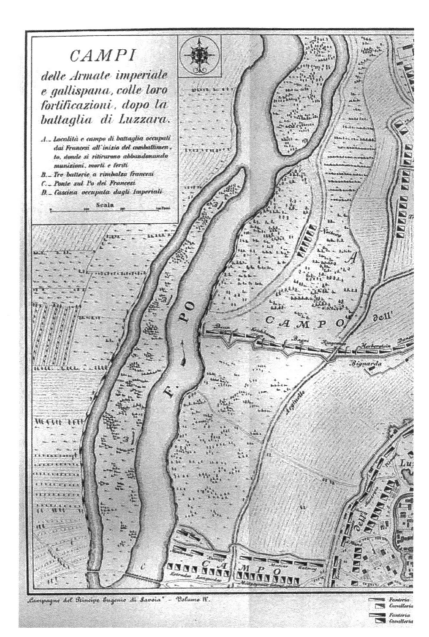

CAMPI

delle Armate imperiale e gallispana, colle loro fortificazioni, dopo la battaglia di Luzzara.

A.. Località e campo di battaglia occupati dai Francesi all'inizio del combattimento, donde si ritirarono abbandonando munizioni, morti e feriti

B.. Tre batterie a rimbalzo francesi

C.. Ponte sul Po dei Francesi

D.. Cascina occupata dagli Imperiali

Scala

F. PO

CAMPO dell'

CAMPO

Campagne del Principe Eugenio di Savoia - Volume IV.

Fanteria
Cavalleria
Fanteria
Cavalleria

Guidento
Commissariato

Villa
di Sie

Berbeitie

Paff
Corbelli
Fda Vigna

Quartiere
del Bosque

Darmstadt

Riva

Parky
d'Artiglieria

Segarba

ARMATA IMPERIALE

Guido Starhemberg Italia

D

ARMATA

FRANCESE

Chiesa della Spedale

Lauteur Prop Francais

la Tomba

L'originale trovasi nell'i.r. Archivio di guerra Campagna 1702. N. 7.

118078

imperiale

francese

emerging from it, mastered, without difficulty, the Margherita gate, and admitted Mercy's horsemen. These then rode at full speed for the Po gate. Eugene, who was close at hand with the remainder of the force, entered the city on their footprints. Nasary and Kufstein duly performed the parts allotted to them.

Marshal Villeroi had returned to Cremona the previous evening from Milan, and had gone to bed tired. At 1 o'clock on this eventful morning he was awakened by the sound of three musket-shots. Before he had time to enquire the reason of this firing, his valet rushed into his room exclaiming, "The Germans are in the town!" Villeroi sprang at once from his bed, ordered his horse, and hastily put on his clothes, whilst he directed his secretary to burn all his papers.

As soon as he had finished dressing, he ran downstairs, leaped on his horse, and, followed by a single page, galloped to the main-guard. But the main-guard was already occupied by Nasary, and, before he was aware of it, the French Marshal was surrounded by Imperialist soldiers. These tore him from his horse and made him prisoner. His evidently high rank earned him no little danger, for each of his many captors claimed him as a personal prisoner. Whilst he was being hustled by them all, there dashed through the crowd an Irish officer in the Imperial service, Macdonnel by name. Macdonnel took the prisoner to Starhemberg, refusing on the way an offer made to him by Villeroi of ten thousand *pistoles* and the command of a regiment in the French Army, if he would connive at his escape. Starhemberg received the prisoner courteously, and, taking his sword, had him conveyed to a house close to the Margherita gate. There he was visited by Eugene, who, fearing lest the French troops should make a desperate effort to recapture him, despatched him at once, under escort, to Ostiano.

Matters, however, were not progressing favourably for the assailants within the town. Mercy had reached the Porta Po, but had found no Vaudemont ready to enter. His numbers were few, and, before he could be reinforced, an Irish regiment in the service of France, forced him to relinquish his hold. In the contest which followed he and several of his officers were taken prisoners. Nor were the Imperialists faring better within the city. As soon as the first feeling of surprise had worn off the French recognised that their assailants were but a handful in comparison with themselves.

The Marquis d'Entragues, whose regiment had been under orders for parade that morning, made resistance so resolute that the remaining French troops had time to rally. Soon the officer who succeeded to the command on the capture of Villeroi, Count Revel, found himself at the head of a force greatly superior to that of the assailants. His rear secured by the firm occupation of the Porta Po, he assumed the offensive, recovered the lost positions, drove the Imperialists from street to street, and finally forced them to quit the town. The casualties on both sides were considerable, the French losing twelve hundred men, and the Imperialists about half that number Eugene had tried a bold stroke, and had nearly succeeded. He had failed because one of his generals, Prince Charles Thomas Vaudemont, had not been able to keep his engagement. That officer had been so delayed by the sticky state of the roads that he had reached the Porta Po only at 2 o'clock, to find it strongly guarded.

In one respect, and that a most important respect, the expedition produced consequences very unfavourable to the Imperialists. The captured Villeroi was replaced by the brilliant and skilful Vendôme.

The new French general was not unworthy, indeed, of being opposed to Eugene, to whom he was, on the maternal side, first cousin. The royal blood of France flowed in his veins, for his grandfather was a natural son of Henry IV and the beautiful Gabrielle d'Estrées. Voltaire, a severe critic, thus described his qualities as a commander—

> Vendôme had not the reputation of bestowing upon his plans the same deep consideration as did Prince Eugene. He neglected details too much; he did not enforce strict military discipline, he allowed the table and sleep to absorb too much of his time, . . . but, in the days of battle, he repaired everything by a presence of mind and by inspirations of genius which danger always roused within him, and he was ever seeking those days of battle.

Though the attempt on Cremona had failed, the fact that it had so nearly succeeded spread consternation and distrust amongst the French commanders before Vendôme had arrived. They hastily evacuated the strong places they had till then held on the Oglio. Eugene advanced, occupied these, and forced the French to retire behind the Adda. The only fortified places they now possessed to the east of that river were Cremona, Soncino, and Sabbionetta. Eugene was able, therefore, to maintain the blockade of Mantua and Goito with a comparatively small number of troops. His communications by way of Lake Garda and Tirol with the hereditary dominions were undisturbed, and he might now hope to receive the reinforcements, and

BATTLE OF LUZZARA

especially the supplies, of which he stood so much in need.

Instead, however, of reinforcements, Eugene received a despatch from Vienna requiring him to despatch from his already too weak army a corps of ten thousand men, under Prince Commercy, to recover Naples for the Imperial House. At a council of war, summoned by him on receipt of this order, at which Commercy was present, the unanimous opinion was expressed that the despatch of such a corps to Naples before he should be reinforced would force him to renounce all the advantages he had gained, and would render it extremely difficult for him to defend even the passes.

The council reported in this sense to Vienna. Their contention was the better grounded, inasmuch as the French king was despatching considerable reinforcements to serve under his new commander. The decision caused, nevertheless, great disappointment at Vienna, and for a considerable time the promised troops and supplies were withheld.

Meanwhile Louis of Vendôme had reached Milan, 18th February, 1702. The reinforcements which followed him increased the strength of the French Army in northern Italy, by the beginning of May, to eighty thousand men. Eugene could not then count more than twenty-eight thousand, and of these five thousand were employed in blockading.

The problem Eugene had to solve was how, with so small a force, to make head against a large army led by a capable general. Finding the solution beyond his power, Eugene wrote to Father Bischoff, confessor to the King of the Romans, and a man of great influence, urging him to press his necessities on the King and on the Emperor. When this letter and other letters addressed to high official personages produced no result, the prince despatched to Vienna Count John Pálffy, a Hungarian nobleman of the highest consideration, to urge his necessities.

During Pálffy's absence, Eugene fell so ill that his life was despaired of. He recovered, however, and then devoted all his energies to make up, as far as possible, for the want of the much-needed troops and supplies. He hemmed in Mantua, strengthened the garrison of Brescello in the Modenese—which Vaudemont had taken during his retreat from Cremona—evacuated Bozzolo as under the circumstances not necessary to maintain, threw a bridge over the Po at Borgoforte, and collected his army on the left bank of that river.

Vendôme, meanwhile, all his reinforcements well in hand, set out, on the 4th May, to relieve Mantua. He made, however, as though he would attack Brescello, for, crossing the Po near Cremona, he marched in the direction of that fortress. Then, suddenly retracing his steps, he recrossed the Po, and turned his course towards Oglio, ascended that river, and crossed it at Pontevico, on the 15th and 16th of May. Eugene had not been deceived, but, too weak to prevent the passage of the Oglio, had taken up a strong position at Canneto. To press more closely the operations against Mantua, he now evacuated that position, and took another close to that fortress.

Meanwhile Vendôme, marching slowly forward, had taken Ostiano and the other places evacuated by the Imperialists, and on the 19th May reached Canneto. He was still there on the 20th when Eugene stormed the strong redoubt which the French had built to protect one of the four gates of Mantua, the Porta Ceresa. The news of this loss came as an inspiration to Vendôme. Crossing the Chiese he forced Eugene to abandon his position on the left bank of the Mincio, and with it the blockade of the fortress. Thus, without losing a man, he had reopened communications with, and had effectually relieved, Mantua.

This movement had rendered the position of Eugene still more difficult. He had always declared that, were he forced to relinquish his hold on the Po, he must think of abandoning Italy. He now took up a strong position between Curtatone and Montanara, his left communicating with the Po, his right resting on the Mincio, both wings secured by bridges across those rivers. Vendôme then encamped within a cannon-shot of him, separated only by the marshy ground of the Mincio and the "*fossa maestra.*"

Vendôme was determined to drive Eugene from his position, Eugene was equally resolved to hold it. He clung to it, therefore, with all the tenacity of his strong character, and, whilst so designing, devised a plan which, had it succeeded, might have changed the fortunes of the campaign.

Eugene held that his most dangerous opponent was less the French Army than Vendôme himself. He resolved, then, to make himself master, if possible, of his person. Learning that Vendôme occupied a solitary house in Rivalta, close to where the Mincio flows into the Upper Mantaun Lake (Lago Superiore), he determined, being well acquainted with his lazy habits, to despatch a party by water to surprise him and bring him a prisoner into the Imperial camp.

He entrusted the carrying out of this enterprise to Adjutant-General Marquis Davia. On the night of the 11th June that officer and two hundred men embarked on twelve boats on the Mincio. Unobserved, the boats crossed the upper lake, and touched the land near the solitary house. Disembarking only a few men, Davia replied to the challenging sentries that he was bringing sick men from Mantua. Under this pretext he approached the sentinels intending to cut them down. Success seemed assured when suddenly one of Davia's men imprudently fired upon the sentry and killed him. This shot was fatal. The men left in the boats took up the fire. A general alarm succeeded all around, and Davia was compelled to renounce the enterprise. He managed to reach the Imperial camp in safety.

This carefully planned enterprise thus failed in consequence of the imprudence of one man. Eugene placed the entire party in confinement, and ordered a searching inquiry into the conduct of each one of them. He doubted whether the "imprudence" might not have been designed, but he could obtain no proof that it was so.

Meanwhile Vendôme, startled by the greatness of the danger from which he had so narrowly escaped, was planning revenge. On the 10th June he caused a number of guns to be mounted at a distance of six hundred paces from Curtatone, the headquarters of Eugene. He then cannonaded that place so fiercely that Eugene was forced to transfer his position to Montanara. There Vendôme, warned by the experience of Villeroi at Chiari, would not attack his enemy. He endeavoured, however, by all the means in his power, to annoy him by constant sorties from Mantua. To protect his camp Eugene took a firm post near Porta Pradella (the western gate of the city), and threw up three redoubts covered by a ditch to prevent egress from it. Though severely attacked the 27th June, whilst these works were in progress, Eugene completed them.

Just at that time the enterprising nature of Vendôme received a fresh impulse by the arrival in his camp of the young King of Spain, Philip V, at the head of a considerable following. The opportunity for the destruction of the Imperialists was tempting. To compass it Vendôme divided his army, leaving one-half in the camp at Rivalta, whilst with the other he threatened Guastalla and Brescello. He hoped thus to entice Eugene across the Po, and then interposing the army at Rivalta between him and that river, to force him to surrender.

Eugene watched the movements of his adversary with some anxiety. He was resolved to hold his position as long as possible, and when it should become untenable to fall back on an entrenched camp he had prepared at Borgoforte. He despatched, then, the Marquis Visconti with three cavalry regiments, numbering fifteen hundred men, to the Enza to observe the enemy, and if possible, to cover the part of the Modenese traversed by that tributary of the Po. Subsequently he despatched Count Auersperg to act with Visconti. Upon both generals he impressed the necessity of acting with the greatest prudence and caution.

But in this respect Auersperg and Visconti paid no heed to the orders they had deceived. They neither planted sentries nor even kept watch. Informed by his spies of their carelessness, Vendôme fell suddenly upon the Imperialist detachment as it lay near Santa Vittoria, between the Crostolo and the Tassone. The surprised soldiers had but time to mount their horses when the enemy came upon them. Visconti did all that a brave man could do to save the day several times he repulsed the French cavalry, but, when their infantry arrived and opened a murderous fire, he felt that all was lost and took to flight. In this flight many men lost their lives in the waters and marshes of the Tassone. The remainder owed their safety to the gallantly of the dragoon regiment Herbeville, which on the first sound of the fight, galloped to the spot and checked the enemy's pursuit.

Eugene heard of this unfortunate affair at 11 p.m. of the day on which it had occurred. He mounted his horse at once, reached the Crostolo half an hour before daybreak, and made there the necessary preparations to repair the disaster. During his long ride he had thoroughly considered the position. It was clear to him that the enemy were separated in three divisions, any one of which he might attack with hopes of success. He resolved, then, to quit his position near Mantua, to leave about five thousand men in the entrenched camp at Borgoforte, and with the remainder to seek out one of the divisions of the enemy's army.

His resolution once taken, he delayed not a moment in carrying it into effect. By the 1st August he had crossed to the right bank of the Po, and made his headquarters at Sailetto. Vendôme, meanwhile, not suspecting any movement on the part of Eugene, was pressing his incursion into the Modenese with one-third of his force. His task was remedied easy by the panic which had communicated itself to the garrisons of the Imperial fortresses. Reggio and Modena, both of which might have offered a solid resistance, surrendered at the first summons. Vendôme then marched to take a position between Luzzara and Guastalla, with the view of attacking one of other of those towns. On the night of the 14th August, he approached Luzzara.

The information of Vendome's march towards Luzzara reached Eugene that same night. He at once broke up his camp, marched in the direction of the enemy, and came in sight of him at 3 o'clock in the afternoon of the 10th.

Vendôme, meanwhile, had summoned Luzzara, and had forced the garrison to take refuge in the tower which dominated the town. He was pressing it there when the news reached him that Eugene was advancing. Believing that he would be attacked the same day, he formed his army in order of battle. The left wing he rested on a strongly fortified building; the right on the Po, his front, which had a natural covering of dams and ditches, he proceeded to strengthen with abattis.

Eugene halted about a mile and a half from Luzzara until all his troops should come up. This happened at half-past 4. Meanwhile, he had examined the ground and the enemy's position, and had decided on his plan of attack. At 5 o'clock his guns opened fire. Under cover of their smoke, Prince Commercy led the Imperialist right wing with great firmness and dash against the French left. They were received with a steady file, two bullets finding their way into the body of Commercy, who fell mortally wounded. The fall of their leader checked for a moment the advance of the Imperialists; but Eugene, whose eyes were everywhere, despatched on the instant three regiments to support them. Three times were they repulsed. Then Eugene dashed forward to lead them to a fourth attack. This attack succeeded. The enemy were forced to let go their hold and fell back into their camp.

Meanwhile the fight was raging with extraordinary fury on the Imperialist left. There Guido Starhemberg commanded, opposed to King Philip and Vendôme. Almost simultaneously with Commercy, Starhemberg had made his attack. At first nothing could withstand his dash. He drove the enemy before him with such fury that they were about to break, when Vendôme rushed forward, and, taking advantage of a brief pause which, the nature of the ground caused in the Imperialist attack, rallied his men, and led them on himself. For a moment this gallant conduct restored the battle. A charge of cavalry, opportunely made by the young Vaudemont restored the superiority of the Imperialists, and, after a stubborn resistance, the French were forced back into their camp.

The day, then, seemed gained. It only remained to storm the camp. But it was now too late. Not only had the sun set, but a thick mist rising from the river obscured the ground. A further advance was impossible. The Imperialists, however, remained in possession of the field of battle, and, covering it with an entrenchment, they occupied it during the night. The French, at the same time, drew a little further back, and spent the night in entrenching their new position.

Neither party cared, when day broke, to renew the attack. The days following the battle were spent in cannonading from both sides, each waiting for the other to move. Vendôme was able to force the surrender of Luzzara and Guastalla, and on these grounds, and on the ground that Eugene's loss had been greater than his own, he claimed the victory. But if the proof of victory be the baffling of the main plan of the enemy, then most decidedly that of Luzzara belongs to Eugene.

For three months the two armies looked each other in the face, the skirmishing parties on both sides, especially on the side of the Imperialists, being extremely active. Vendôme was the first to give way. On the 3rd November he fell back to put his army into winter quarters. The same day Eugene joyfully reported to the Emperor that he had attained his end by, "lasting out Vendôme."

In his retreat Vendôme took Borgoforte and Governolo, and then placed his army in quarters along the Adda, near Cremona. Eugene lodged his troops in the country, not yet desolated, along the Secchia and the Tartaro. He had reason to be content. With a small army he had maintained his position in Northern Italy against vastly superior numbers, directed by one of the greatest generals of France.

CHAPTER 6

Blenheim

When he had placed his army in winter quarters Eugene returned to Vienna, which he had not visited for two years. He found affairs there in a critical position. Max Emanuel II., Elector of Bavaria, had definitively cast in his lot with the French, and had taken Ulm. General Villars had gained his marshal's staff by his victory over Prince Louis of Baden at Friedlingen. On the Lower Rhine and in the Netherlands, however, Fortune had smiled, for on the former Kaiserwerth had been taken by the Prussians and Dutch, whilst in the latter Marlborough had become master of the Meuse as far as the heart of Flanders, having taken the fortresses which had secured France from invasion in that quarter.

To counterbalance this advantage, Hungary, always an open sore in a very vulnerable part of the Empire, had, at the instigation of Prince Francis Leopold Rákóczy, risen in revolt. Warned by experience, Rákóczy had avoided decisive action, and engaged only in that guerilla warfare which, nevertheless, necessitated the employment against him of large bodies of the Imperial forces.

Such was the political situation in the early part of 1703. Eugene found the Emperor and the court alike discontented with the existing state of affairs. An entire reorganisation of the ministry was insisted upon. In the new arrangements the Presidency of the Council of War was conferred upon Eugene This appointment placed him at the head of the army, in direct communication with the Emperor.

The condition in which Eugene found the War office was of a nature to make the boldest tremble. Everything had to be created. After an expedience of some months he thus wrote to Guido Starhemberg (30th October, 1703).

I can assure you that had I not been present myself, and seen everything with my own eyes, no one would believe how matters were. In fact, if the monarchy had been in such a bad state as to require fifty thousand *gulden*, or less, to save it from destruction, it would have been impossible to procure those *gulden*.

Still, he worked hard, the harder because stinted by want of money, at the organisation of the army. Political circumstances came to help the Emperor in his need. On the 16th May, 1703, Portugal acceded to the alliance against France; and on the 9th November of the same year the Duke of Savoy bound himself by treaty to contribute fifteen thousand men to the common cause.

In Hungary, however, matters were going badly. The Imperial commander, Count Schlick, had, indeed, beaten a considerable body of the rebels at Ocskay, but a few days after, during the absence of Schlick at Neufohl to celebrate the Emperor's birthday, another body of rebels, led by the Counts Bercsenyi and Karolyi, fell upon and completely defeated the Imperialists. Schlick fell back, then, slowly on Pressburg, leaving the entire country between the Waag, the March, and the Danube in the possession of the Hungarians. Karolyi then despatched his hordes to ravage Lower Austria and Moravia. The cruelties committed in these raids scarcely bear to be mentioned.

The terror was at its height. There were no troops available, and, even if there had been troops, there were no guns, no ammunition, no store of provisions. Buda lay in ashes, and the other towns, except Pressburg, were incapable of offering resistance. Above all this, there was not a *stiver* in the treasury.

It was under these circumstances that the Emperor summoned Eugene to the field to take command of whatever troops were in Hungary and Transylvania. Eugene proceeded at once to Pressburg, there to organise resistance, and to check as much as possible the progress of the Hungarians.

The first care of Eugene was to protect the right bank of the Danube against the depredations of the rebels. But, even then, the danger which threatened the Imperial interests was enormous. Pressburg itself was so insecure that Eugene despatched the Hungarian crown for safety to Vienna. The means at his disposal were absolutely inadequate. Whilst, then, endeavouring to protect Lower Austria by means of entrenchments on the March, whilst encouraging the commanders in Transylvania, in Asia, and in other fortified places to exert themselves, he sent pressing letters to Vienna for troops and money to enable him to meet the enemy in the field. To this end he wrote letters to the Emperor, painting in glowing terms the absolute necessity of compliance with his requisitions. He urged even the advisability of applying for aid to Poland.

Meanwhile, in spite of all his efforts, he could not efficiently check the forward march of the insurgents. Before the trenches on the March could be completed a band of them dashed into Lower Austria, burned the Imperial castle of Hof and the village adjoining, and returned laden with booty.

At length, however, his representations produced some slight results. Count Czernin contributed one hundred and fifty thousand *gulden*, in payment for the office of Chief Burgrave in Bohemia. The Imperial riding-school in Vienna supplied one hundred and fifty, the University, eighty horses. Citizens who had no horses contributed money. Others fitted out soldiers, some by companies, some by tens. But these aids were as a drop in the ocean in comparison with the necessities of the case. To urge these with greater force Eugene resolved to return to Vienna. Having seen, then, that the castle of Altenburg was placed in a state of defence, that the frontier as far as Neustadt was covered, and that the troops in Pressburg were ready for offensive action, he made over command to Count John Pálffy, and proceeded to the capital.

The events which had occurred in Italy, in Alsace, and the Palatinate, on the Danube, and in the Netherlands, in the year 1703, had been scarcely more favourable to the House of Austria than had been Eugene's efforts in Hungary. On the Danube Marshal Villars had beaten the Imperial Army under Count Styrum at Hochstadt, 21st September, and, but for circumstances into which it is foreign to the subject to enter, might have marched on Vienna. In Alsace and the Palatinate, Tallard had defeated the Duke of Hesse-Cassel at Speyer (15th November), and had taken Landau. In the Netherlands Marlborough, pitted against Villeroi, had taken Huy, but in other respects the timidity of the Dutch deputies had powerfully contributed to render the campaign somewhat barren. In Northern Italy the Imperialists had been reduced to the defensive. On the whole, then, the advantages lay with the French.

This was more especially the case on the Danube. The idea which filled the mind of Villars, the idea of finishing the war by marching on Vienna, had met a hearty recognition at Versailles. Villars himself had been recalled because he could not agree with Max Emanuel of Bavaria. His idea, however, remained, and, on receiving the news of the victory gained by Tallard at Speyer, the French Court had despatched General Marchin, with a considerable force, escorting a large convoy, to join the Elector of Bavaria on the Danube. On the very day of the junction, at Donauworth, the Elector presented Marchin with a patent, signed by Louis XIV, nominating him to be Marshal of France. Marchin at once marched upon and captured the city of Augsburg, whilst the Elector, filed with the hope of taking Vienna, proceeded down the river to Passau, and occupied that place early in January 1704.

This, then, was the position when Eugene arrived, the same month, in Vienna. France had one army in the Netherlands, under Villeroi, a second in Northern Italy, under Vendôme, a third on the Rhine, under Tallard, a fourth, under Count de Coigny, on the Moselle, a fifth under Marchin in the heart of Southern Germany. Co-operating with this last, Max Emanuel of Bavaria occupied the entire country between the Inn and the Lech, as well as Passau, Kufstein, and several places in Upper Austria. A Franco-Bavarian corps likewise occupied the Upper Palatinate. France had also troops in Spain, and others employed in suppressing the insurrection of the Protestants in the Cevennes.

An examination of the situation made it clear to Eugene that the great danger to the Empire would arise from the combined action of France and Bavaria. He counselled, then, the Emperor to confine himself in Hungary to a defence of the position whilst he should co-operate with his allies in meeting the assault directed at the heart of the Imperial dominions.

To meet that assault the allies, not counting the troops employed in Spain and Hungary, possessed one army, that of Marlborough, in the Netherlands, a second, commanded by Margrave Louis of Baden, in the Black Forest; a third, recently commanded by the Duke of Hesse-Cassel, but now destined for Eugene himself, on the Rhine and Moselle, a fourth, under Starhemberg, in the north of Italy. These, in the opinion of Eugene, would be sufficient provided unity of action could be secured.

Observing that whilst the armies of Tallard and Coigny were virtually one army, and those of Marchin and Max Emanuel were also in all respects one, yet that between those two there was a space which, commanded by the army of Louis of Baden, prevented their communicating with each other, it became clear to him that the Court of Versailles would endeavour to bridge that space by separating the army of Tallard from that of Coigny, and sending it to join Marchin and Max Emanuel. When that were accomplished, the French Army on the Danube, having only Louis of Baden to deal with, would experience no difficulty in marching on Vienna. He wrote these ideas to Marlborough, and, pointing out to him that the Empire would be totally unable to aid him in the Netherlands so long as the sword was directed at its very heart in Germany, urged him to unite with himself in an attempt to baffle the enemy by meeting him on the very ground he had selected. The idea coincided entirely with the views of Marlborough, and he at once applied for and obtained permission from England and the States-General to execute it.

Events were soon to prove how clearly Eugene had read the enemy's designs. On the 13th May Tallard crossed the Rhine with a large convoy at Breisach, and, outmanoeuvring Louis of Baden, effected on the 19th a junction with, and made over the convoy to, Marchin and Max Emanuel between Villengen and Donaueschingen. He then fell back and recrossed the Rhine into Alsace (2nd June). Max Emanuel then took post at Ulm, whilst Louis of Baden, recovering from the surprise caused him by the eruption of Tallard, marched to Ehingen, twenty miles to the south-west of that town.

Marlborough, meanwhile, acting in consort with Eugene, crossed the Rhine the 26th May, the Neckar the 3rd June, and entered Mundelsheim, nine miles south of Heilbronn, on the 10th. There Eugene, accompanied by a small escort, met him. The interview which followed laid the foundation of the esteem, admiration and regard which ever after existed between the two men. Three days later, riding in front of the troops, they met Margrave Louis of Baden at Gross Heppach (on the Rems), a village on the direct road to Nordlingen. Under a tree, still living, in front of the Lamm Inn, still used as a hostelry, the three commanders deliberated over the plan of the campaign. The first matter to decide was as to the regulation of the command.

On this point the least capable of the three, Louis of Baden, displayed the greatest obstinacy. He insisted that he should command in chief the allied armies. When it was made clear to him that such an arrangement was impossible, he agreed that he and Marlborough should command on alternate days. On the conclusion of this arrangement, Eugene proceeded to his command on the Moselle.

The two allied commanders, anxious to possess a strong place on the Danube, then marched against Donauworth, and arrived before it the 2nd July. Marlborough, reconnoitring, saw that to delay the attack

105

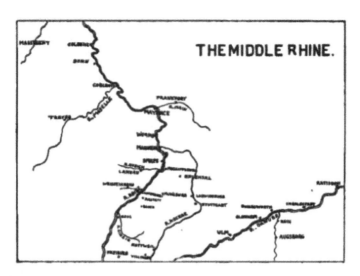

THE MIDDLE RHINE.

would give the enemy the opportunity of greatly strengthening his position. In spite, then, of the fact that his men were tired, he ordered an immediate attack on the Schellenberg, a conical hill, with a flat surface on the summit half-a-mile in diameter, which covered the town on the north, and was held by Count Arco with eight thousand men. So strong was the position that the defenders beat back three assaults. The fourth, however, succeeded, and Max Emanuel fell back on Augsburg.

The day before the attack on the Schellenberg Tallard had again crossed the Rhine with twenty-six thousand men to effect a junction with Max Emanuel. To replace and support him Villeroi came a few days later with an army of about the same strength and took post at Ottenburg. Coigny still held his old position, between Fort Louis and Drusenheim, threatening always an attack on the lines of Stollhofen. Those lines were occupied by Eugene with an army which he had not proved, and which, as yet, knew him not. Its component parts were contingents from Brandenburg, Denmark, the circles of Westphalia and of the upper Rhine, and from the Palatinate. The Brandenburg, or Prussian Contingent, was commanded by Prince Leopold of Anhalt-Dessau, a man stern in his manners, but just, capable, and honest and beloved by his men. The relations between him and his commander soon became most cordial.

Eugene could not prevent the march of Tallard, for he had Coigny in front of him, and Villeroi marching to take a position in the Palatinate. But, determined to prevent the allied army on the Danube from being overwhelmed, he disposed twenty thousand men of his army in such a manner as to impose upon Coigny, then hurried with the remainder, fifteen thousand, in the track of Tallard, fully resolved to attack that general should opportunity offer. Fortune did not so far favour him, for Tallard effected his junction with Max Emanuel, the 4th August, at Augsburg. Two days later, the 6th, Eugene pitched his camp at Hochstadt. The same day he rode to Aichach, sixteen miles from Augsburg, to concert measures with the allied commanders, who, after having taken Rain, on the Lech, had encamped there, and were engaged in ravaging the country as far as Munich.

Eugene found the two commanders divided in opinion Margrave Louis was bent on besieging Ingoldstadt, Marlborough objected to the employment of his own troops for such a purpose. The difficulty was solved by a proposal made by the Margrave to undertake himself the siege if Marlborough and Eugene would cover his operations. To this the two friends joyfully acceded, and it speaks much for the total absence of self-seeking from the character of Eugene that he, the conqueror of Zenta, the hero of Chiari and Luzzara, offered on the spot to place himself, for the carrying out of the common purpose, under the orders of the Englishman.

Eugene stayed three days in the English camp, assisting in the preparations for covering the siege of Ingoldstadt, and then returned to his own troops. Just after he reached Hochstadt, the 9th August, he received information that a portion of the Franco-Bavarian Army had crossed the Danube at Neu-Offingen, and was in full march on Dillingen, five miles from his own position. Instructing Leopold of Anhalt-Dessau to keep a strict watch on the enemy's movements, and to retire behind the Wernitz should he make any indication to advance beyond Dillingen, Eugene rode to Marlborough's camp, explained to him the position, solicited and obtained a promise that he should at once be reinforced by the troops under the Duke of Würtemberg, then returned to find that a portion of his army had fallen back on the Schellenberg, the defences of which they were engaged in restoring.

Eugene then despatched the remainder of his infantry and a portion of his cavalry to Donauworth. But, convinced that it was the intention of the enemy to despatch at once the remainder of his army to the left bank of the Danube, he determined not to give up his strong position on the Kesselbach, but to await there, between Munster and

Oppertshofen, the Würtemberg troops, and possibly the whole English Army.

With twenty squadrons, the horses saddled and the men in readiness, Eugene kept watch through that night on the Kesselbach. Late in the evening he was joined by the Würtemberg cavalry, and this addition of strength gave him confidence to be able to hold the position should he be attacked. But he was not attacked, and during the 11th, and up to the early morning of the 12th, he was joined by the English Army.

The neglect to attack Eugene on the Kesselbach was one of the first faults committed by Marshal Tallard and Max Emanuel. Those generals had crossed to the left bank on the 10th, and had resolved to attack Eugene before he should be reinforced. But learning that Hochstadt was but weakly occupied, they directed their first attack on that place. As they approached it—the morning of the 12th—their attention was attracted by the dust caused by a considerable cavalcade. This consisted of Eugene and Marlborough, who, accompanied by two thousand cavalry, had ridden to the front to reconnoitre. It was the first intimation the enemy received that the junction had been effected.

The enemy took Hochstadt the same day, and, advancing, occupied a position behind the Nebelbach. Tallard, who commanded the right, held the village of Blindheim or Blenheim, almost touching the Danube. Marchin, who commanded on the left, rested on Lutzingen and the slopes of the Goldberg. Max Emanuel, with the cavalry of his guard, occupied Sondernheim, a short distance in rear of Blenheim.

Marlborough and Eugene, meanwhile, had arrayed their army on the ground close to the spot where the junction had been effected. Marlborough placed the left wing, which constituted two-thirds of the entire strength, and which he commanded in person, close to Munster, the left, commanded by Eugene, occupied Oppertshofen, the touching point was the village of Bragstetten.

The reconnaissance made by the two allied commanders, and which they had conducted, we have seen, as far as Hochstadt, had given them a very fair idea of the nature of the ground between them and the enemy. They had noticed that to the south-west from Donauworth, along the left bank of the Danube, there extended a plain, which, covered by wooded hills to the north, sloped imperceptibly towards the river, that this plain was intersected by many rivulets, ditches, and water-courses, and was in many places marshy, covered with coarse reeds and grasses; that on the other hand, it bore on its surface some villages, and many isolated houses and mills. They judged that its greatest breadth—that, for instance, between Lutzingen and Blenheim—was about four and a half English miles; whilst at its narrowest part, that about Schweningen and Tappheim, the wooded hills were not more than two thousand paces from the river. They noticed that between the two positions the Danube made many turnings; that it was dotted with islands and sandbanks; that many brooklets ran into it; and that its banks were in many parts covered with bushes.

It had been the intention of the two generals, when they returned from their reconnaissance, to advance on Hochstadt. But ascending, the same afternoon, the church tower of Tappheim, they beheld the masses of the enemy taking up the position I have described behind the Nebelbach. They resolved, then, to lose no time in attacking them before they should have time to strengthen their position. They at once despatched fatigue-parties to the front to fill up as much as possible the inequalities of ground there existing, and made every preparation for an advance on the morrow.

At 2 o'clock on the morning of the 13th the allied troops were silently awakened and ordered to fall in. The men, drawn up in the order in which they were to advance, stood impatiently awaiting the signal for their forward movement. They numbered fifty-two thousand men with sixty-six guns, and they were composed of the contingents of many sovereigns. Germany was not then a nation, and the troops from Prussia, from Hanover, from Hesse, from the Palatinate, and from Würtemberg, were virtually foreigners to each other. Besides these, there were Danes, Dutch, and, last but not least, the stalwart sons of the British Isles.

The French and Bavarians mustered fifty-six thousand men with ninety guns. Of these, fourteen thousand were Bavarians. In point of leadership they were inferior to their enemies, for whilst Marlborough and Eugene were united by ties of mutual respect, and Eugene had, for the common good, resigned the supreme control to Marlborough, Tallard, Marchin, and Max Emanuel each exercised a separate control. This was a disadvantage which was far from being counterbalanced by the small numerical superiority of the Franco-Bavarians.

At 3 o'clock in the morning Marlborough gave the signal to advance. Eugene's corps, which consisted of nearly eighteen thousand men, was ranged in four divisions two of infantry and the like number of cavalry. The infantry led, then came the guns, the cavalry brought up the rear. The left wing, composed of nine thousand English, nine thousand five hundred Dutch, nine thousand five hundred Hanoverians, four thousand five hundred Hessians, and fifteen hundred Danes, marched in similar order.

A thick mist covered the plain. No sound from the enemy's camp reached the ears of the advancing soldiers. They pushed on till, at 6 o'clock, they reached the ground about Schweningen. Here they halted whilst Marlborough and Eugene rode forward to reconnoitre. But the mist was still dense, and nothing was to be seen. Again, then, the troops pushed on until, at 7 o'clock, the advance-guard gained the high ground near Wolperstetten. Here the mist suddenly lifted, and the enemy's position, stretching from Blenheim to the woods between Lutzingen, and covered in front by the Nebelbach, burst upon the view. It seemed very formidable.

The village of Blenheim, its right covered by the Danube, was evidently strongly occupied. In front of it, on the Nebelbach, were many mills and detached buildings, all, apparently, held by troops. Nor did the centre seem to offer a better chance of attack. There the village of Oberglauheim, its front covered by a marsh—the made paths across which were strongly guarded—commanded in its rear by batteries placed on the hillocks using above its level, and linked on its left to the troops commanded by Marchin and Max Emanuel, presented a very formidable appearance. The extreme left rested on the wooded heights and the village of Eichberg. There seemed to be but one weak spot in the position, and that was between Blenheim and Oberglauheim. The distance between the two villages was considerable, and the ground was apparently weakly held. But the weakness, covered as the ground was by a line of cavalry, did not, at the moment, attract the observation of Marlborough.

The generals of the enemy's army were not at all expecting an attack. The sound of the reveille had indeed reached the ears of Tallard, but he believed it announced a retreat in the direction of Nordlingen. Not till the mist had cleared away and the morning light displayed to his astonished gaze the allied army marching in battle array to the attack, did the deception vanish. Then, for a few minutes, all was confusion. The trumpets and bugles sounded to arms. Three cannon-shots recalled to the ranks the forage parties started, or about to start, on their daily errand. There was the rush to arms, the hurry to take up the appointed position. It is on such occasions that the French soldier is seen to advantage. His natural intelligence was not wanting on this eventful morning; and, before the allies could approach sufficiently near to fire a shot, their opponents were ready to receive them.

Tallard regarded Blenheim as the key of the position. To secure it absolutely he had concentrated in it sixteen thousand of his best troops. But in his eagerness to secure Blenheim he had weakened the thin line which connected him with Oberglauheim, and had thus given a chance to an adventurous enemy to cut him off from that place. The small space between Blenheim and the Danube he had secured by filling it up with a barricade of wagons, guarded by four regiments of dismounted dragoons. The front of Blenheim was protected by palisades and abattis.

To the left of that village, following the course of the Nebelbach, but drawn back a little distance from its swampy bank, was ranged the French cavalry of the right wing, five thousand five hundred strong, supported in the centre by two weak infantry brigades, numbering five thousand four hundred. Baron Zurlauben, who commanded this line, had received instructions to allow the enemy to cross the brook unopposed, that he might crush them the more completely on his own side of it.

The left of his long line of cavalry nearly touched Oberglauheim. This village was defended by the Marquis de Blainville with seven thousand men. It and the village of Lutzingen, further to the left, formed the pivots of the left wing, which likewise stretched further to the left front and occupied the ground as far as Eichberg. These three villages were connected by bridges with the country which the allies were traversing.

Marlborough had not, I have said, detected at the moment, the weak spot in the French line between Blenheim and Oberglauheim. He believed, with Tallard, that Blenheim was the key of the French position, and he had arranged that whilst Eugene should operate against the enemy's left, he should hurl his masses against that village.

At 9 o'clock, the English column of attack, composed of five English and one Hessian battalion under General Rowe, supported by eleven battalions and fifteen squadrons led by Lord Cutts, who commanded the column, advanced against Blenheim. Under a very heavy fire directed from that village, Rowe stormed two detached mills in its front, and then dashed against the palisade. The French infantry behind them reserved their fire until the assailants were well within distance, and then delivered a volley with murderous effect, following it up with an increasing file fire. Still the English pressed on, striving to reach the palisades. They reached, but could not force them.

Vainly did the men, seizing them with their hands, endeavour to tear them from the earth or to break them down. They resisted all their efforts, whilst the steady fire of the French infantry diminished every moment the numbers of the assailants. Still the remnant clung on, their leader badly wounded, the two next senior officers killed, hoping that their pertinacity would ultimately prevail. Just then a charge of the French cavalry on their flank threw them into disorder for a moment they lost their colours and though an opportune charge of the fifteen squadrons in reserve enabled them to recover these, yet the chance was gone, and they fell back, beaten and baffled, threatened by larger masses of hostile cavalry, to their original position.

The failure of this attack convinced Marlborough that the enemy's right was secure against assault. Reports from his own right satisfied him that Eugene was about to absorb the attention of the enemy's left centre and left. He resolved then to make his second attack on the thin line which guarded the long stretch between Blenheim and Oberglauheim. He was convinced that by piercing the enemy's line there he should have the enemy's line there he should have the two wings at his mercy.

As a preliminary to this attack he detached an infantry division commanded by Lord Churchill to drive the enemy from Unter-glauheim, a small village between Blenheim and Oberglauheim, on the centre of a bend made by the Nebelbach towards the English position. Before, however, Churchill could reach it, the French set fire to it and fell back. This incident did not much retard the advance. The English pressed forward as best they could, crossed the Nebelbach by the bridge, and re-formed on the other side. They were followed by the Hanoverians, commanded by the Prince of Holstein-Beck, who had orders to attack Oberglauheim. As soon as these troops had crossed, Marlborough ordered his cavalry to advance across the rivulet. The difficulties they encountered in carrying out this order were very great, for the rivulet divided itself, in many places, into channels, and the banks as well as the beds were soft and marshy.

It was only by great exertions, by casting into the stream fascines and boards, that the horses were able to struggle through. Even then they reached the opposite bank in twos and threes, without order or arrangement, thus offering a splendid chance to the enemy to deal with them in detail. But Tallard, though he directed a continuous fire from the somewhat too distant Blenheim, neglected this great opportunity. He thought himself, as I shall now proceed to describe, too sure of victory.

Tallard, in fact, wishing to destroy rather than to repulse, purposely waited till the whole of Marlborough's cavalry—the Danish and Hanoverian squadrons excepted—should have crossed the Nebelbach. Then, whilst they were struggling to re-form, he directed against them an attack of the entire French cavalry at his disposal. That charge had nearly decided the day. The French horsemen overthrew the struggling line of Marlborough's cavalry, and forced their left wing more and more under the fire of Blenheim. Their defeat seemed absolutely certain, when Lord Churchill wheeled his infantry to the left, and from the whole of his line poured in a musketry fire so severe that the French relinquished their grasp on the cavalry to turn to this new enemy. Marlborough utilised the respite thus gained to bring across the Hanoverian and Danish squadrons. Just then the French cavalry, recovering, renewed the attack, once more threw the allied cavalry into disorder, and were again prevented from annihilating them solely by the musketry fire of another division of infantry, which had crossed the bridge in support of Churchill. Marlborough took advantage of the momentary cessation of the attack to form his cavalry in solid order on the right bank of the rivulet.

Scarcely had he done so when information reached him that the Prince of Holstein-Beck, whom he had ordered to attack Oberglauheim, had been attacked by Blainville with the entire garrison of that village defeated, and taken prisoner. Marlborough felt that the enemy's advantage, if followed up, could not but prove most dangerous to him, for a rent had been made in the very centre of his army, which, unless closed up, would be fatal.

For a moment it seemed as though the French were about to improve their advantage to the utmost; for Marchin, though engaged with Eugene in the manner presently to be described, directed some squadrons to gallop to the spot and aid Blainville as he might direct. But Marlborough had been too quick for the French marshal. As soon as he heard that the Hanoverians were beaten he put himself at the head of Bernstorff's brigade, four thousand strong, and led it towards Oberglauheim. Blainville had not yet received the cavalry sent by Marchin, and, content with his success, was falling back into Oberglauheim.

Marlborough had just reached the scene of the Hanoverian defeat when Marchin's cavalry galloped up. Marlborough formed up his men to resist them, and, seeing that the fate of the day depended upon the ability of Bernstorff's brigade to resist the attack till he should obtain assistance, directed an officer to gallop at full speed to Eugene to beg him for instant aid in cavalry. I propose now to turn to the right wing and ascertain the position in which Eugene found himself when this messenger reached him.

The difficulties which Eugene had had to encounter before he could reach his enemy were greater than those which had hindered the progress of his English colleague. Numerous tributary streams, running from the high ground covered with bushes, and in many places, sticky and marshy, prevented a direct advance. Forced, then, to give his flank to the enemy, he had reached, coming every moment more under their fire, only at 11 o'clock, a position whence he could attack. The line of the enemy was supported in its centre by Lutzingen, well in the rear, and on the left by Eichberg. Resting as its right did upon Oberglauheim, it was so long, that to assail it with any chance of success Eugene was forced to bring all his reserves into line. Noon, then, arrived before he was ready to begin.

The task before him was no light one. He had under him seven thousand four hundred Prussians and five thousand Danish infantry and five thousand cavalry. Opposed to him, in a strong position, were the troops of Marchin and Max Emanuel, numbering sixteen thousand infantry and ten thousand cavalry. Having formed his troops in order of attack, Eugene waited until two batteries should have taken a commanding position he had assigned to them. Then, under the fire of these, he despatched the Prussians to attack the central position of Lutzingen, and the Danes to force the extreme left at Eichberg. These attacks succeeded. The length of the enemy's line made Eugene superior for the moment at both points of attack.

The enemy's front line was driven back, the batteries in front of Lutzingen were stormed; the French were forced to evacuate Eichberg. To improve these advantages Eugene then ordered a charge of cavalry. But here he was not so successful. The front line of the French did indeed fall back upon its supports. But it was only to entice the Germans. The device succeeded. Assailed in front and on both flanks by superior numbers, the Imperial cavalry were driven across the rivulet. Under cover of this success Max Emanuel regained the lost batteries in front of Lutzingen.

It was at this moment, when fortune seemed to frown upon him, that the messenger from Marlborough asking for cavalry reinforcements reached Eugene. With a chivalrous devotion which stamps him as a great man as well as a great soldier, Eugene promptly despatched his best squadrons, led by Count Fugger, at full gallop to the aid of his colleague. Then, confident that he could best assist him by keeping the enemy in front of him fully occupied, he launched against him a second attack. This, too, after one glimpse of success, shattered before the greatly superior numbers of the enemy. Realising, then, that unless he were reinforced he could not force the hostile position, and noting that Marlborough had restored the battle on his side, Eugene despatched to him, in his turn, an orderly officer urgently demanding aid.

Whilst the officer was speeding on his errand, Eugene re-formed his men, and went through the ranks, speaking to them words of encouragement. Then, before the expected reinforcements could arrive, impatient of delay, he directed a third attack. Leopold of Anhalt-Dessau formed his Prussians on the slopes of the wooded heights to attack the left flank of the Franco-Bavarian array, whilst the cavalry received orders to divert their attention by a front attack. But again, did the superior numbers of the enemy baffle Eugene. Before the Prussians could make their attack felt, Max Emanuel, concentrating his horsemen, charged upon and drove back the Imperial cavalry. Vainly did Eugene try to rally them. They were so panic-stricken that, though Eugene shot two of the fugitives, they were not to be turned.

Leaving, then, to their own officers the care of rallying them, Eugene dashed to the Prussian infantry. He found them steady, unshaken, their faces to the foe, ready to obey his orders. Without a moment's delay he dashed them furiously against the left flank of the enemy, who, on that extreme point, were Bavarians. The shock was terrific. The best soldiers of North Germany were pitted against the experienced veterans of the South. Feeling that everything depended on the result, Eugene fought in the front ranks like a common soldier. His example was electric. Every man felt that he must do or die. The Imperial commander almost paid with his own life the forfeit of his daring. But his daring triumphed. With stupendous efforts he at length forced back the enemy. Had his cavalry been at hand he could then and there have completed his success, but, as it was, with only two squadrons at his disposal, he was forced to be content with establishing himself firmly on the edge of the wood beyond Eichberg.

That position, however, would have been full of danger had Marchin and Max Emanuel been able to concentrate against him all their resources. But the splendid efforts of Marlborough, in the interval, against the French right and centre had so shaken them that they were forced to concentrate all their energies against him. We left Marlborough threatened by Marchin's cavalry, whilst, at the head of Bernstorff's brigade, he was endeavouring to repair the mischief occasioned by the defeat of the Hanoverians, and despatching a messenger to Eugene for aid. We have seen how Eugene replied by sending to him at full gallop the Imperial *cuirassiers* led by Count Fugger. Fugger arrived in time to throw himself on the flank of the French horsemen just as they were pressing Bernstorff's men very hard. This opportune charge enabled the latter to hold their ground till the arrival of fresh squadrons and of a battery from the left gave Marlborough the strength he required to establish his position.

The English general now felt himself able to make a supreme bid for victory. Of the French Army the bulk of the infantry was shut up in Blenheim, the greater part of the remainder was in, and on the left of, Oberglauheim; he himself stood, with his whole army, on the ground beyond the Nebelbach, facing the weakest part of the enemy's position, that between Blenheim and Oberglauheim, defended by his cavalry and two weak brigades of infantry. Could he pierce that line the battle would be assuredly gained, for the enemy's right would be cut off from his centre.

Full of hope that he could do so, Marlborough drew up the infantry he had in hand, composed mainly of Danes, Hessians, and the rallied Hanoverians, and led them, supported in the centre by his guns, and on his flanks by the cavalry in two lines, up the gentle slope on the summit of which stood the two brigades I have referred to. These brigades, those of Robuq and Albaret, were formed in good order, their guns in the centre, their cavalry likewise, on their flanks. As the allies advanced, the French poured upon them a fire of artillery and musketry so hot that the Hessians and their comrades recoiled, and fell back some sixty paces. Then offered the last and greatest opportunity for the sons of France! Tallard saw it. "I saw," he wrote in his despatch, "an instant in which the battle was gained by the brigades of Robuq and Albaret, if"—if his cavalry had done their duty!

For a moment, indeed, it seemed as though that duty would be gallantly performed. The French cavalry, encouraged by the recoil of the allied infantry, advanced with the apparent intention of securing victory by a charge. Had they charged boldly who can say what might have been the result? But, tired as they were, the firm attitude of the English horsemen, who, far from awaiting, rode forward to meet them, dissipated their courage, they shrank from the shock, and, turning rein, rode to the rear, leaving the gallant infantry to their fate. Vain were the efforts of Tallard to rally them. Single files, even single squadrons, here and there, responded to his call, but the mass were not to be reformed. Marlborough used the propitious moment to send his cavalry over the crest of the ridge. The abandoned infantry made a noble resistance. But they were overpowered, and the men were, for the most part, cut down where they stood. Then was Marlborough undisputed master of the ground between the two villages.

Tallard saw that the battle was lost, but he might yet, he hoped, save the infantry shut up in Blenheim. Hoping to delay the advance of the victorious enemy against that village, he vainly endeavoured once again to rally his cavalry. Failing in that, he sent to Marchin for aid. But Marchin was, as we shall see, too much occupied by Eugene to respond favourably. Then he despatched the older to the Marquis of Clérembault, who commanded there, to evacuate Blenheim, and fall back on Sondernheim. Unfortunately, his messenger was taken prisoner, and when Tallard, disturbed at seeing no sign in the direction of Blenheim, whilst Marlborough was hurrying to attack it, rode thither to carry his own order, his short-sightedness carried him into the midst of the allied cavalry, and he, too, was captured.

We left Eugene having established his position on the edge of the wood beyond Eichberg. The position, I have pointed out, would have been full of danger if Max Emmanuel and Marchin had been able to mass their forces against him. But by this time the fierce onslaught of Marlborough on the centre had made itself felt all along the Franco-Bavarian line, and the two commanders, recognising the danger of their own position if Marlborough should succeed in establishing himself upon their right whilst Eugene was attacking their front and left, had now no other thought but to draw off their men.

To check the advance of Eugene, they set fire to the hamlets and isolated houses on the rivulet, and, drawing to them all their troops, began a movement in three columns in the direction of Mörshlingen. Max Emanuel, brave as a lion, commanded the rear-guard in person, and displayed so much skill and conduct as to effectually baffle the pursuers. He was much aided by the circumstance that for a long time Eugene could dispose, in cavalry, only of two squadrons. When, at last, the bulk of his horsemen, aided by some squadrons sent by Marlborough, joined him. Max Emanuel had occupied a position behind the Brunnenbach strong enough to resist attack.

The field was now cleared of the enemy. The last two French bat-

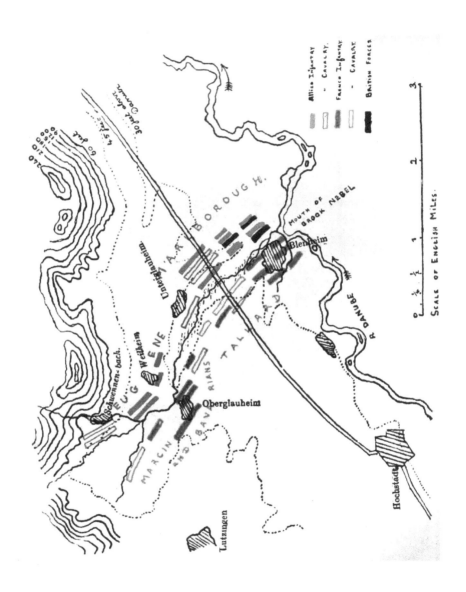

Allies Infantry
" - Cavalry.
French Infantry
" - Cavalry.
British Forces

SCALE OF ENGLISH MILES.

0 ¼ ½ ¾ 1   2   3

240
210
180
150
120
90
60 feet.

4.5 feet
slope of Conway.
slope of.

MARLBOROUGH.

MOUTH OF
BROOK NEBEL

Blenheim

R. DANUBE

Unterglauheim

Z
E
U
G
E
N
E

Weilheim

Schwennen-bach.

TALLARD.

MARCIN

AND BAVARIANS

Oberglauheim

Hochstadt

Lutzingen

talions which had maintained the fight had just laid down their arms to General Hompesch. Blenheim alone remained in their hands and Blenheim, uncovered. was now exposed to the assault of all the troops of Marlborough.

Up to this time the Marquis of Clérembault had been content to maintain his position at Blenheim, which he had made very strong. But as he noticed the later events of the battle, the flight of the French cavalry, the overthrow of the two brigades, his heart sank within him, and, seeing that all was over, he resolved to leave his troops to their fate and escape. With this object he spurred his horse to the Danube, and attempted to swim to the further bank. But fortune would not aid the man who had barely abandoned his own soldiers. His horse sank, and he was drowned. Count Blansac, who succeeded him, was, likewise a man incapable of forming a plan or accepting responsibility. He might yet, by a timely retreat, have saved to France a considerable portion of the garrison. But, left without orders—for Tallard and his messenger had both been captured—he preferred to accept his fate rather than act for himself. Thus, it was that when Lord Cutts and his division again attacked Blenheim, it was as firmly held as on the first occasion.

But this time the morale strength was with the assailants. The French knew that they were doomed. They nevertheless defended with intrepidity the outer works, and even twice repulsed the assailants. At length Cutts carried the churchyard—the strongest of those defences. Even then the defenders for a long time refused to hear of surrender, and it was only when a herald from without informed Blansac that Marlborough had ranged in front of the village forty battalions and sixty guns, that he had more battalions in reserve, that the place was no longer defensible, that the rest of Tallard's army, and the armies of Marchin and Max Emanuel were in full flight, that the French commander unwillingly gave the order to lay down arms. The greater part of the French soldiers obeyed in angry despair, but the men of the regiment of Navarre, a regiment grown grey in victory, displayed their deep mortification by burning their colours and destroying their muskets!

All was now over. The armies of Marchin and of Max Emanuel had been defeated; that of Tallard had been annihilated. Whilst the loss of the victors in killed and wounded reached twelve thousand men, that of the French and Bavarians exceeded fourteen thousand. In addition, the latter lost thirteen thousand men taken prisoners, fifty-seven pieces of cannon, twenty-five standards, and ninety colours.

First Foot Guards at Blenheim

Such was the Battle of Blenheim. It was one of the decisive battles of history, and it changed the character of the war. Up to that moment, the action of France against Germany had been aggressive, thenceforward it became purely defensive. Blenheim, in fact, dashed to the ground the hopes of Louis XIV and Max Emanuel of Bavaria. It saved the House of Habsburg in Germany, and helped it greatly in Hungary. It showed likewise that it was possible to inflict a crushing defeat on the armies of Louis XIV. In bringing out such results, Eugene had borne a great part. His dash across the Rhine to join the allied army, his perfect understanding with Marlborough, his forgetfulness of self on every occasion, had combined with his skill as a commander to render the efficient aid without which Blenheim could not have been fought.

The victory having been gained, it devolved upon the allied commanders to make it fruitful. But there ensued a delay for which it is difficult to account. The day after the battle they made a short march to Wittislingen, and then halted for four days between that village and Steinheim. These four days might have been better employed than in giving repose to the army. Had they only pressed on, Landau must have fallen, and the seat of war been transferred at once to French territory. Other counsels, however, prevailed. On the 19th August, six days after the battle, the army reached Guldenfingen, seven miles from where it was fought. It proceeded thence, in two marches, to Ulm— and there the two commanders remained nine days, till 30th August, in consultation. They had, in the interval, been joined by the Margrave Louis of Baden, who had been ordered from Vienna to raise the siege of Ingolstadt.

At Ulm the three commanders arranged to despatch their troops in five columns to the Rhine, to lay siege to Landau, and then to invade France. Eugene, for his part, hastened as quickly as possible to Rottweil, to take in hand, first the troops left there, and then those he had left in the lines of Stollhofen, so as to make head against Villeroi should he attempt to break into Würtemberg. Whilst he is travelling thither, I must glance for a moment at the movements of Marchin and Max Emanuel, and of Villeroi.

The armies of the two former had, on their defeat by Eugene, retreated with all haste on Ulm. A discussion took place here between the two commanders, Max Emanuel wishing to halt there and call up to them the army of Villeroi, Marchin insisting that it was necessary to join Villeroi on the Rhine. The views of Marchin prevailed, and Max Emanuel, refusing an offer made to him by Marlborough and

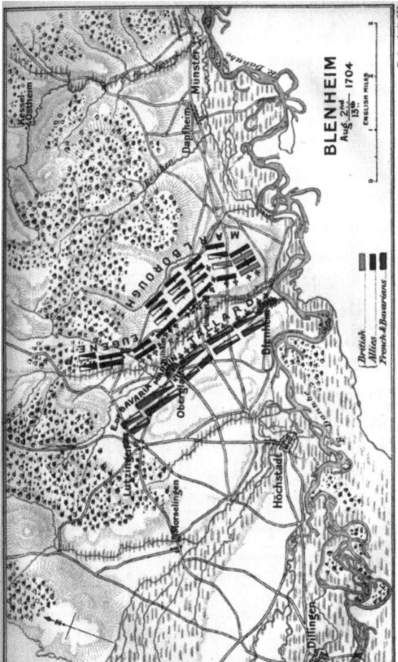

BLENHEIM
Aug 2nd 1704
13th

ENGLISH MILES

British
Allies
French & Bavarians

Kessel-Ostheim

R. Reichen

Dapfheim Munster

R. Danube

MARLBOROUGH

EUGENE

TALLARD

BAVARIA MARSIN

Oberglau

Blenheim

Lutzingen

Morselingen

Höchstadt

Dillingen

Eugene—to secure him in possession of his dominions, to obtain for him from England and Holland a subsidy of four hundred thousand crowns if he would join the alliance against France and put eight thousand men into the field—made over to his wife, a daughter of John Sobieski, the care of his dominions, and marched, in company with Marchin, to the Rhine. On the 25th August they effected a junction with Villeroi at Hüfingen, not far from Donaueschingen.

Villeroi had been despatched by his master to the Rhine, to keep in check Eugene. We have seen how Eugene, leaving half his army in the lines of Stollhofen, had eluded the vigilance of that commander. So little diligence, indeed had Villeroi used, that he only learned of Eugene's departure on the morning of the day on which Blenheim was fought. Then he bestirred himself to range his army to attack the troops left to defend the lines. But, before he was ready, the news of the defeat on the Danube reached him. Feeling it, then, his duty to lend a hand to the beaten armies, he marched with all haste into the duchy of Baden, and effected the junction, as we have seen, at Hüfingen.

The three united armies then marched, under the direction of Villeroi, to Kehl. They crossed the Rhine the 2nd September. Max Emanuel then left them, with his household troops, for Brussels, to take up there the post confided to him by the influence of Louis XIV., of Stadtholder of the Spanish Netherlands! The same day Eugene, who had taken Rottweil on his way, arrived at Philipsburg, and began to throw bridges across the Rhine.

The bridges were ready on the 6th, and the same day Eugene moved to the left bank the troops he had left at Stollhofen. The same day he was joined by Marlborough, and two days later by the Margrave. Louis Villeroi, meanwhile, had occupied a very advantageous position behind the Queich, whence he was able to cover Landau. From this position the allies resolved to drive him. Villeroi, however, did not wait their attack, but fell back behind the Hotter. Margrave Louis then, the 10th September, laid siege to Landau, Marlborough and Eugene covering the siege. As Landau was defended by one of the best officers in the French Army, Count Laubanie, and the siege threatened to be of long duration, it was, a few days later, agreed upon between Marlborough and Eugene that, with the view to carry the war into France on her weakest side as soon as possible, Eugene should remain to cover the siege whilst Marlborough should capture the strong posts on the line of the Moselle.

Left with but an inconsiderable army, Eugene could not think of attacking Villeroi, who had fallen back behind the entrenched lines, extending from Drusenheim ("the home of Drusus") on the Rhine, to Chateau Lichtenberg in the Vosges. He ventured, however, repeatedly to alarm him, and, under cover of his movements, formed a plan for the surprise of the fortress of Alt Breisach. The plan, ingeniously conceived, failed through the stupidity of one of the soldiers of the party, who prematurely gave the alarm. This failure was compensated for by the surrender of Landau after a siege of seventy days. On the 26 November Count Laubanie and his garrison marched out with all the honours of war and returned to France. The defence is one of the most famous defences known in history. "There is true glory in conquering such enemies," said to Count Laubanie—who had been blinded by the bursting at his feet of a bombshell—the King of Rome, afterwards Emperor Joseph I, who had joined the besieging army. On his arrival at Paris Laubanie was presented to the king by the Duke of Burgundy with the words "Sire, here is a poor, blind man, who has need of a staff (*bâton*)" meaning the *bâton* of a marshal. Louis XIV was silent. The silence of his sovereign produced a result which the enemies of France would never have been able to accomplish it broke the old man's heart.

With the capture of Landau, the campaign on the Rhine ended Marlborough had in the meanwhile taken Trier, and the Crown Prince of Hesse-Cassel Trarbach. The armies on both sides then went into winter quarters. For Bavaria the fight of Blenheim had been fatal. On the 11th November the diplomatic agents of the Emperor signed at Ildesheim a treaty with the Electress, whereby all the fortresses and military establishments in the Electorate, with the exception of a guard of four hundred men, were made over to the Emperor, who was likewise to receive the entire revenues, with the exception of those derived from Munich, Ingolstadt, Rain, and Kempten, which were reserved for the Electress. The Emperor nominated Eugene as his administrator to carry out this convention.

The task was a difficult one, for the convention wounded the pride of the Bavarians. At Ingolstadt, where the garrison numbered twelve thousand men, the tumult was so great that the commissioners fled in dismay. Ingolstadt, often besieged, had never been taken, and the garrison, resolved that it should not be surrendered, resisted even the solicitations of the Empress. At last Eugene was forced to march towards it with thirty-five battalions and seventy-three squadrons. Halting at Grossmöhring, he sent a message to Ingolstadt giving the garrison twenty-four hours in which to make up their minds. This message, supported by the loyal Electress, produced its effect, and on 7th December Ingolstadt was evacuated. The other strong places followed its example, and the bulk of the Bavarian soldiers joined the army of Eugene. Having laid down stringent rules for the protection of the life, the property, and the industries of the inhabitants, having, in fact, secured to them the same rights as those of the other peoples of the empire, having seen that confidence was everywhere restored, and finally, having indicated Count Wratislau as the fittest man upon whom to bestow the administration of the country, Eugene returned to Vienna to receive the thanks of the Emperor for his great services, and to plan new combinations for the year which had already opened.

CHAPTER 7

Cassano

Eugene found the Emperor Leopold sickly, undecided, and disheartened. Affairs had not prospered in Hungary. Never had the audacity of the rebels been so marked, or their ravages on the Austrian lands so unpunished as in the year 1704. On the 28th May they had beaten and taken prisoner, at Schmölenitz, the Imperial general von Riczan, and from that time Vienna itself had not been safe from their attacks. In fact, on the 9th June Count Karolyi had appeared with four thousand men before its walls and had caused the greatest alarm. It is true that Karolyi did not attack the city itself, but, to cause annoyance to the Emperor, he destroyed the new building outside the walls which contained the Imperial menagerie, and killed all the animals. Amongst these were two tame hunting-leopards, a present from the *Sultan*, upon which Leopold placed great store.

Enraged at this insult, the Emperor had sent Count Heister, a hard, even a cruel man, with all the troops he could spare, to repress the Hungarians. Eugene had earnestly advised Leopold not to entrust such a mission to a man so merciless and so little capable as Heister, but Leopold had not listened to him. Heister was sent, and, careless of maintaining his communications with Vienna marched into the depth of Hungary. Fortunately for him he met and defeated the rebels at Raab. Instead, however, of pushing his success, he returned at once to Altenburg to await there reinforcements, which were not forthcoming. Satisfied that he would receive none, Heister marched without plan into Hungary, devastating the country, plundering the people, and thus diminishing the adherents of the Emperor.

Whilst he was at Stuhlweissenberg, Hungarian partisans appeared in the Marchfeld, and again threatened Vienna. Vain were the efforts made to restore peace. Heister subsequently came to Vienna and submitted plans, of which Eugene—to whom they were sent—approved. Sent, against the expressed opinion of Eugene, to carry these out, Heister again defeated the insurgents, 26th December, this time at Tyrnau. Again, he neglected to profit by his victory. Count Rabutin had long successfully held Transylvania for the Emperor, but the time had now come when he, beset by the rebels, was cut off and in danger, and, at the close of the year, great preparations were being made to relieve him.

Nor had matters gone much better in Italy. There, after the departure of Eugene, two corps had been formed, one under Starhemberg acting with the Duke of Savoy in Piedmont, the other, under Trauttmansdorff, posted in reserve at Revere and Ostiglia. As Trauttmansdorff refused, from jealousy, to obey the orders of Starhemberg, the command was taken from him and conferred upon the young Prince Vaudemont, with whom the reader is acquainted. Unfortunately, Vaudemont died of fever at Ostiglia on the 12th May. The command was then offered to Count Leopold Herberstein, but on his modest refusal of it, it was given to Count Leiningen, who proved an utter failure.

In the campaign which followed, Vendôme proved more than a match for the combined forces of the Duke of Savoy and Starhemberg. He captured, in succession, the strong places of the country. Crescentino, and Susa surrendered to him after a faint resistance. The defence of Ivrea was more prolonged, but in the end, he captured Ivrea, and then laid siege to Verrua, twenty-three miles east-northeast of Turin. He continued this siege all the winter. Its preservation was of the greatest importance to the Duke of Savoy, for were Verrua to be taken, Turin alone would remain to him of all the cities in his dominions.

Such was the condition of affairs in Italy when Eugene returned to Vienna from his successful campaign. Where he had commanded, there had success been achieved. Evidently, he was the man to be despatched where the danger was the greatest. Should it be to Hungary or to Italy? The consideration that the further progress of the French in the latter country would probably induce the Duke of Savoy to re-purchase his territories by an alliance with them, induced the Emperor to decide in favour of sending Eugene to Italy.

Before he had been commissioned to proceed thither the news arrived (16th April) that Verrua had fallen (9th April). The following day Eugene set out and reached Roveredo the 23rd. He found his troops in a most deplorable condition. He was anxious to relieve Mirandola, then invested by the enemy, he wrote:

To do this, with my starved and half-naked soldiers, without a *kreutzer*, without tents, without bread, without carriage, seems to me an impossibility.

Under circumstances such as these the campaign commenced. Arrived at Roveredo the 23rd April to find his army in a deplorable condition, Eugene had, in the first week of May, led it by Pescantina over the Adige, and had endeavoured to cross the Mincio at the point where he had made the passage four years before. But the enemy was on his guard. Endeavouring, then (11th May) to bridge the river at Salionze, he was baffled by the superior fire of the French guns. He then worked his troops back with the view of uniting them to the army-corps posted at Gavardo. The cavalry went round the lake of Garda by land, whilst the infantry marched along its eastern face as far as San Vigilio, embarked there, reached Salo the 18th May, and Gavardo three days later. At that place the army gradually reunited, and in the meanwhile Eugene threw up entrenchments to make his position impregnable. It was whilst engaged in these operations that Eugene received news (14th May) of the death of the Emperor on the 5th. The next day brought him information that Mirandola had fallen.

Vendôme, meanwhile, had joined the French Army. He had promised his sovereign that he would make short work of Eugene. All material things combined to promise him success. To use the expression of the English Minister, Hill:

He had possession of the cities, the passes, and the rivers; on the other side lay the superiority in genius.

On the 23rd May, Vendôme marched in two columns against Gavardo. Riding in front to reconnoitre, he saw the greater part of the allied infantry strongly entrenched, their cavalry, weak in number, drawn up in battle array between the entrenchment and some hills which lay behind it, likewise held by the infantry. Behind the position was a steep and unassailable wall of rock.

Recognising at once that the position was too strong to be attacked, Vendôme sought, then, how to post himself so as to hem in his enemy and cut him off from Lombardy. Under a heavy fire of artillery, he encamped his army about a cannon-shot from Eugene's position, his right resting on a hill very difficult of approach, his left on the Chiese. Here he entrenched himself, and then hurried back to Piedmont to superintend the siege of Chivasso; begging his brother, the Grand Prior of Vendôme, whom he left in command, to keep a careful watch on Eugene, and should he, as he hoped but did not think he would, move towards the Oglio, to follow him along the Naviglio as far as Brescia.

The grand prior did not possess sufficient patience to carry out literally these instructions. Irritated by the persistently quiescent attitude maintained by Eugene, he marched the 31st May, with four companies of grenadiers, took up a commanding position between Goglione and Garvardo, not far from the stone bridge over the Naviglio, and thus became master of the road leading from Gavardo to the plains of Lombardy.

Eugene saw at a glance the importance of this position. On the night of the 31st May, then, he despatched Alexander of Würtemberg, with 2,500 men, to drive the enemy from it. But the fierce resistance of the French gave their leader time to bring up reinforcements, and the attack was repulsed. The grand prior, more than ever satisfied of the importance of the position, caused it to be much more strongly occupied, and to be coveted with entrenchments.

Eugene was resolved to gain the plains of Lombardy. Seeing himself blocked up on the one side, he proceeded quietly to arrange so as to reach Brescia by the other. He waited only till the troops promised from the Palatinate should join him. Then, the evening of the 21st June, leaving a few men behind as a blind, he suddenly evacuated his entrenched position with the remainder about twenty-five thousand in number, and fell back on Sopraponte, whence a mountain-path led in a westerly direction to Nave, five miles to the north-east of Brescia.

Whilst he was making his hurried march, the men left behind as a blind under the direction of a Colonel Zumjungen, did their duty to perfection. Wooden cannon had been placed in the part of the position which lay under the eyes of the French. Sentries were relieved, watch-fires burned, at break of day the bugles sounded. Suspicion only began to be aroused when, about 10 o'clock, the French guns opened fire and the fire was not returned. Still, fearing a stratagem, the French did not dare to approach sufficiently near to convince themselves. It was only at mid-day that the truth was discovered.

The movements of the French Army showed then very plainly that the great Vendôme did not command them. Instead of following his brother's directions and hurrying along the Naviglio to Brescia, there to bar the way to Eugene, the grand prior followed the course of Chiese northwards as far as Montechiaro. Before he could reach that place Eugene, unpursued, had gained the plains near Brescia and was in full march towards the Oglio. The evening of the 27th June he arrived on the left bank of that river, close to Urago. Without a moment's delay he placed his artillery on the heights of that name, to disperse a small party of Spanish troops who occupied Calcio on the opposite bank, embarked a detachment of grenadiers in boats whilst the cavalry regiments Savoy and Herbeville crossed the river at the swim. In attempting this feat, they lost their commander, Count Szerenyi, and six dragoons who had tried to save him, but they accomplished it. At the same moment Eugene ordered his engineers to commence at once the construction of a bridge.

At break of day the bridge was ready and the infantry began to cross. The passage of the river was completed before night. Eugene, meanwhile, had made prisoners of the Spanish detachment, and had fixed his camp at Calcio. He had completely outwitted the Grand Prior, who, on the discovery of the fact, had marched with more haste than in good order to the Oglio, had crossed that river near Orzinovi, and had taken up his post at Soncino, due south of Calcio, after Eugene had well established himself at the latter place.

Not wishing to undertake any further forward movement until he had assured his communications with Tirol, Eugene sent from Calcio a strong division, under the Marquis Visconti, to drive the Spaniards from Pontoglio and Palazzuolo both on the Oglio, and between his position and the point where that river issues from Lago d'Iseo. On hearing of the approach of the allies, Toralbo, who commanded the two Spanish detachments, cast all his stores into the Oglio, and hurried towards Bérgamo. Visconti despatched the two dragoon regiments, Savoy and Herbeville, in pursuit. These caught him on the way, held him and his men fast till the infantry came up, when Toralbo, with eleven hundred men, besides officers, surrendered. Only a few Frenchmen, under Louvigny, escaped into the mountains. The next day Pontoglio and, Palazzuolo were occupied by the allies.

The grand prior, meanwhile, blamed by his brother, blamed even by his own generals, had left only a small garrison in Soncino, and fallen back on the Adda. As soon as Eugene heard of this he marched on Soncino—then a strongly-fortified place—and took it (12th July). Not quite resolved whether he should march thence on the Adda or the Po, but making preparations for either movement, he advanced to Romanengo. Here he came, in contact with the enemy. Two days after the fall of Soncino Vendôme had returned from Piedmont and, reassuming command of the army, had at once led it back towards Soncino. As the two armies approached Romanengo their vanguards came in contact. Eugene did all in his power to bring about an engagement, but Vendôme fell back at once, and, as the ground was unfavourable for fighting, being intersected with ditches and water-channels, Eugene could not well force it on. He determined, then, to halt where he was and to watch for a favourable opportunity.

But the capable Vendôme was resolved not to give him that opportunity. As earlier in the season, so now, he entrenched himself in a position close to that of Eugene, a position so well chosen that it was impossible for the latter to reach either the Po or the Adda, to the south, without risking a battle under unfavourable conditions. It became from that moment a trial of skill between two great captains.

From Soncino Eugene had despatched General Wetzel to the Po, to collect boats there and to bring them back to Soncino. Wetzel had returned with the boats. Eugene, resolved, in spite of Vendôme, to accomplish his purpose, now caused these boats to be placed upon carts. Then he despatched his sick and wounded up the Oglio into Tirol. This done, he marched north-westward, on the 12th, to Prembate, in the fork between the Brembo and the Adda. He found the latter river so swollen as to render the passage apparently impossible. He sought diligently to find a place where he could bridge it higher up, and at length found one near the Villa Paridiso. Meanwhile Vendôme had discovered the route taken by his adversary, and had followed him with all speed, leading the way himself, with a regiment of dragoons. At Lodi he crossed the Adda, then, ascending the stream, reached the joint near the Villa Paridiso where Eugene was engaged in bridging it. He then encamped just out of cannon range, and, sending his guns to the front, opened a heavy fire on the workmen.

Convinced that he was baffled at that point, Eugene did not, however, renounce the idea of securing the passage. On the night of the 15th August he demolished the work he had begun, and before the day broke the next morning started by forced marches towards Lodi. On his way he learned from a prisoner that the road thither was barred by the grand prior with ten thousand men, opposite to Cassano, his position, a strong one, covered by the Ritorta canal. Resolved to attack and, if possible, destroy that enemy, Eugene placed his army in battle array, and marched in three columns against him. Count Leiningen, who commanded the right, had orders to direct his efforts to the seizing of the bridge of Cassano, the centre and left commanded respectively by Baron Bibra and Prince Leopold of Anhalt, were to wade through the canals which lay in their way, attack and force the enemy's position, and cast the enemy, if possible, into the Adda.

But, before the attack could take place, a great change had occurred. When Vendôme glanced towards his enemy's position on the morning of the 16th August he was surprised to find it had been evacuated. On the instant he divined the truth, and, well aware of Eugene's activity, and of his brother's carelessness, started at full gallop for Cassano, accompanied by a handful of officers and dragoons, and followed by his army. When he reached Cassano, Eugene was forming his columns of attack. No preparation was being made on the French side to meet it, his brother, the grand prior, though informed of the enemy's approach, lay still in bed. Instantly Vendôme took upon himself to dispose the troops. His chief force he ranged behind the Cremasca and Pandina canals, he caused the island formed by the Adda and the Ritorta canal to be strongly occupied, and the massive building called the Osteria, which commanded that island and the stone bridge across the Ritorta, to be firmly held.

The clocks were striking one when the guns of Eugene opened fire upon the French troops. Under cover of the smoke, the Imperialists rushed to the attack. So impetuous was their charge that the stone bridge and the Osteria were alike carried. The engineers had just succeeded, as a preliminary to the next advance, in closing the flood-gates of the canal, when the French returned to the charge, recovered the Osteria and the bridge, and re-opened the sluices.

This first attack had been led by Count Leiningen. Eugene, noting its repulse, galloped to the right wing, and himself led the men in two columns to the assault. One of these waded through the Ritorta canal, and the other threw itself on the bridge. The bridge, indeed, was gained, but the overwhelming force of the enemy from the high right bank of the Adda prevented him from pushing across the island. In the endeavour to do so, Leiningen was mortally wounded. A third time Eugene made the attempt, and on this occasion more successfully. He forced the enemy's dragoons to flee, then advancing in extended order across the island, he drove the French before him into the Adda, and formed his men to attack the entrenchments which covered the bridge of Cassano.

Here Vendôme commanded in person. The struggle which ensued here was one of the bloodiest and most hotly-contested in the war. On both sides the troops were fighting under the eyes of their leader, on both the leader possessed the confidence and affection of his soldiers. Not a man flinched, each felt that on his individual exertions depended the fate of the day. Already had the Imperialists, Eugene at their head, dashed through the barricade of wagons formed round the entrenchments, already had some grenadiers planted the Imperial Eagle on the summit of the parapet, when reinforcements, pouring in across the bridge, caused the fight to be renewed. To hold the entrenchment was indeed all-important for Vendôme, and he risked everything to beat back the enemy. His supply of troops, hurrying down from the position he had occupied in the morning, seemed inexhaustible, whilst Eugene had no supports to fill up the gaps in his line. For a few moments, then, Eugene renounced the attack. Only, however, for a few moments. Re-forming his troops once again, he led them once more to the charge. But once again had he to fall back before superior numbers.

Whilst the attack was thus proceeding to the Imperialist right, the centre and left were endeavouring to carry out the programme. Leopold of Anhalt had led his men through the canals, the water of which reached in many places up to their shoulders. Arrived on the opposite bank, their ammunition rendered useless by the immersion, they had recourse to the bayonet. For a moment they drove two French brigades before them, but the latter, opening fire, forced Leopold to retire.

It was just at this period that a musket-ball grazed Eugene, who had just failed in his last attack, on the neck. Though he did not quit the field, yet he found it impossible to exercise the functions of command. He made over change of the army, then, to Bibra. Bibra fell back in good order across the island, and made a great effort to hold the stone bridge. Whilst gallantly exposing himself he was severely wounded. Similarly placed *hors de combat* were Count Reventlau, Leopold of Anhalt, Alexander of Würtemberg, and Joseph of Lorraine. Eugene, somewhat recovered, now resumed command, and, at half-past five in the evening, fell back on Treviglio. His retreat was so orderly and well-conducted that Vendôme was content to send a cavalry division to observe, he did not venture to attack, him. At Treviglio Eugene entrenched himself.

The Battle of Cassano was the bloodiest of the whole war. It was the most fruitless of results. The quickness of Vendôme had repaired the faults of his brother, and had baffled, by equalling, the quickness of Eugene. In other respects, the situation of both the contending parties was unchanged. Eugene had been prevented from crossing the Adda, and that was all. He entrenched himself at Treviglio, whilst Vendôme encamped at a distance of ten miles from him, between the Adda and Aguadello, a position which he thought barred his enemy from access either to the Po or to the Adda.

But it was a necessity for Eugene to cross one or other of those rivers. Chivasso, long besieged by the French, was evacuated by its defenders the 30th July. Victor Amadeus of Savoy and Starhemberg fell then, with the remnant of their forces, only seven thousand men on Turin, the last city remaining to the duke. Here, unless Eugene could effect a diversion, he might momentarily expect an attack from the French.

Four weeks did Eugene remain in his position at Treviglio engaged in collecting carts to send his sick and wounded into Tirol. During this time, he was incessantly watched by Vendôme. Once, indeed, did Eugene send a detachment to seize the fort of Trediciponti, but the commander found Vendôme too much on the alert. But Eugene did not despair. He was expecting money from Vienna, and when that reached him he set to work to execute the plan which he had formed.

On the morning of the 10th October Eugene broke up from Treviglio, and marched, in a southerly direction, through Crema to Montodine, with the view there to cross the Serio, and then to take Castiglione and Goito. But before he could collect the materials necessary for building a bridge Vendôme appeared on the opposite side of the river. It seemed scarcely possible to cross in the face of such an enemy. But unwilling to return without, at least, making the attempt, Eugene sent two battalions across (16th October), and began to make the bridge. On the first alarm, however, Vendôme came down in force, and compelled the two battalions to recross. He baffled a similar attempt made by Eugene two days later at Crema.

But Eugene still persisted, and his efforts were at last crowned with success. Discovering that the Serio was fordable just beyond Mozzanica, he hurried thither, crossed without opposition, then pushed on to Urago, crossed there the Oglio (3rd November), and thence, despite heavy falls of rain, passed by Brescia, crossed the Chiese, reached Montechiaro, and thence threatened Castiglione. Vendôme, who, on the passage of the Serio by his enemy, had retaken Soncino, and drawn to himself there some reinforcements, now hastened to march towards Lonato, a very favourable position, as, situated on the extreme southwest point of the Lake of Garda, it cut Eugene's communications with Tirol.

But Lonato was the very place which Eugene had determined to occupy. This time he won the race, and Vendôme, finding the place held in force, entrenched himself in the neighbourhood. A few days later, the two armies went into their winter quarters, the Imperialists occupying the country from Brescia and Lonato, and from Lonato to the banks of the Adige, with the headquarters at Gavardo and an advanced post at Montechiaro, the French from Castiglione to Mantua. Eugene then proceeded to Vienna, to arrange for money and men for the next year's campaign, leaving Count Reventlau in command.

The task was a hard one—harder even than the task of fighting Vendôme. But Eugene had powerful friends Starhemberg had preceded him, an eye-witness of the state of destitution of the army and of the utter helplessness of the Duke of Savoy. The new Emperor, Joseph I, was, too, an admirer as well as a friend of the great captain. Promises were abundant. But Eugene would not quit Vienna until the reinforcements had set out and the money he had stipulated for had been actually provided. Thus, it was that, although, in consequence of the vast preparations made in France, he was anxious to set out for the army the first week of March, he did not actually take his departure till the 7th April, and before that date hostilities had broken out.

CHAPTER 8

Turin

The preparations in France had indeed been made with a view to ensure a decisive result Louis XIV was resolved that Turin should fall. He had, therefore, in consultation with Vendôme, placed on foot two large armies. One of these, led by Vendôme in person, was to fall upon the Imperial troops in their winter quarters, the other, equally strong, led by the Marquis de la Feuillade, the same who had taken Chivasso the year preceding, was to advance upon and capture Turin.

Vendôme, full of his enterprise, reached Mantua the 6th April. There he learned that the Imperial Army still occupied its winter quarters; that it had received but a very small portion of the intended reinforcements, and that Eugene had not quitted Vienna. Determined to succeed, he resolved, in the first place, to invoke the aid of stratagem. General Medavi, who had commanded the army up to the time of his arrival, had, in pursuance of instructions, gradually filled the magazines and sent his best troops to occupy the posts nearest to the Imperialists. When Vendôme arrived, he caused the report to be spread that he was extremely dissatisfied with the condition of the army, that he was seriously ill, and that it was impossible for him to undertake or even to think of any military undertaking till after the middle of May.

When he thought that his adversary, fully impressed with the truth of this rumour, had relaxed his watchfulness, Vendôme, who had quietly concentrated his troops at Castiglione, set out on his enterprise. It was the night of the 18th April. Before daybreak the following morning he reached and crossed the Naviglio—the canal which flows from Caneto to Montechiaro. Here he took prisoner an Austrian dragoon, who assured him that Reventlau occupied an entrenched camp, his right resting on Montechiaro, his left on Calcinato, and that he had no suspicion whatever of the movements of the French. Vendôme therefore pushed on rejoicing.

But in one respect he reckoned without his host. Reventlau had perfect information of the designs of Vendôme. Over and over again had he been told that he would be attacked before Eugene could arrive. The 16th April had even been noted as the day fixed by Vendôme for striking his blow. The Imperialists, then, were not taken by surprise. On the other hand, Reventlau was wanting in capacity as a commander, was apt to lose his head under fire, and was, above all, a procrastinator and careless.

Vendôme, as was his custom, had ridden in front of his army to reconnoitre. Examining the position of his enemy, he recognised that it was too strong to be attacked. He formed, then, the resolution to turn it, and by threatening to cut off Reventlau from Gavardo, to force him to fall back from his strong position, when he would take an opportunity of smiting him.

It would seem that on the 19th April Reventlau took no special precautions either to ward off attack or to watch the movements of the enemy. When at length he divined the turning movement which Vendôme was making, he hastily ordered out his men, and to prevent Vendôme, proceeded to occupy the heights of Calcinato with his cavalry and part of his infantry. The remainder he ordered to follow from Montechiaro. He thus fell into the trap which Vendôme had prepared.

Vendôme, noting this, resolved to attack him before the main body of his infantry could arrive from Montechiaro. With praiseworthy celerity he ordered his columns to the assault, and then led them up the heights, forbidding them to fire a shot. Reventlau allowed them to approach well within musketry-fire, and then saluted them with a volley from his whole line. The intrepid Frenchmen winced not under this discharge, but, pushing the more quickly forward, dashed against the ranks of the enemy. The charge was irresistible. The Imperialists had no confidence in a leader whose contradictory orders betrayed his incapacity.

The household troops of the Emperor displayed, indeed, their wonted valour. But the assault was not to be withstood. Then Reventlau, seeing the day lost, ordered a retreat. The retreat, at first orderly, soon became a rout, and the sight that met Eugene as he was hurrying from Roveredo to the camp was that of his own soldiers in disordered flight! Eugene had quitted Vienna the 7th April, and journeyed hastily to Roveredo. He had stayed there a few days to hurry on his reinforcements, and now arrived just one day too late to prevent a disaster!

But he had arrived and the presence of one man, if that man be a great man, is sufficient to repair a greater disaster even than that of Calcinato. Eugene made his presence felt. The troops gathered round him, he inspired them with confidence, the orderliness of the retreat was restored; the pursuit was checked; and Eugene, rallying his army, took up a strong position on the heights of Gavardo.

The next day he led them somewhat nearer to the enemy, to a position which he had caused to be marked out. Here he designed to remain until he should be joined by his reinforcements. With respect to these, the affair of Calcinato was so far helpful to his views in that it convinced the Court of Vienna of the necessity of aiding him still more largely with men.

The same day on which Eugene changed his camp, Vendôme approached within three miles of him. Vendôme did not offer battle. He hoped rather to force Eugene from Italian ground by easier means. He knew well that the Lake of Garda served as a connecting link between Eugene and Tirol. The boats sailing or propelled on its surface brought him all his supplies. By manoeuvring so as to force Eugene to let go his hold on that lake, Vendôme would compel him to retire into the mountains of Tirol. He laid his plans accordingly. Eugene recognised his object, and unable with his actual strength—less than one-half of that of his enemy—to prevent it, he decided to evacuate the Brescian territory, and fall back on Riva, nearer to his communications. This he did accordingly, his retrograde movement being successfully covered by his rear-guard, commanded by Colonel Zumjungen.

No sooner had he seen his army securely entrenched than Eugene hastened to the valley of the Adige to select there a position which should be at once the rendezvous for his reinforcements and a gate through which he would, re-enter Italy. He selected Ala, below Roveredo, and connected by a good road with Riva, for this purpose, and directed General Harrach to occupy the heights of the Montebaldo with his brigade. This order Harrach, despite the fierce opposition of the French, successfully carried out.

As his reinforcements came up, Eugene proceeded to occupy the heads of the several narrow valleys which lead from Tirol into the Veronese territory, just as, under circumstances not dissimilar, he had acted in 1701. He had but one main object—the relief of Turin—and he had pledged his word to the Emperor to effect that at all costs. Whilst he was so occupied, Vendôme, well acquainted with his enterprising character, had formed between the Lake of Garda and the

Adige, and southwards along that river, strong works covered with ditches and palisades. These, he thought, would hinder the advance of his enemy sufficiently long to enable him to concentrate his army at the decisive point of attack. Having done this, and thereby curbed in his imagination the ambitious promptings of the heart of his rival, Vendôme fell asleep!

Meanwhile, the other French Army, under La Feuillade, had advanced to besiege Turin. The few troops to whom the defence of that important city was entrusted, seven thousand in number, were all insufficient for the purpose. The character of their commander compensated to a certain extent for this paucity, for Count Wirich Philip Laurence Daun—father of the opponent of Frederick II of Prussia—was a man possessing courage, steadfastness of purpose, and a firmness which his enemies called obstinacy. The French Army, forty thousand strong, had appeared before the city the 13th May, and had opened trenches the night of the 26th. From that moment the siege was carried on with energy, whilst the place was defended with resolution. To save it was the set purpose of Eugene.

Non-military readers seldom realise how much soldiers are affected by morale influences. From a mathematical point of view, it would have seemed impossible that Eugene, shut up in the mountains of Tirol by a superior force under Vendôme, should be able to relieve Turin, besieged by another superior force under La Feuillade. And yet, at this period, two circumstances happened which produced an extraordinary effect on the minds of the soldiers on both sides—an effect which went far to compensate for the difference of numbers. One of these was the repulse of King Philip V from Barcelona and his consequent departure from Spain; the other, the victory obtained by Marlborough over Villeroi at Ramilies the 23rd May. These events produced something more than a morale result. They disposed the Republic of Venice, which till then had seemed to favour the French to come to an understanding with the Emperor. For the moment its rulers did not dare to proceed further.

At length all the reinforcements, except the Hessians, had reached Eugene, and that leader, gathering his troops, prepared to redeem his promise to the Emperor. Having, by a series of manoeuvres, fully persuaded Vendôme that he designed to attempt the passage of the Upper Adige, he suddenly, on the night of the 4th July, despatched Colonel Battée, with a strong detachment, to seize the position of Rotanuova, on the Lower Adige, whilst he threw himself upon the enemy at Masi.

The French, overpowered, fell back on Badia, and thence to Canela and the Canale Bianco. Then Eugene threw a bridge across the river and gained the right bank at Badia, whilst Battée did the same further down, and took post at Lusia and Boara.

On the 14th July Eugene, now firm on the right bank, sent back General Wetzel to give a hand to the Hessians, then, the day following, he crossed the Canale Bianco at Castelguglielmo, forcing the French before him. Marching straight to the Po, he threw a bridge over it at Polesella, crossed over it, pressed on past Ferrara, reached Santa Bianca, on the Passaro, on the 21st, and three days later, stood with his army, twenty-five thousand strong, at Finale!

Vendôme had promised his master, only a few weeks before, that the last man of his army would perish before Eugene should cross the Adige! But shortly before Eugene had made his spring Vendôme had to replace Villeroi, and the Duke Philip of Orleans, assisted by Marshal Marchin, had been nominated to succeed him. The duke, a man of rare capacity, abler far than the adviser who had been sent to instruct him, had assumed command just at the moment when Eugene made his dash at the Lower Adige. He had not had time to master the position before Eugene had crossed the Po. But when he had mastered it, the measures which he took were not unworthy of his predecessor.

Divining at once the meaning of Eugene's movements, the Duke of Orleans, leaving General Medavi on the Mincio to watch Wetzel, strengthened the garrisons of Mantua, Governolo, Ostiglia, Mirando- lo, Modena, Reggio, and Guastalla, then, throwing two bridges across the Po, he sent pressing orders to La Feuillade to send all the troops he could spare to occupy the defile of Stradella, which Eugene must traverse if he would reach Piedmont. He then established his head- quarters at Volta. A few days later he broke up with about twenty-five thousand men to follow Eugene, hoping to take him in rear whilst he was forcing the Stradella pass.

Fortune, however, was adverse. On the one side La Feuillade wrote to say that he could not spare the troops to send to Stradella, on the other, Eugene was far more bold and adventurous in his movements than the duke had contemplated.

Eugene, in fact, had expected that the enemy who had allowed him to cross the Adige, the Canale Bianco, and the Po, without op- position, would certainly not give him the same immunity when he should attempt the Secchia. Ever thinking the worst to be possible, for he was, in point of fact, in an enemy's country, away from his communications, possessing neither magazines nor even a piece of arms, and dependent greatly for his supplies on his foraging parties, he was forced to act with caution. Yet with that caution was mingled a boldness, a fertility of resource, an adventure, which makes this campaign, of all campaigns, antecedent to that marvellous campaign of 1796, the most worthy of study and admiration. To supply one of his wants, that is, to gain a strong place in which he might safely leave his sick men, he attacked, after having, to his surprise, made the passage of the Secchia unopposed the fortified town of Carpi, nine miles from Modena. On the third day Carpi surrendered. Pushing on thence, he took Reggio. His mind, however, being bent upon one object, the relief of Turin, he resolved to attempt no other conquests until that should have been accomplished.

His difficulties were very great. The season was noted even then for its extraordinary heat. Not only, then, were the smaller streams and the wells dried up, so as to make it impossible to obtain water in anything like sufficient quantities, but the power of the sun made itself felt, especially amongst the contingents from North Germany. These causes augmented his sick. Then the Duke of Orleans was on his right flank, whilst an army stronger than his own was besieging the city he was marching to relieve. There was but one fact which prevented the task from being impossible—and that was the fact that it was Eugene of Savoy who commanded the smaller army.

Pushing on, Eugene approached Piacenza. The Duke of Parma had previously intimated to Eugene that be was favourably disposed to the Imperial cause. No sooner, however, did Eugene enter his territory than he threw off the mask, and endeavoured by all the means in his power to increase the difficulties in his way. But, with Turin as his watchword, Eugene overcame them. If he had required any stimulant, he would have found it in the urgent letters he received from the Duke of Savoy and Count Daun.

One circumstance had occurred which had considerably perplexed the Duke of Orleans, and had prevented him from taking any decisive action against Eugene. I have mentioned that when Eugene broke up from his position about Ala, and had made thence his dash to the Lower Adige, he had sent back General Wetzel to give a hand to the Hessian troops, when they should arrive. The Hessians joined Wetzel just after Eugene had crossed the Po and reached Finale. Wetzel then commanded a force on the right rear of the Duke of Orleans sufficiently strong to cause him embarrassment. To ward off all danger from it, he was compelled to reinforce the corps which he had left on the Mincio, under Medavi, to observe it.

Medavi was not strong enough, however, even when reinforced, to prevent Wetzel from attacking Goito. The news of this action on his part caused the duke to hurry back to save the place. But he was too late. The *commandant* of Goito had capitulated. Too soon, indeed—for his weakness cost him his head!

It will readily be gathered how much this timely diversion encouraged Eugene and his soldiers, how it gave them hope, strength, even wings to hasten to the relief of the beleaguered garrison. A detachment sent on in front occupied, without opposition, the dreaded passes of Stradella. Then, to add to their encouragement, rain fell, and the heat diminished. Hastening on, they passed by Tortona and Allesandria, and on the 29th August, crossed the Tanaro, just beyond Isola (d'Asti). From Isola, in order to have only fighting men, entirely unencumbered, with him, Eugene despatched his entire camp equipage with the sick to Alba, further up the river on the same side.

As soon as he had crossed the Tanaro the same day, he galloped in front to have an interview with the Duke of Savoy, who had managed to escape from the city with some troops of cavalry. From him he received the joyful information that the two French armies had united before Turin, and that an attempt to storm the citadel the same morning had been beaten back. Three days later he effected a junction with the cavalry of the Duke of Savoy at Villa Stellone, about fourteen miles south by south-east from Turin.

The boldness of this wonderful march had completely imposed upon the French commanders. Marchin, placed at the side of the Duke of Orleans as his councillor, continued to insist that it was impossible that Eugene could cherish the design of relieving Turin, that his object must be to make a diversion in Parma or in the Milanese. La Feuillade was of the same opinion. Even if they should be wrong in their calculations, they argued, it would be easy to unite before Turin, and their strength, then, would be sufficient to crush their adventurous enemy. The Duke of Orleans, then, had marched on a line almost parallel to that of Eugene, latterly a little in advance of him, and had effected a junction with the besieging army of La Feuillade, the 28th August, the day before Eugene crossed the Tanaro. The following morning, they attempted the storming of the citadel, the repulse of which the Duke of Savoy announced to Eugene.

As soon as they heard of the arrival of Eugene at Villa Stellone the French commanders held a council of war. The Duke of Orleans pronounced himself in favour of massing all the troops which should be available after providing for the maintenance of the siege, and of marching against, and forcing a battle on the enemy. Marchin opposed the plan.

★★★★★★

This has been denied, and, as a proof, the opinion given by Napoleon at St. Helena, and the last words of Marchin himself, addressed to the English Minister at Turin, "*Croyez au moins, Monsieur, que ç'a été contre mon avis que nous avons attendu dans nos lignes,*" (Believe at least, sir, that it was against my opinion that we waited in our lines) have been cited to support the denial. But there is extant a letter from Marchin to Chamillard, Controller-General of Finances and Minister of War at Versailles, dated the 6th September, the day before the battle, which proves that Marchin had entirely lost his nerve, that he expected to be killed, and that he was most anxious to avoid a battle. Further, it is certain that the Duke of Orleans was desirous to march in full force against Eugene, but that he was controlled by his councillors

★★★★★★

He was for waiting for the enemy's attack. La Feuillade and all the other generals, with the exception of Albergotti and d'Estaing, supported Marchin. The resolution was then adopted to await Eugene's attack.

Meanwhile, Eugene had not been inactive. On the 2nd September he had ridden to the summit of the Superga, accompanied by the Duke of Savoy, to reconnoitre the enemy's position. Viewing the want of plan, betraying, as he thought, irresolution and disorder in the enemy's lines, he turned to his cousin with the words:

Il me semble que ces gens là sont à demi battus. (It seems to me that these people are half-beaten.)

Victor Amadeus replied by vowing that, if his prognostications should prove true, he would erect on the spot where they stood a church in honour of the Virgin. Visitors to Turin know how truly Victor Amadeus kept his vow.

The day of the 3rd September was spent by Eugene and the duke in making the last preparations for the inevitable battle. On the 4th they broke up their camp at Villa Stellone, crossed the Po between Carignano and Moncalieri, attacked on the 5th a large convoy on its way under a strong escort to Turin, drove the escort in headlong flight to Pianezza, and, pushing on across the Dora Riparia, captured that place, full of supplies, the same evening. Thence, the following day, they marched to the Veneria Reale, three miles due north of Turin. Since the 4th they had marched round the city—from Villa Stellone.

Eugene had resolved to attack the enemy on the face nearly opposite to which he now stood, between the Dora Riparia and the Stura, where they were entrenched less strongly than on the other points. With this view he moved his right wing on to the Dora, just where that tributary flows by Collegna, whilst he rested his left on the mills of Altezzano. He had under him about thirty thousand men, one-fifth of whom were cavalry. About one-half of the entire army was composed of Austrians, nearly the whole of the other half of the troops from Northern and Central Germany, for the Piedmontese, few in number, who had joined with the Duke of Savoy, had been despatched on the 2nd to Chiari to endeavour to introduce thence provisions into the beleaguered city. The Duke of Orleans had commissioned General Albergotti to observe this detachment.

In the grey dawn of the morning of the 7th September the Imperialists advanced to the attack. The infantry was formed in two lines each composed of four columns. Grenadiers selected from the several German nationalities, linked to the Prussians, led by Leopold of Anhalt Dessau, Eugene's trusted comrade at Blenheim, had the place of honour and danger on the left, the centre was formed of Austrians and a few troops from the Palatinate, the right of the bulk of the Palatinate contingent and Saxons. The second line was similarly composed, with the exception that the Austrians also formed the right wing, all the Saxons being in front. Prince Alexander of Würtemberg commanded the left wing, the Prince of Saxe Cobourg-Gotha the right, General Rehbinder the centre, of the front line. The command of the second line was entrusted to a Frenchman, the Marquis de Langallerie, who, for personal motives, had but recently deserted his country's service.

★★★★★★

He was thus described by the Duke De Noailles in a letter addressed to Louvois, "*C'est un homme enivré de lui-même, qui veut un commandement en chef, il n'est pas permis d'avoir un autre avis que le sien, sans s'exposer à ses emportements.*" (He is a man intoxicated with himself, who wants a command in chief, he is not allowed to have another opinion than his, without exposing himself to his outbursts.)

★★★★★★

The cavalry were commanded by Baron Kriechbaum, Marquis Visconti, and Philip of Darmstadt. Eugene and his cousin held themselves free to proceed to the spot where their presence was most required. It remains to add that Eugene had succeeded in conveying information of his movements to Count Daun; and that officer was prepared to hold his entire garrison in readiness for a sortie the moment the sound of Eugene's guns should announce to him that the propitious moment had arrived.

Meanwhile, the information that the Imperialists were in movement had reached the Duke of Orleans and Marchin. Instantly they rode to make what dispositions were possible to repel the attack. Their guns at least were in position, and these opened a heavy fire, alike to damage the assailants and to give them time for their own formation. That was then hurriedly completed. The right wing, which rested on the Stura, was commanded by Count d'Estaing, the centre by the duke in poisons, assisted by Marchin, the left, which touched the Dora and rested on Castle Lucento, by General Saint-Fremont.

Eugene had halted his line within half cannon-shot of the entrenchment, and, after speaking to them a few words of encouragement, had ordered his guns to open fire. For two hours the artillery fire continued, to the disadvantage, in so far as slaughter was concerned, of the Imperialists, who had no earthworks to cover them. Then the order to advance was given. The Grenadiers and the Prussians advanced then without flinching to within ten paces of the entrenchment. Here the terrible fire stopped, them. The centre and right had been delayed by the inequalities of the ground, and these gallant men had to bear the whole weight of the enemy's fire. After struggling for a time to advance, their leader drew them back in good order.

Eugene had not remarked the retreat of his left wing when he hurried up with the centre and right. The left then renewed their advance, and the fire became general along the whole line. It continued for more than half an hour, with heavy loss on both sides. The Imperialists could not reach the entrenchment, but they yielded no ground. A supreme effort was required to give one side or the other the advantage.

Feeling this necessity very strongly, and confident that the gallant Brandenburgers would respond to any call he might make upon them, Eugene galloped to his left wing, and, calling to the Prussians to follow him, dashed, accompanied by their own daring leader, Leopold of Anhalt-Dessau—"the bull-dog," as Eugene was wont to call him—through the thick musketry shower to the entrenchment. The men, full of enthusiasm, followed, stormed the entrenchment, then reforming, charged so furiously that the French yielded to the shock. Whilst Eugene thus pushed the enemy before him, he directed some of his men to level the entrenchment so as to allow the cavalry to enter. Then, not wishing to compromise himself further, till his centre and right should have followed the example of his left, he ordered his men to halt where they were. But their blood was up, and they were not to be held back. At last, and before they had gone very far, Eugene brought some gunners to the front and turned on the enemy the guns which had fallen into his hands when he carried the right of the entrenchment.

He was just, and only just, in time, for the French meanwhile had rallied, and, strongly, supported, had forced back the Prussians and the cavalry which had come, by the way made level by Eugene's order, to their support. Just at the moment the unexpected artillery-fire checked the re-advancing French. Just then, too, the Imperialist centre, to the encouragement of which the Duke of Savoy had rushed, succeeded, after three repulses, in forcing the entrenchment in front of it. The fight here had been most bloody. The French were fighting under the eyes of their two leaders, and they exacted blood for blood. Nor was it till Marchin had been mortally wounded, and the Duke of Orleans forced, by two wounds, to quit the field, that the Imperialists made good their attack.

On the French left the defence had been still more prolonged. The possession of the castle of Lucento gave the defenders here an enormous advantage. For a moment, indeed, they seemed to have made that advantage decisive, for their cavalry issued from the entrenchment and charged the flank of the Saxons. But before they could get home, Baron Kriechbaum, ever on the look-out, dashed at them, and catching their flank before they could reach the flank of the Saxons, rolled them over in disorder. It was a magnificent charge—an inspiration of genius. Then the Saxons, pushing forward by the opening made by the French cavalry, penetrated within the entrenchment, stormed the work which protected the bridge over the Dora, and took prisoners a whole French battalion

The entrenchment had now been forced, and the Imperialists, infantry and cavalry, were drawn up beyond it. But the French were not yet beaten. Still more numerous than their assailants, they re-formed and sought to regain the lost ground. Eugene waited till the whole of his second line had come up, then, charging the enemy, threw them into complete disorder. They had now no leader, no inspiring genius to rally them. They fled, then, in different directions. Some tried to gain a bridge over the Dora; others, the most numerous, to fall back upon a second line of entrenchments behind the Po. But as these last reached the bridge across that river they were set upon by Count Daun, who, sallying with his garrison, cut them down or made prisoners of them. A third and smaller body of fugitives, who had fled to the Po by way of the royal park, were pursued and cut down by the cavalry.

There remains now only to account for the fugitives who fell back on the Dora. These succeeded in crossing that river, and, taking up a position on the high bank, their left resting on Lucento, maintained themselves for some time. But soon the castle was evacuated as, under the circumstances, untenable. Then the Imperialists crossed the Dora and completed their victory by dispersing, killing, or making prisoners of the last considerable body of the enemies whose position they had stormed.

But there was another portion of the French Army which had taken no part in this decisive battle. This was the besieging corps of the Marquis de la Feuillade. That general had not ceased, during the battle, to maintain a hot fire against the city from the trenches. It was only when he saw the battle lost that he ordered a retreat. This was conducted in the greatest disorder. One portion of his troops fell back on Cavaretto, another on Moncalieri. On their way they fired their magazines, and the explosion of these caused much damage to the houses in the vicinity.

The defeat of the French was now complete. Wounded as he was, the Duke of Orleans summoned then a council of his chief officers to advise him. He, himself, was of opinion that it was advisable to fall back by way of Moncalieri on Alessandria, to unite there with the Viceroy of Milan and General Medavi. A false report that Moncalieri was occupied by the Imperialists decided him, however, to fall back on Pignerol. There he hoped to find magazines and to receive rein-forcements from Dauphine. It was a fatal decision, for which the duke himself, and those who gave him the false report about Moncalieri, were responsible.

The military student, examining the map, and noting how, whilst the position at Alessandria would have secured Piedmont whilst that at Pignerol renounced it, will understand and sympathise with the exclamation of Eugene when he learned the duke's decision:

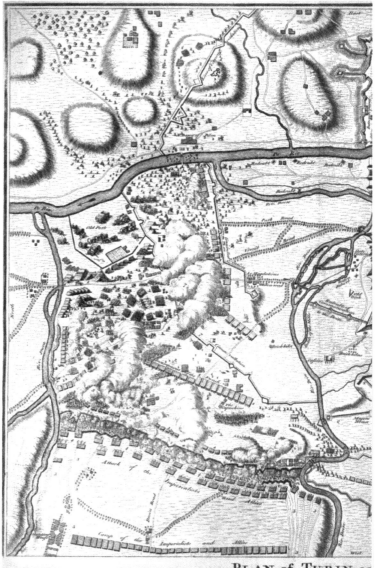

PLAN of TURIN as

For Mr. Tindal's Continuation of

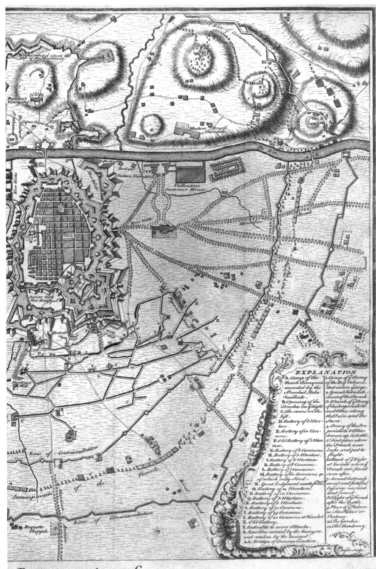

EXPLANATION

A. Camp of the
French Dragoons
wanted by the
Marshal Tolo
Souillade.
B. Opening of the
Trenches on Right
C. The same on the
Left.
D. Battery of Mor-
tars.
E. Battery of six Can-
non.
F. Old Battery of Mor-
tars.
G. Battery of 3 Cannon.
H. Battery of 2 Mortars.
I. Battery of 2 Mortars.
K. Battery of 6 Cannon.
L. Battery of 3 Cannon.
M. Battery of six Cannon of
which rally Road.
N. Great Lodgment made from
O. Battery of a Mortars.
P. Battery of 12 Cannon.
Q. Battery of 2 Mortars.
R. Battery of 5 Mortars.
S. Battery of 30 Cannon.
T. Battery of 34 Cannon.
V. Battery of six Cannon at Sunset.
X. Old Battery.
Y. Redoubts to cover Attacks.
z. Raveline carried by the Besiegers
and retaken by the Besieged.
AA. Bridge of Communication.

1 Camp of the
the Do... Ordanan
that even ...ing.
2 Grand S... which
stood the French
3 March of ...ting
of the troops reached
and ... along
the ...Raine and the
Hurst.
4 Army of the Am-
periales in villages
drawn up in battle.
5 First place where
the French were
broke and put to
flight.
6 March of 2 ...Right
at Canopic where of
broke were forced
soon after.
7 Second ...ily
most and first full
Infantry carried
and forced.
8 Right of the French
after the Battle.
9 Place of Battle.
10 Men Palace or
Chateau.
11 The Garden.
12 The Academy.

Whilst the French were retreating Eugene and his cousin had galloped into the besiegers' lines to save what stores and provisions were yet to be saved, and to take measures against plundering. Then, at 4 o'clock in the afternoon, amid the shouts of the populace, they entered the city. Their first act was to proceed straight to the cathedral and to thank God for the great mercy he had vouchsafed to them. They had indeed effected a great deliverance. In one day, with forty thousand men, including those of Count Daun and of the Duke of Savoy, they had virtually freed Italy from the French. Of the thirty thousand who had marched that morning to the battle under Eugene they had lost three thousand, or one tenth, in killed and wounded. If the French did not suffer more from their enemy's fire, their loss, in other respects, was far greater. Six thousand of their men were taken prisoners, they lost almost all their guns, their munitions, their supplies, and three thousand horses.

More important still was their loss of prestige. The united armies of the Duke of Orleans and La Feuillade, amounting together to sixty thousand, had been routed by—including the garrison—forty thousand Germans! The Battle of Turin deposed France from the high position which, during the reign of Louis XIV., she had occupied in northern Italy! For Eugene was not content with having relieved Turin. Not wishing to throw any obstacles in the way of a French retreat upon Pignerol—a retreat which meant the evacuation of Piedmont—he remained quiet until the duke was well on his way thither, contenting himself with sending parties to hang on his rear. He was the more encouraged to do this because he had now to deal with Medavi.

On the 9th September that general attacked and badly beat the Crown Prince of Hesse-Cassel at Castiglione (delle Stiviere)—the Castiglione which was to become so famous in 1796. On the 15th, then, after he had seen Turin well provisioned, Eugene crossed the Dora Battea and marched on Chivasso, which surrendered with twelve hundred prisoners. Marching, then, through the Milanese he took Vercelli, Novaro, and Crescentino. On the 23rd he crossed the Ticino, and on the following day received the keys of the city of Milan, and entered the place in triumph on the 26th. Contenting himself with blockading the castle, which was garrisoned by two French and four Spanish battalions, he despatched Daun against Pavia—which surrendered to him—and then marched to recover for the Duke of

Savoy the places still occupied by the enemy.

His progress was a triumphal march. Como, Lodi, Ivrea, Pizzigh-etone, Alessandria, Asti, Mortara, fell with but slight opposition into his hands. General Wetzel took Modena. Tortona was taken by storm, and, finally, Guastalla and Casale surrendered. Meanwhile the Duke of Orleans, finding neither magazines nor supplies at Pignerol, had fallen back to the French frontier and had been ordered by his sovereign to place his army in winter quarters. The Spanish Governor of the Milanese was likewise commissioned to arrange with Eugene for the withdrawal thence of all the Spanish and French troops still remaining in the Duchy.

When this had been accomplished Eugene placed his army in winter quarters. He was conscious that he had deserved well of his adopted country and of his cousin. He had made a campaign which will forever remain a model and a study for soldiers, he had gained a great victory over superior numbers, and had used that victory to expel the French from northern Italy, to gain the Milanese for the House of Austria, to recover Piedmont for the Duke of Savoy. The Emperor whom he so truly served, Europe (without France) whose cause he was fighting, even France whom he defeated, hastened to give him proofs how greatly was appreciated the genius which had conquered the impossible.

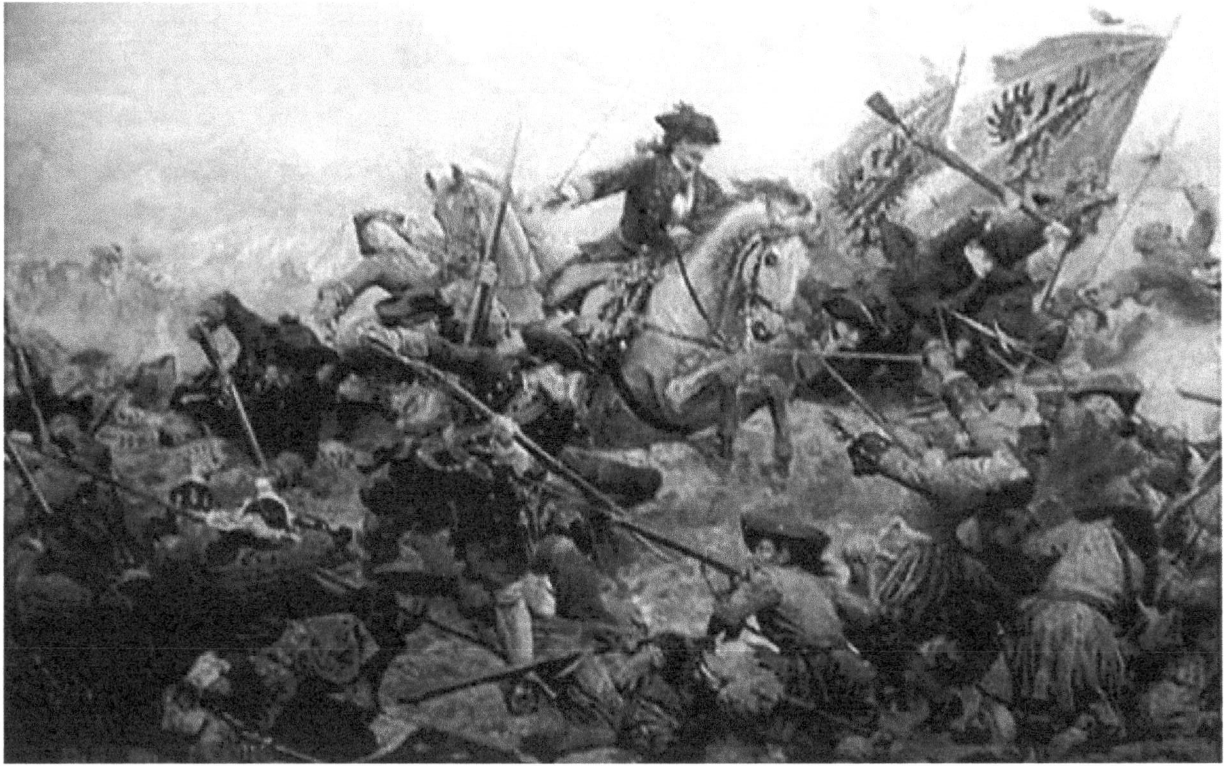

Battle of Turin

CHAPTER 9

Toulon and Susa

In the winter of the following year, 1707, Eugene was nominated Lieutenant-General and Field-Marshal of the German Empire. He had cherished the wish to command the Imperial Army combating on the Rhine, but, during the winter, the Court of Vienna, in conjunction with the Sea-Powers, England and Holland, strongly urged the advisability of retaliating upon France by crossing her southern frontier and attacking the important town and naval arsenal of Toulon, and they begged that the carrying out of such a scheme should be entrusted to the victor of Turin. With his usual self-abnegation Eugene gave way.

Under his auspices, and by the exercise of his eminently practical common sense, the castle of Milan and the other fortresses held by the French in northern Italy had been evacuated, and by the end of April not a single man of that nation remained on Italian soil, Savoy, the valley of Susa, Perosa, and Nice excepted. It had been the Emperor's wish, as a small recompense for Turin, to appoint Eugene Governor of the Milanese. Considerations of the public weal, into which it is hardly necessary here to enter, had prevented Eugene from accepting the high dignity at the moment, but in the spring of 1707 those difficulties had disappeared, and on the 16th April, he made his public entry into Milan as Governor of the territory of which that city was the capital.

The recovery of Naples lay very close to the heart of the Emperor Joseph. In that city the House of Austria had a strong party, and the Emperor wished that that party should be supported in such a manner as would enable it to regain there the upper hand. To carry out the Emperor's wishes Eugene despatched Count Daun, the defender of Turin, with ten thousand selected troops and selected superior officers.

153

The beginning of June had arrived before Eugene had placed in the field the army which he was to lead against Toulon. It was above all necessary that the enemy should be kept in the dark as to his intentions. The French commander on the frontier was Marshal Tessé who had succeeded the Duke of Orleans, despatched to Spain. Tessé, and, through him, the Court of Versailles, had been at first led by Eugene's preparations to believe that his adversary's real object was the recovery of Savoy. He had placed, then, Medavi with a strong army corps in that duchy, whilst, guided by his instinct, he guarded with the rest of his troops the passes leading into Provence. On the 15th June, Tessé learned that his instincts had rightly influenced him. On that day Eugene, having divided his army into four corps, marched, accompanied by the Duke of Savoy, from Cuneo, and entered the mountains.

Penetrating the Vermegnana Valley he marched by way of Limone to the Col di Tenda. On the 5th July he reached land occupied the village of Tenda. Pushing on in a south-westerly direction he occupied Sospello. There, on the 8th, he halted his tired troops, as well to give them rest, as to allow the *impedimenta* to come up. On the 9th he resumed his march, resting on account of the heat during the day, and moving in the early morning and late afternoon. Avoiding, to gain the time which otherwise would have been spent in taking it, the fort of Montalban, Eugene reached on the 11th the River Var. Along its banks the French had thrown entrenchments of considerable extent and some strength, and behind them stood a French force, capable, though not numerically strong, of offering a stout resistance.

Eugene, after reconnoitring the entrenchment, thought it might be possible, with the aid of Sir Cloudesley Shovel, the English admiral, who, with a combined English and Dutch fleet, was supporting the enterprise against Toulon, to compel the French to evacuate it without much fighting. Sir Cloudesley, whose fleet was off St Laurent, readily assented, and despatched Rear-Admiral Norris, with nine hundred sailors and marines, in boats up the Var, escorted by ships of light draught. On his side Eugene had crossed the river by a ford, at a point beyond the entrenchment. The contest was very short. The French, fearing to be hemmed in, beat a hasty and disorderly retreat, rendered very disastrous by the repeated charges of cavalry sent in pursuit of them.

At a council of war held after this action on board the English admiral's ship, the plan for the further prosecution of the enterprise was settled. Eugene marched by Cannes and Fréjus, left Antibes unattacked and unhappily unblockaded, and, his force suffering much from the intense heat and from want of water, often even from paucity of food, reached, the 26th July, Valetta, about a mile and a half from Toulon. His army was thoroughly exhausted.

Toulon was not then the strongly-fortified town, considered by French engineers to be impregnable, which it is at the present day. It consisted then of a series of narrow streets descending towards a wide quay. These were covered towards the land by eight bastions connected by works in the form of a half-moon, both ends of which rested on the sea. On the sea face the town was protected by a great and a little roadstead. Both of these were provided with solid works, towers, and strand batteries. Behind the roadstead were two harbours, the one, the Darse Vieille, to the east, for ships of commerce, the other, the Darse Neuve, to the west, for ships of war.

Marshall Tessé hastened on the first alarm to Toulon, and, in anticipation of the attack, had formed three entrenched camps outside the town. The easternmost of these leant, to the right, on the fortifications of Toulon, to the left, on the heights of St Anne. It was occupied by General Guébriant with twenty-six battalions. Another was laid out to cover the valley of Favière and the road running through it. This was occupied by eight battalions. To the west, covering the town near the sea, was the third, occupied by sixteen battalions. These camps were connected by broad roads with the town. The land defences were not, in the opinion of Tessé, strong enough to defend it for any length of time.

Eugene held a different view. His first examination of the place, from the high point of Mount Phiran, whence he had easily driven a small detachment placed in observation, convinced him that with the means at his disposal the task was difficult if not impossible. With a small force, badly provided with provisions, severed by a hostile country from communications, to attack a place so strong and so strongly occupied as Toulon would be madness. He expressed these views to the Duke of Savoy and to Sir Cloudesley Shovel.

The English admiral replied drily that his orders were to attack, and that, if it should be necessary to retreat, the infantry and artillery would find their base on his ships, whilst the cavalry could cut their way by land. A further conversation with the admiral showed Eugene that in his opinion the place could only be taken by a land attack. Against his better judgment, then, he resolved to persevere.

Before daybreak of the 30th July the Imperial Grenadiers, led by

Baron Rehbinder and Count Königsegg, stormed the heights of St. Catherine, driving out in great disorder the French who had held them. Eugene entrenched himself on these heights, and caused to be conveyed thither his heavy guns, with which to play on the camp of St Anne and the city. Two days later he gained the heights of La Malgue, placed there likewise a strong battery, connecting it by a formidable line of defence with the Chapel of St Catherine. From these points an effective fire was opened as soon as possible.

Notwithstanding the success thus achieved, Eugene felt then as he had felt from the first, that the allied force was not strong enough in numbers to storm the enemy's lines. He was not able, indeed, to occupy the position he had gained in strength sufficient to insure them against a sortie in force. In this sense he wrote to the Emperor, the 14th August, adding that he only persisted because the officers of the fleets, "who do not understand land operations, still consider it practicable."

His forebodings were soon realised. On the night of the very day on which he wrote the letter from which I have quoted, the French sallied forth, attacked the heights of St. Catherine and Mount Pharon, drove out the Imperialists, destroyed their batteries and spiked their cannon, and then withdrew as quickly as they had come. In this affair the Prince of Saxe-Coburg Gotha, a young soldier of great promise, was killed.

Notwithstanding this, Eugene opened from the heights of La Malgue so heavy a fire on the forts St. Margaret and St. Louis that the first surrendered, and the other, after having been abandoned, was blown up. As these forts had commanded the entrance of the passage into the great roadstead, it now became possible for the fleet to approach sufficiently near to bombard the town. The bombardment had scarcely begun, however, when information reached Eugene which, in the opinion of the English admiral, rendered the continuance of the siege impossible.

Louis XIV. had been roused to the utmost indignation by the invasion of the sacred soil of France. Without any delay he had recalled troops from Spain and the Rhine to march to the relief of Toulon. General Medavi, who commanded a force superior to that of the besieging army, had seized the line of land-communication with Italy so that Eugene's only safe base was the fleet. Every day the situation was becoming more dangerous. It being clear, then, that the place could not be taken before a hostile army should close on the rear of the

Imperialists, the raising of the siege became imperative.

The fleet had begun to bombard the town. Under cover of its fire, first the sick and wounded, then a portion of the heavy artillery, were shipped. By degrees all the men and material that it was intended to send on board had been despatched thither, and on the 22nd August the army began its retreat in five columns. Marching in good order, the rear-guard suffering only from the repeated attacks of the peasants, who had been levied in mass and armed, the army reached St Laurent the 30th. At this place it crossed the Var and entered Italy. Thence it continued its retreat across the mountains, still in five columns, until, on the 16th September, Eugene reunited them in a camp he had selected at Scalenghe, on the Lemnia, seven miles to the east of Pignerol. The fleet had accompanied the army as far as Nice. It sailed thence for Lisbon.

This successful retreat through a hostile country, in the face of two hostile armies, contributed not a little to increase the reputation of Eugene. It was as masterly as the famous retreat of Massena from the lines of Torres Vedras. Like that most illustrious commander, Eugene had to fall back through a territory which had been purposely wasted; he had to carry with him his supplies, to present a firm front to the army of Tessé on his rear, to protect his flank from that of Medavi, and to repulse the continuous assaults of the armed peasantry. He accomplished his aim with a loss practically inconsiderable.

More than that although he failed in his main object, he caused the campaign to result in a manner favourable to the aims of his master, for, as Marlborough wrote to Count Maffei—28th September—the expedition to Toulon acted as a powerful diversion in favour of the Allies. In Spain it prevented the French from taking any advantage whatever from a victory which, if followed up, would have had decisive results—the victory of Almanza—whilst in southern Italy it enabled Daun to conquer Naples without the opposition which would otherwise have been sent to confront him.

Dissatisfied with these results, Eugene, after a rest of two days at Scalenghe, marched against Susa, the 19th, and appeared before it the 21st September, the French general, Vraignes, who occupied an entrenched camp outside the town, abandoning it and retreating within the citadel on his approach. The town surrendered to Eugene the 22nd. Fort Catinat was stormed the 29th, and the citadel surrendered the 3rd October. Marshal Tessé, who had marched with but little diligence to relieve the place, was, at the time of the surrender, in its vicinity. But, immediately after it, he received orders from Versailles to confine himself to guard the frontier of Provence against invasion.

Such an invasion was no longer possible. The crests of the mountains were covered and the passes were blocked with snow, and Eugene was not prepared to renew in winter, and unsupported, an advance which had failed under more favourable circumstances. Leaving, then, a strong garrison in Susa, he fell back on Turin, and, whilst he placed the troops of the Duke of Savoy in winter quarters in the country about Mantua, Ferrara, and Bologna, he despatched the Palatinate troops by sea to Catalonia, the Hessians by land to Germany.

He then proceeded to Milan, to exercise there the administrative functions which devolved upon him as Governor. Having accomplished all that was possible, and having confided to a trusted officer, Marquis Visconti, the task, with the command of the army, of carefully watching the proceedings of his cousin, the Duke of Savoy, whom he always mistrusted, and bidding him on no pretence to supply him with troops, Eugene proceeded to Vienna, where he was received as the Liberator of Italy.

CHAPTER 10

Oudenarde and Lille

At Vienna Eugene found, as usual, many different cliques and many
diverse opinions. The campaign of 1707 had not been very eventful.
In the Netherlands Marlborough had been unable to effect anything
against Vendôme, whilst on the Rhine Villars had driven the Margrave
of Baireuth from the lines of Stollhofen, and, but for the obstinacy
of Charles XII of Sweden, would have marched on Vienna. Refused
his concourse, and fearing to be cut off, he had ultimately re-crossed
the Rhine, Hungary and Transylvania had been overrun by the insurgents, and Starhemberg had had the greatest difficulty in barring to
them ingress into the two Austrias. In Spain matters had resulted still
more unfavourably for the House of Austria, for Charles, who had at
one period of the year entered Madrid, was confined at the end of it,
to a corner of Catalonia. Positively the only advantage the Allies had
gained had been achieved by Eugene, for he had gained Susa, and Susa
was one of the gates of Italy!

The Austrian affairs in Spain being, it was considered, in the most
critical condition, an influential party at the Court of Vienna desired
to send Eugene thither. England, Holland, and Charles, titular King of
Spain, supported this party. But the Emperor Joseph could not spare
Eugene. His interests were on the Rhine, in the Netherlands, in Italy.
Eugene was the only general in whom he felt absolute confidence,
and he could not, in justice to his own territories, lend him, at the
crisis which was then existing, even to his brother. Instead of Eugene,
then, he despatched Starhemberg to Spain. Eugene received orders
to proceed to The Hague, to consult there with Marlborough and
the Grand Pensionary Heinsius regarding the plan for the coming
campaign.

Eugene reached the capital of Holland on the early morning of

BATTLE OF OUDENARDE

the 8th April (1708). Marlborough arrived a day or two later, and the discussions then seriously commenced. The subject was simply how best to compass the humiliation of France—to free the Spanish Netherlands. Two plans were finally resolved upon, the one working into the other. The first of these required the formation of an army to be commanded by the Elector of Hanover, on the Moselle, and to attempt with it an invasion of France through Lorraine, the second, and more important, the constitution of a second Imperial Army under Eugene, which by a rapid march should join the Anglo-Dutch Army under Marlborough, the united armies should then force a battle on the French, and, in case of victory, should capture the frontier fortresses, and thus wrench the Spanish Netherlands from France.

To render these plans workable Eugene and Marlborough proceeded to Hanover. They found the Elector—a dull, heavy-minded uninteresting man, afterwards George I of England—full of jealousy of Eugene, and quite indisposed to operate in any scheme which would rob himself of the laurels which he had gained—in his sleep. Convinced, then, that if the whole scheme was confided to him he would decline the part allotted to him, the two allied generals wisely made no mention of it, and the Elector then, first refusing, finally accepted the command of the Army of the Moselle. The two generals then separated, each to carry out his allotted task, Marlborough returning to Holland, Eugene visiting in turns, on his way to Vienna, the Grand Duke of Baden, the Landgrave of Hesse, the Elector of Saxony, to urge upon them, in the name of the Emperor, the necessity of an early despatch of their respective contingents.

At Vienna Eugene found the financial necessities, and the consequent difficulties in the way of fitting out an army, at least as great as ever they had been. To surmount these Eugene devoted every moment of his time, but the second day of June had arrived before he was able to quit Vienna to join his army. He took, on his way, the cities where he could meet the princes of the Empire, and, by dint of urgings, of solicitations, even of upbraidings, succeeded at last in inducing them all to fulfil their obligations.

Meanwhile he received letter after letter from Marlborough, whose army was already in the field, urging him to join, painting in somewhat dark colours his own prospects, attacked by the peace party in the English Parliament, and opposed in the Netherlands by an army superior in numbers and led by the illustrious Vendôme, by the side of whom served the king's grandson, the Duke of Burgundy.

161

His situation was indeed critical, for whilst the English commander and Eugene had formed the plan to unite and overwhelm Vendôme, the Court of Versailles had, on its side, contemplated the despatch of a portion of the Army of the Rhine, commanded by the Elector of Bavaria and the Duke of Berwick, so to reinforce Vendôme that he might overwhelm Marlborough, and Berwick was actually on his march to carry out his portion of the plan.

Berwick's action had not escaped the keen-sighted Eugene, and he hastened his preparations all the more. But, as in 1706, so now again in 1708, he had to wait till the Hessian contingent should arrive. At length it joined, and then, on the 28th June, he crossed the Moselle, reached Duren the 3rd July, and, learning there that affairs were critical, hastened with an escort of hussars, in advance of his army, to Brussels. On his arrival there, the 6th, he learned that the French had attacked and occupied the city in Ghent, and were then besieging the castle!

Marlborough's joy was great when, under these untoward circumstances, he heard that Eugene, though accompanied only by a few hussars, had reached Brussels. The two commanders met at Assche. The progress of the French had caused Marlborough the greatest alarm, and had caused a dejection which he found it difficult to conquer, even with the aid of the assurances of Eugene. He did, however, conquer it, and separated from Eugene with the determination to join him again as soon as possible and carry out the original programme. Meanwhile, they both threw a reinforcement into the fortress of Oudenarde, then besieged by the French, and, convinced now that the conquest of that fortress by Vendôme would give him an unassailable position, they pushed forward their troops with all diligence to save it.

The two armies united on the 8th. On the 9th they set out for Oudenarde, and crossed the Dender on the 10th. Before daybreak of the 11th Marlborough despatched General Cadogan with a strong corps to the Scheldt, to throw bridges over that river near Oudenarde and to reconnoitre the enemy. The main army followed at 7 o'clock Cadogan did his part to perfection, crossed the Scheldt at Oudenarde, and began the bridging of it at five other places.

The two commanders had correctly divined the projects of Vendôme. The capture of Bruges and of Ghent had encouraged him to attempt that of Oudenarde, because then he could easily guard the line of the Scheldt, cut off the enemy from Menin and Courtray, and possibly expel him from Brabant. Unfortunately for Vendôme, the

Duke of Burgundy, who possessed a voice in the direction of the army, really, though not at the time nominally, equal to his own, and who was under the influence of a very incapable *entourage*, held other views. The duke permitted himself to lay but slight stress on the capture, in the first instance, of Oudenarde. He was for crossing at once to the left bank of Scheldt, cover the points where that river could be crossed with entrenchments, at the same time that Oudenarde should be attacked likewise from the left bank, and for sending a detached corps to besiege Menin.

Unfortunately, this diversity of opinion caused uncertainty in action. Berwick had not arrived, or it is scarcely to be doubted but that the voice of the victor of Almanza—alike the son of James II and the nephew of Marlborough—would have exercised a preponderating influence on the general plan. As it was Burgundy's idea was carried out, though in a very perfunctory manner. The French Army slowly approached the Scheldt, and made as though it would cross it at Gavere, their generals being confident that the entrenchments that they had already thrown up would prevent the passage of it by the enemy.

To return now to Cadogan. That intrepid officer, after obeying, as I have described, his orders, had taken up a safe position in the plain of Oudenarde, on the left of the river. Here twenty French squadrons, despatched in advance of the army crossing at Gavere, suddenly approached him.

It seemed impossible to avoid a conflict, and, certainly, Marlborough and Eugene, who had ridden in front to reconnoitre, were most anxious that it should take place. They did all in their power, then, to hasten the march of the main body. Thanks to their exertions, the allied cavalry came on at a smart trot, and at midday began to cross the Scheldt by the bridges. Meanwhile the French party had been joined by some infantry, and, fearful lest the opportunity should pass, Marlborough ordered Cadogan to attack them without further delay Cadogan carried out his orders with coinage and success. He completely overthrew the French cavalry of the seven battalions which had come to their support, and, with that object, had occupied the village of Eyne, three retreated before Cadogan had charged home, but of the remaining four scarcely a man escaped, those who tried to get away, being cut down, were made prisoners.

That Cadogan had thus been able to strike so severe and so successful a blow was due mainly to the fatal division which existed between the French commanders. For, in point of fact, the French occupied,

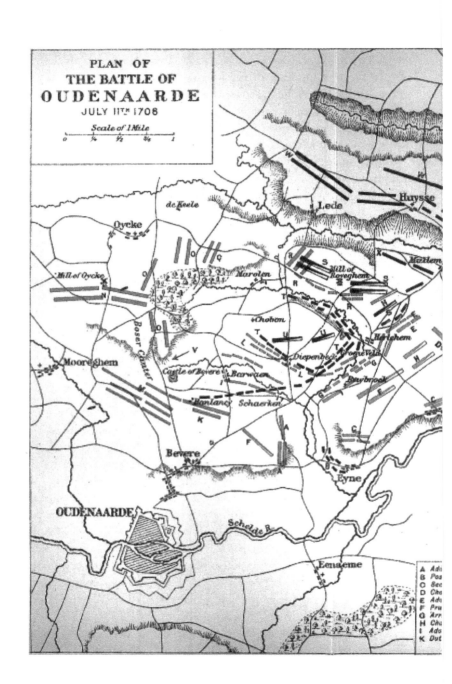

PLAN OF
THE BATTLE OF
OUDENAARDE
JULY 11TH 1708

Scale of 1 Mile

0   ¼   ½   ¾   1

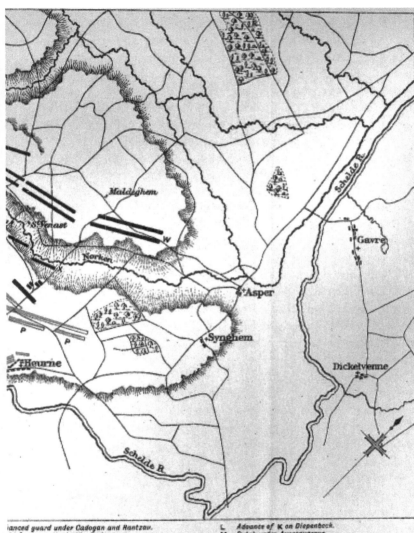

Maldeghem

St Ernast

Norken

Asper

Gavre

Synghem

Hourne

Dickelvenne

Schelde R.

Schelde R.

at that moment, a far better position than did the Allies. The entire French Army had then crossed at Gavere and stood on the left bank of the Scheldt; of the allied army, besides the division under Cadogan, the cavalry only had crossed or was crossing that river; whilst the infantry had not reached the right bank. Vendôme, who recognised all his advantage, requested then the Duke of Burgundy to make a strong attack with the left wing, which he commanded, on the allied cavalry. The duke, however, influenced by men who hated Vendôme, made an excuse for not obeying, then, instead of pushing forward, began to entrench himself on the ground he occupied, thus giving the allies time they required for the full development of their plans!

Of this inaction on the part of the duke, Marlborough and Eugene proceeded to take the fullest advantage. One after another the regiments crossed the bridges to take position on the flat lands where the first combat had taken place. No sooner had a sufficient number arrived than the allied leaders launched them against the enemy. Eugene, who commanded the right wing, was the first to reach the hostile line. Marlborough was not long behind him. Then the battle joined. There was but little manoeuvring. It was a direct attack on the enemy's front, illustrated by many isolated combats; the difference being that whereas those conducted by the Allies formed part of one general scheme, on the side of the enemy each divisional leader fought for his own hand.

Far different would have been the battle had Vendôme had the supreme control of the French Army. But with a prince of the blood royal, possessing no military talent whatever, remarkable mainly for his bigotry and the ease with which he was led by incompetent flatterers, occupying a position equal to that of the nominal leader, and refusing obedience to orders, the genius of Vendôme availed but little. One after another the positions occupied by the French soldiers were carried. Then these took advantage of the falling night to make a retreat as hurried and disorderly as their defence had been wanting in tenacity. In no pitched battle, indeed, have the French soldiers less distinguished themselves than at Oudenarde. Fighting under a divided leadership, they were fighting virtually without leadership, and they knew it. The Duke of Burgundy contributed as much as either Marlborough or Eugene to gain the Battle of Oudenarde for the Allies.

★★★★★★

"They were beaten at Oudenarde, it was not a great battle, but it was a fatal retreat. There was a multiplicity of errors. Regiments went where they could, without receiving any orders

After Oudenarde Marlborough visiting French prisoners

More than four thousand men were taken by the enemy some miles from the field of battle"—Voltaire.

Gamache, one of the gentlemen (*menins*) of the Duke of Burgundy, thus candidly stated his opinion to his prince "*Je ne sais si vous aurez le royaume du ciel, mais, pour celui de la terre, le Prince Eugene et Marlborough s'y prennent mieux que vou.*" (I do not know if you will have the kingdom of heaven, but for that of the earth, Prince Eugene and Marlborough do it better than you.)

★★★★★★

The Allies followed the retreating French during the early part of the night, greatly augmented the disorder of the retreat, and took many prisoners. In their misfortunes Vendôme and the Duke of Burgundy forgot their differences. They both rushed to the post of danger, and so greatly exposed themselves that they narrowly escaped capture. At length the pursuing troops were called back, and the French pursued their way, still in great disorder, as far as Ghent. There they rallied, and Vendôme and the duke—for the fatal division of command was allowed to continue—strove to reorganise their army, still very numerous.

The Allies, meanwhile, prepared to take advantage of their victory. They were within a circle commanded by three hostile fortresses, Ypres, Lille, and Tournay. After some consideration it was resolved, on the proposition of Eugene, that Lille should be besieged.

As a preliminary the Allies destroyed the entrenchments which the enemy had thrown up between Ypres and Warneton, to cover the country between the Lys and the Scheldt. They took, likewise, Warneton, Commines, and Werwick. Then Eugene proceeded with a strong corps to Brussels, to obtain from the Dutch the siege-train necessary for the leaguer of a place so strong as was Lille.

The French never believed for a moment, all reports to the contrary notwithstanding, that the Allies would venture on so perilous an undertaking as the siege of Lille. Vendôme went so far as to declare that Eugene was too able a commander to make so great a departure from the rules of war as such a siege would necessitate. For Berwick was on the point of joining him, and with Berwick his army would at least equal that of the Allies.

It was, indeed, a perilous task, but Marlborough and Eugene brought to the carrying out of it all the resources of experience directed by genius. At length the siege-train was collected at Brussels. It consisted of fifty heavy pieces and three hundred powder-wagons, and covered in its length thirteen miles. This train had to be conveyed to Lille in the face of an enemy such as Vendôme, who had always shown himself enterprising, active, and audacious. Eugene commanded the escort; Marlborough the covering army. They managed so well, assumed a front so bold, and made dispositions so adapted to circumstances, that the French did not dare to attack them. On the 13th August they arrived before Lille, and Eugene began, the following day, to mark out the lines of circumvallation.

Lille, the capital of French Flanders, had been made by Vauban one of the strongest fortresses belonging to France. Its advantageous position between the lands watered by the Lys and the Scheldt gave it great importance, whilst the fact that through it flowed the Deule, navigable by small ships, and fed by numerous marshy streams, greatly increased its defensive power. The garrison consisted of 10,000 men. Its *commandant* was Marshal Boufflers, Governor of French Flanders, a man of remarkable daring, great self-confidence, and of unsurpassed loyalty, who had learned his trade under Turenne.

Whilst Eugene was engaged before Lille in making preparations for the siege, the King of France sent orders to his grandson, the Duke of Burgundy, to break up from Ghent, with a hundred battalions and a hundred and thirty squadrons, and approach the threatened fortress. To enable him to carry out this order, the Duke of Berwick was directed to join him.

The Allies had disposed their forces in the following manner; Eugene, with his troops, stood before Lille, to besiege it, Marlborough, with the Anglo-Dutch Army, occupied Helchin. It had been arranged between the two commanders that, if Marlborough should be threatened by the Duke of Burgundy alone, he should deal with him unassisted, but should Berwick, as well as the duke, menace him, then Eugene should despatch fifty squadrons to his assistance. When, then, on the 1st September Marlborough discovered that Berwick was marching with the duke against him, he rode to Eugene's camp and demanded the promised aid in men, and, what he valued even more, the presence of Eugene to reconnoitre the enemy.

On the morning of the 2nd of September Eugene proceeded to Marlborough's camp, and then rode with him to watch the movements of the enemy, and to select a good position to check his advance. He found that the French had marched from Ghent to Tournay, that, on leaving Tournay, they had proceeded westward, by way of Orchies, towards Lille. Remaining with Marlborough a few days longer,

RYSSEL, *door de GRAAF MERDE den 22 Aug en 8 Bet BARD, met de LOBEN van Circumvallatie, Attaques, Nieuwen en Regimenten, enz. door een kundig ingen. tekst gen.*

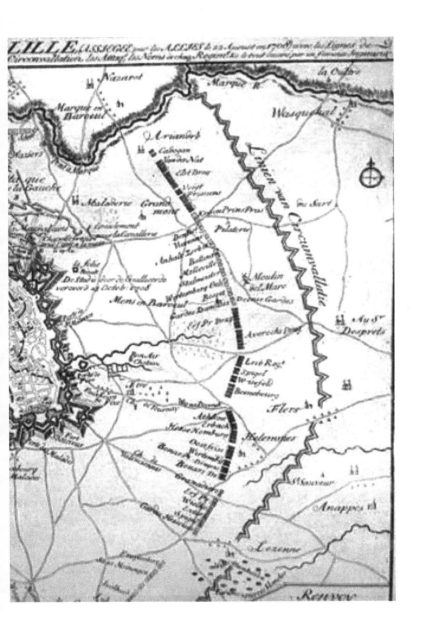

he noticed that from Orchies, which is fourteen miles from Lille, they marched to Mons-en-Pevèle, between two and three miles nearer, and there took up their position. It was a position extremely well chosen for the purposes of attack.

Meanwhile the two allied commanders had selected a position very advantageous for defensive purposes, and this position they now caused to be occupied. Their right rested on Seclin, then left on Fretin, their centre was covered by the village of Ennetières.

The 5th September was the birthday of the King of France, and the Allies expected, they even hoped, that his grandson would celebrate that day by endeavouring to gain a victory which would change the fortunes of the campaign. The idea had presented itself to the French commander. But here, again, a great difference of opinion had been manifested, and an altercation, more violent even than that before Oudenarde, had ensued. Since that battle a special order from the king had freed his grandson from any sort of dependence upon Vendôme. Berwick had also joined, and he, seeing how affairs were tending, seized the pretext to declare that he would take orders only from the Duke of Burgundy, over whom he had managed to gain a considerable influence.

The position of a weak man like the duke, between two opposing forces such as Berwick and Vendôme, was not enviable. Vendôme, when, from the heights of Mons-en-Pevèle, he beheld the allied army in the position I have mentioned, was all for an attack, and even pressed forward with the left wing against them. Berwick, on the contrary, whose sharp eyes recognised at once the excellence of the allied position for defence, and who—to use his own expression in a letter addressed to the War Minister—thought that, though it would be a misfortune to lose Lille, it would be a misfortune ten times greater to lose the only army the king had in Flanders, strongly advised against a battle.

The duke, secretly agreeing with Berwick, did not like to decide against Vendôme. He sent, therefore, a courier to Versailles for orders. The same courier carried the resignation of Vendôme in the event of his advice being rejected.

Before the answer of Louis could arrive, the allied position had been greatly strengthened, Eugene, too, returning to his lines, stormed, 7th September, several of the outlying works of Lille. The same day he escaped an attempt made by some unknown hand to poison him. On opening a letter, he discovered within it a paper smeared all over

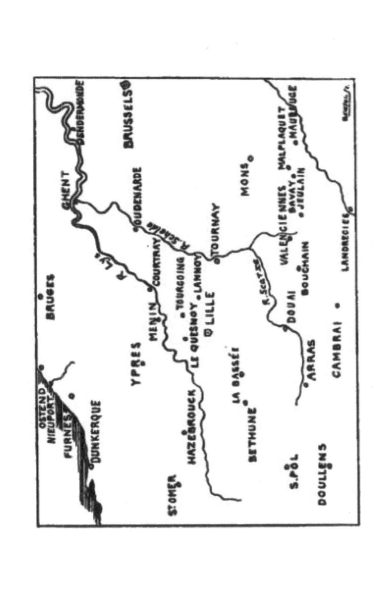

with fatty, sticky substance. He at once threw it from him, but curious, when his business had been transacted, to ascertain whether it were harmless or otherwise, he caused it to be attached to a collar encircling a dog's neck. The animal died within twenty-four hours. The author of the audacious attempt was never discovered.

Meanwhile the King of France had been thrown into a great state of perplexity by his grandson's reference. Unable to solve the question himself, he despatched his Minister of War, Chamillard, to examine the situation and report upon it.

Chamillard was the most unfit man possible to despatch upon such a mission. He was, in the first place, not a soldier. In other respects, he is thus described by Saint Simon:

> Chamillard possessed a very narrow intellect, and, like all men of small minds and few ideas, was very obstinate, very head-strong, bitter against all who opposed reasons to his views, and entirely incapable of understanding them, consequently always duped in his friends, in affairs, in everything.

This representative of his sovereign reached the French camp the 9th September, when the situation had greatly altered for the worse. It was at once apparent, even to his limited intellect, that the time had passed when an attack could succeed. Yet, as he knew the king was bent on the relief of Lille, he gave his opinion that something should be attempted. It was resolved, therefore, to approach the enemy in the hope that the latter would make a movement of which they could take advantage.

But Marlborough was on his guard. When, on the morning of the 11th, he observed the enemy on the move, he despatched a messenger to Eugene. Eugene responded not only by coming, but by bringing all the troops he could spare from the siege. For two whole days the allied army stood under arms, expecting the attack. But the attack was never made. The French contented themselves with a cannonade, and then fell back to Orchies. Even Vendôme admitted that the position of the Allies was now unassailable. Eugene then returned to his lines to press the siege.

On the 20th the trenches were pronounced practicable, and Eugene resolved to storm. At 6 o'clock that evening the troops told off for the purpose, assembled in the trenches; at 7 o'clock, under a heavy fire from all the batteries, Eugene himself gave the signal to advance. Bravely as his soldiers pressed on, as undauntedly were they met by the gallant soldiers of France. Three times was the storm repulsed. Then Eugene, fired at the sight, rushed with his drawn sword to the front, and, speaking a few stirring words to his men, led them to the fourth attack. His troops, animated by his example, dashed on with enthusiasm. Fierce was the struggle, terrible the carnage. It was hard to say which side would prevail, when suddenly the leader of the Imperialists was struck on the head by a bullet and fell to the ground.

A few seconds had not elapsed when he rose and endeavoured to resume his place in the van. But his strength failed him, and he had to be carried to the rear. The wound, fortunately, was not serious. The bullet, discharged in an oblique direction, had caught the head at the angle just above the left eye, and had slanted off the bone. The attack continued after the prince had quitted the field, and resulted in the assailants establishing themselves in some only of the defensive works. They lost, however, nearly two thousand men. The next morning Marlborough rode over to see his wounded colleague. He found him on the point of mounting his horse, in order personally to superintend the progress of the siege. At Marlborough's earnest request he agreed, though very unwillingly, to rest till the effect of the wound should have worn off.

The place continued to be heroically defended by Marshal Boufflers. He did not surrender an inch of ground without contesting it to the last. Thus, every defensive work had to be stormed. The loss to the assailants was always greater than that of the assailed. Meanwhile, great as had been the quantity of *matériel* brought from Brussels, the rapid expenditure of shot and shell threatened at a not very distant period the failure of supply. Added to which, Eugene had daily experience of the mistake of the Imperial war system—a mistake remedied after this campaign—in not training a distinct corps of officers to serve as engineers. Provisions, too, were becoming daily more scarce.

Nor, on the other hand, had the Duke of Burgundy and his councillors given up the idea of forcing the Allies to raise the siege. True it was that they had recognised the impossibility of attacking Marlborough in position, but there was another ready mode of forcing him to move. This was to cause a diversion to be made on Brussels, and to reconquer that capital. Expresses were sent to the Elector of Bavaria, who was opposed to the Elector of Hanover, on the Moselle, urging him to march on Brussels. Should he succeed in enticing Marlborough to march to the defence of that capital, it was agreed that Vendôme should attack Eugene in the trenches.

Meanwhile the two allied generals had arranged to procure a convoy of supplies from Ostend. This convoy set out from that place. It had reached, under a large escort, the vicinity of the old castle of Wynendaele, some sixteen miles from Ostend, when the escort was attacked by a strong detachment from the French Army. The action, which was one of the bloodiest of the campaign, terminated in the complete defeat of the French, and, on the 18th October, the convoy reached the lines of the besieging army.

Eugene now prepared for the final storm. On the 21st he opened a terrific fire on the place. This fire, which continued during the night and the following day, destroyed, for all practical purposes, the remaining defences of the city. At 4 o'clock on the afternoon of the 22nd, Boufflers, recognising the impossibility of further defence, offered to surrender the city, provided that he might be allowed to retire with his garrison, reduced now to four thousand men, to the citadel. The terms were agreed to and carried out. The prisoners on both sides were at the same time exchanged.

Eugene then attacked the citadel. This was a regular pentagon to the north-west of the city, and on that face offering easy approaches. Whilst Eugene was endeavouring by all the means at his disposal to crown his work by its capture, the French were attempting the scheme they had devised.

Fortunately for the French, the combined ineptitude and jealousy of the future King of England had rendered the contemplated expedition easy. The Elector of Hanover, disappointed at seeing all the glories of the campaign monopolised by Marlborough and Eugene, had, at a comparatively early season, broken up his army and gone back to Hanover. Left free to act, Max Emanuel hastened to carry out the programme allotted to him, and to march on Brussels. He appeared before that city the 22nd November, and summoned it to surrender. But General Pascal, who commanded there, seeing that the general feeling leant strongly towards the Allies, announced his intention to defend the city to the last, at the same time that he despatched messengers to Marlborough and Eugene to inform them of his danger.

The allied generals, on receiving these messengers, met in hasty council. They were both of one mind. Marlborough set out with his army on the 24th. Eugene, leaving a force sufficiently strong, started with the rest of his troops on the 25th, and caught Marlborough at Oudenarde. Vendôme was on the right bank of the Scheldt, prepared, it was believed, to oppose their passage. He fell back, however, without striking a blow, and the Allies crossed the river. Marlborough then pressed on towards Brussels, whilst Eugene returned in all haste to Lille to defend his position there against a possible attack on the part of Vendôme. The attack was not made; and whilst Marlborough rescued Brussels, without striking a blow, from the grasp of Max Emanuel, Boufflers, unable to defend his position longer, surrendered the citadel of Lille on the 9th December. The French marshal and his garrison were allowed to march out with all the honours of war.

The capture of Lille was not, however, the last act of the campaign. No sooner had the citadel been evacuated than Marlborough marched against and invested Ghent. This time Eugene covered the operations. On the 18th December the investment of the city was completed. Twelve days later, the *commandant*, La Mothe, announced his readiness to capitulate provided that he should not be succoured within four days. No succour did arrive, and the place surrendered on the 2nd January. It was a shameful capitulation. So numerous was the garrison that the evacuation, which began in the morning and continued all day, was not concluded till 6 o'clock in the evening. Bruges opened its gates to the Allies the day following.

The brilliant and successful campaign of 1708 was now concluded. It is probable that under any circumstances the campaign would have resulted favourably to the Allies. But it cannot be denied, that, brilliant as were their plans, and exact as was the execution of those plans, they were greatly aided by the disunion which existed amongst the French commanders.

The campaign concluded, Eugene accompanied Marlborough to The Hague, stayed there till the middle of January, and then proceeded to Vienna. I have omitted to mention that on the 10th October he had lost his mother, the Countess of Soissons. She had enjoyed the satisfaction before her death of seeing the humiliation of her enemy, Louis XIV., at the hands of her son.

CHAPTER 11

Malplaquet

The winter of 1709 was spent mainly in negotiations. Louis XIV was humiliated, and he offered peace on terms which the Allies would have done well to accept. But when they insisted that he should, if required, employ the strength of France against his grandson, he replied, with a noble indignation:

> If I must make war, I prefer to wage it against my enemies rather than against my children.

And the war continued.

It had been decided that the campaign in the Netherlands should be continued under the same skilful generals who had brought that of 1708 to so successful an issue. In anticipation, then, of the refusal by the French king of the hard terms insisted upon by the Allies, Eugene had proceeded to Brussels to be near his troops. The letter announcing Louis's final resolution was despatched from Versailles the 2nd June. On the 23rd of that month the allied army, consisting of an hundred and ten thousand men, was assembled between Courtray and Menin. Marlborough commanded the left wing, about seventy thousand strong; Eugene the right, about forty thousand.

Louis, on his side, had made extraordinary efforts. But even with these he had been able to put in the field an army only eighty thousand strong. That army was, however, well provided with all the necessaries of war, and the command of it had been wisely given to one who was great in the field of glory, who possessed genius and insight, as well as tactical power—to the illustrious Marshal Villars.

★★★★★★

"His *coup d'oeil* and his coolness in action were remarkable. He made himself beloved by his men, and know how to excite

EUGENE AT MALPLAQUET

their gaiety and their enthusiasm in the midst of the greatest dangers. A strict disciplinarian, he was nevertheless a popular commander. Opposed to generals, circumspect, cool in their calculations, prudent in their movements, and who made war according to the rules as they were known, Villars astonished them by the promptitude of his conceptions, by the rapidity and boldness of his manoeuvres."—*Portraits Militaires.* Amongst great commanders his place is with the highest.

★★★★★★

Villars had occupied a position between Douai and the Lys, and had there thrown up lines, in the strengthening of which he found daily employment for his troops. All the villages and hamlets in or near these lines he fortified, he built, likewise, redoubts, and so arranged that he could overflow the country immediately in front of him.

On the 24th June Marlborough and Eugene rode to the front to reconnoitre that position. If they should find it weak, it was their intention to attack it, if strong, to make a campaign of sieges. They recognised at a glance that the position was impregnable. Not only was it strongly fortified, but, to bring the army before it, many defiles had to be traversed so close to the enemy that the army could only debouch from them under a very heavy fire. They therefore, resolved to besiege Tournai, but, on the advice of Eugene, to conceal their intention as much as possible from Villars by making as though they still intended to attack his lines.

On the night of the 26th the Allies marched towards the French camp, the soldiers believing that they were going to attack the lines. Suddenly, however, the columns wheeled to the left, then moving straight on, appeared early the following morning before Tournai. So little were they expected, that they interposed between the fortress and some cattle intended for the provisionment of the garrison.

Tournai, taken by Louis XIV in 1667, had been newly fortified and provided with outworks by Vauban. The citadel, a pentagon, likewise furnished with earthworks, had been pronounced by the great Condé to be a masterpiece of engineering skill. The fortress was well situated for defence. No envious hills commanded it, whilst a considerable portion of its works were protected by a wet ditch formed by the overflow of the Scheldt. The works were in the best condition, but though the place was well provisioned, and the magazines were full, the garrison was only at one-half its normal strength.

The siege of so strong a place in the face of a powerful hostile

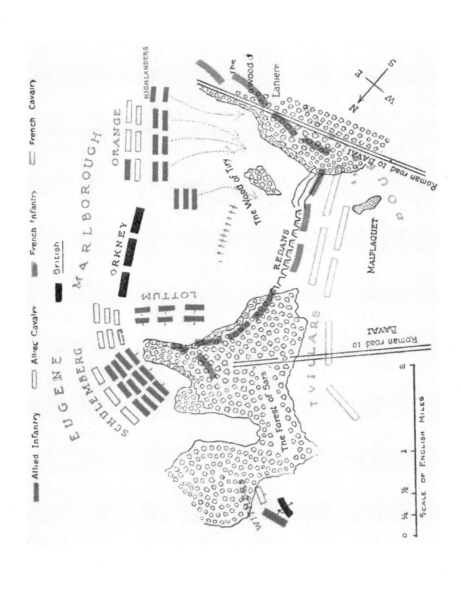

Legend:
- Allied Infantry
- Allied Cavalry
- French Infantry
- French Cavalry
- British

EUGENE

MARLBOROUGH

SCHULEMBERG

LOTTUM

ORKNEY

ORANGE

HIGHLANDERS

The Wood of Tiry

The Wood of Laniere

REDANS

The Forest of Sars

WITHERS

TISNIERS

MALPLAQUET

Roman road to BAVAI

Roman road to BAVAI

SCALE OF ENGLISH MILES

0   ¼   ½   1   2

army would in itself have been no light undertaking, had not Villars, completely deceived by the enemy's movements, and expecting daily an attack, drawn from the fortress one half its garrison. The remaining moiety, consisting of eighteen battalions, was commanded by the Marquis de Surville, a man whose excessive vanity clouded his good qualities. (The necessity devolved upon him during the siege of coining silver pieces. He caused these to bear on one side his effigy crowned with laurels, on the other, his name, with the arms of the town. The king never forgave him.)

Marlborough on this occasion commanded the besieging, Eugene the covering, army. The trenches were opened the night of the 7th July; the batteries were placed four days later. On the 28th Surville sent two officers, one to each of the allied commanders, to offer to surrender the town. The terms were agreed to, and on the 30th the garrison withdrew within the citadel.

Villars, meanwhile, had drawn to himself reinforcements from the Army of the Rhine, and had so extended his lines that they reached from the German Ocean to the Meuse, and severed from France the territory on which the Allies were operating. He had resolved to attempt the relief of Tournai, and had reached a point threatening St Amand, then occupied by Eugene, when the news of the surrender of the place reached him. He then halted, watching for an opportunity to strike a blow.

The Allies meanwhile had attacked the citadel. Mining operations of a most desperate character were conducted, and met with equal courage. Hunger at last forced the garrison to surrender, and on the 3rd September, they evacuated the place, marching out, in consideration of their gallantry, with all the honours of war. The capture of Tournai led the allied commanders to meditate a fresh undertaking. To attack Villars in his lines seemed to promise no favourable result. Valenciennes was covered by the French Army, and, in other respects offered difficulties. Finally, Mons, the capital of the province of Hainault, only thirty-six miles from Brussels, and slenderly garrisoned, was selected as the place to be attempted. The only difficulty in the way of the enterprise lay in the necessity to be beforehand with Villars, to prevent him from reoccupying his former lines, which stretched from the Trouille to the Sambre.

Although, to effect this purpose, the Allies had to cover a longer stretch of ground than would have Villars, had he attempted to anticipate them, they fully succeeded. On the morning of the 4th

September the Crown Prince of Hesse-Cassel, who commanded the advance-guard, marching forty-nine miles in fifty-six hours, gained a position to the south-west of Mons, which interposed between Villars and that fortress. There he was joined, before the French Army could prevent it, by the rest of the allied army. Mons was thus severed alike from France and from the French Army.

A few days before, the King of France had sent Marshal Boufflers, who we have seen defending Lille, to aid Villars with his advice, and, in case of accident, to succeed him. Boufflers was much senior to Villars, but, with an abnegation of self which has been conspicuous by its absence from the French Army during the present century, he willingly consented to serve under him. Villars received him with the greatest delight. The two marshals resolved at any cost to save Mons.

The Allies had taken a strong position in a country hilly, woody, well watered, intersected with ravines. Marlborough's wing, the left, was covered by the wood of Lanière, Eugene's by that of Taisnière. On the right of the latter rose a wooded hill commanding the neighbouring country, called the wood of Sart. Between the woods were many clearings, separated from each other by ravines. The clearings in front of Eugene were called La Louvière, those in front of Marlborough bore the name of Aulnoit, from the village of the same name.

It was through these clearings that Villars determined to advance to attack the Allies. Forming his army into four columns, he set out early on the morning of the 9th September, seized the entrances to both clearings, took then a position behind that of Aulnoit, whilst, with one division he seized the wood of Taisnière, and with another that of Lanière. Having occupied these advantageous positions, he deemed it more prudent to await in them an attack. Renouncing, then, his earlier intention, he employed the spade very diligently to fortify himself where he was.

Eugene and Marlborough had watched these movements with eager eyes. Early the same morning they had met at the mill of Sart, almost exactly opposite the centre point of the enemy's operations. Divining in a very short time the intentions of the French general, Marlborough pushed his wing forward, resting his left on the wood of Lanière, his right on Sart, and advancing his headquarters to Blaregnies behind the centre of his army. Eugene, at the same time, brought up eighteen battalions, and linked them on to Marlborough's right, whilst he sent urgent orders that the remainder should push forward from Quaregnon. The generals then called a council of war.

At this council the opinion expressed by the Dutch deputies was against an attack on a position which, naturally strong, was being made every moment stronger. This argument was combated by Marlborough and Eugene. Undoubtedly, they urged, an immediate attack was preferable to delay, but delay would bring to reinforce them the troops from Tournai, and on their arrival an assault would be imperative. At this result the council arrived. Meanwhile General Dedem was despatched to seize St. Ghislains, thus to open a direct communication with Tournai.

In the course of the next day Eugene's troops came up, and the French completed their entrenchment. Noting, upon examination, that it was strongest in the centre, the allied commanders resolved to make a false attack upon that point and to direct their principal efforts against the wings. Of these, the right was commanded by Lieut.-General d'Artagnan, the left by Lieut.-General Legal. The two marshals, Villars and Boufflers, had taken up their-position at Longueville, a point whence they could command a view of the whole field, and hasten or direct assistance to the part which should be most endangered. At the decisive moment, when the battle was first engaged, they however, separated, Villars taking the supreme direction of the left wing, Boufflers that of the right.

I have already stated that Marlborough commanded the left, Eugene the right wing of the allied army. Under the former served, in the first line, Field-Marshal Claude, Count of Tilly, the nephew of the famous opponent of Gustavus Adolphus, commanding the Dutch troops, the Crown Prince of Hesse-Cassel, the Prince of Orange-Nassau, and General von Bülow, leading the contingents of Hanover and of smaller German princes, in the second line, the English troops, led by Lord Albemarle, the Prussians, commanded by Count Lottum, and a Dutch reserve by Baron Fagel.

The right wing was formed entirely of Imperial troops, a few Danish soldiers, and some Dutch cavalry. The front line, consisting of Saxons and Austrians, was commanded, under Eugene, by General von der Schulenburg (not "Schulemberg," as in Alison's *Life of Marlborough*) and Count Vehlen, the second by Prince Charles Frederic of Würtemberg. Eighteen battalions formed a connecting link between the left of Eugene's line and the right of Marlborough's, whilst Eugene had directed General Withers, the commander of the troops coming from Tournai, to march straight to the farm of La Folie, in the left rear of the enemy's position and to attack their flank and rear at a critical moment. Withers took up his position accordingly.

The night before the battle, Eugene took no rest. Up to one o'clock he was engaged in galloping here and there, seeing that all his orders were being punctually carried out. At one he visited his front line and prescribed to Schulenburg the exact movement he wished him to make. At 3 o'clock the troops were ordered under arms. Prayers were read, and the men then marched to take up their allotted positions.

At the same hour the French soldiers formed their line of defence. Confident in themselves, in the strength of their position, and in their leaders, they were in the highest spirits. Lustily cheered they for the marshal and for the king when Villars rode down their ranks. Through the thick mist which obscured the coming light of day, those cheers penetrated to the camp of the Allies, conveying the assurance that they would meet foemen worthy of their steel, as daring and as confident as were they.

The French, already in their positions, were the first to open fire. The front line of attack marked out by Marlborough and Eugene was within cannon range, and the French guns played upon it as their enemy was forming. Until that formation had been completed there was no reply, but then, from the right wing, where Eugene commanded, there poured upon the defences a general discharge from the heavy guns posted there. Under cover of the smoke Schulenburg led forward forty battalions along the edge of the wood of Sart, against the extreme left flank of the left wing of the enemy, which projected somewhat forward. Across ditches, marshes, and brooks pressed the gallant Saxons, till they reached the hard ground in front of the extended point of attack, then they charged.

Opposed to them was Lieut.-General Albergotti, a very capable officer. Albergotti had noted the approach of the enemy, and had ordered his men to reserve their fire till the Saxons should approach within pistol-range. Then they poured in a fire so deadly and so destructive, that the front rank fell back badly smitten, carrying with it the ranks in its rear.

But Schulenburg was no ordinary leader. Not in vain had he combated against Charles XII. Quickly rallying his men, he re-formed them, and was about to lead them to a second attack when Eugene galloped to the spot. The insensibility to danger of the leader of the Imperial Army, the desire to inspire his troops by his example, caused him often to merge the duties of a general-in-chief into those of a leader of a forlorn hope. It was so on this occasion. Placing himself at the head of the rallied Saxons, he led them forward, carried the first line of entrenchments, then the second. The third line was apparently so weak as to afford little defence to the Frenchmen behind it. These retreated as the Saxons pressed on.

Not, indeed, from want of courage. The plans of the French commander had been deeply laid. Should the enemy carry the first two lines of defence, he designed to lead them on to a position where he could overwhelm them. As the Saxons pressed on they found the forest increase in density. So thick did it become that regiments and companies, even sections, became separated, and it was impossible to distinguish friend from foe.

At last the assailants arrived, scattered and in disorder, in front of an entrenchment stronger than those which they had carried. Here the French had intended to muster in force. But events in other parts of the field came to spoil this intention just at the moment when it might have been made effective, and Eugene, still leading the Saxons, succeeded, after a fierce resistance, in carrying this obstacle also. The carrying of this, combined with the gradual advance of Withers on the left rear, rendered imperative the evacuation of the wood of Sart by the French. Albergotti, on evacuating that wood, led his men to a new position behind the wood of Taisnière.

Whilst matters had thus progressed on the extreme right of the allied army, Marlborough, on the left, had not been idle. There, by his orders, General Lottum, leading twenty-two English and Prussian battalions, had dashed against the front of the French left wing. The men of that wing, animated and encouraged by their gallant commander, received and hurled back the attack. The Prince of Orange, who advanced then with thirty battalions of German and Dutch troops, had no better fortune. It was at this moment that news reached Villars of the success achieved by Eugene against Albergotti. The loss of the wood of Sart rendered his position on the left untenable. As quick as lightning, then, Villars fell back in splendid order to his second line of defence—behind the wood of Taisnière—so as to renew communication with, and give a hand to, the extreme left of his wing.

He had just taken this new position when Eugene fell upon him. The struggle was fierce and bloody, both sides doing all that men could do, the leaders animating their men and exposing themselves like the meanest soldier. Of those leaders Eugene was the first to feel the effect of this daring. A shot grazed the back of his head, causing a sensation as though he had been stunned. Quickly rallying, however, he threw off the effects, and remained mounted, giving orders, refusing even to grant the time for the application of a bandage to the wounded part.

It was now one o'clock. The struggle had continued with swaying fortune, and no one could divine how it would terminate, for, if the Allies had gained the wood of Sart, the French were making the most determined efforts to recover the advantage. Eugene saw that only a supreme effort could win the day. He closed up his battalions, and, moving them into the open, charged vigorously the French line. But Villars, ever quick in thought as in action, and never more so than on the field of battle, had detected his intention, and, realising its importance, moved thirty battalions against him, and at the point of the bayonet drove back the Imperial troops.

To accomplish this result with certainty Villars had drawn to himself the troops which maintained his communication with his right wing. Boufflers was thus as it were isolated, for a gap had thereby been created between the two wings. Villars, in fact, in his eagerness to strike a decisive blow at the enemy's right, had committed a fault which Villars alone could repair. It is possible enough that Villars might have repaired it, but the danger incurred by a man of genius, however consummate, in deviating from rule, lies in the fact that he, too, is liable to all the accidents of life, and that the repairing power dwells in him alone. Thus it was on the present occasion. Villars had repulsed Eugene, as he believed decisively, then his mmd recurred to the fact that to mass the troops necessary to produce this result, he had broken communication with his right, and that that communication must be restored.

He had turned his horse to lead back his reserves to the necessary spot when a bullet struck him in the knee, and he fell to the ground fainting and senseless. His fall, which was perceived by his men, produced a double effect. It disheartened them, and it caused to banish till it was too late the intention to restore communication with the right. Of the first effect Eugene was prompt to take advantage. His warrior's eye detected at once the faltering in the attack caused by the fall of Villars. He rallied his men, and brought them again to the charge. His attack was met this time with so little vigour that he forced back the French left wing, and at length compelled it to abandon all its positions!

Whilst on the allied right matters had taken so satisfactory a turn, Marlborough had been acting not less energetically against Boufflers. When, after repulsing the second attack on the front of his left wing, Villars had fallen back on his extreme left, Marlborough had despatched fifteen battalions under Lord Orkney, supported by twenty-seven squadrons under General Bülow and a reserve of ninety squadrons under the Prince of Würtemberg, to storm the position occupied by the left of the French right—so to speak, their right centre.

The attack was made with great fury, and the first line of the entrenchment was carried. Then, with great promptitude, Orkney turned the conquered guns as well as those of a light battery he had hurriedly brought up, upon the French cavalry posted on the plateau of Malplaquet. Under their fire the Prince d'Auvergne dashed forward with thirty Dutch squadrons to the charge. The French met the attack with their accustomed gallantry, and the fight was yet doubtful, when Boufflers, forming into a column the *élite* of his cavalry, took the Dutch horse in flank, drove them back to the entrenchment, and would probably have retaken it but that at the moment there came galloping to the spot the ninety squadrons of the Prince of Würtemberg. Before their numbers Boufflers fell back.

Meanwhile, the Prince of Orange had re-formed his men after his repulse, and had led them against the entrenchment which covered the approach to Malplaquet. In no part of the field was the fight more fiercely contested than that near the spot which gave its name to the battle. The entrenchment was very strong, and was defended with great courage. But the Prince of Orange was not to be baffled, he led his men again and again to the assault. At last his courage and perseverance triumphed, and the enemy retreated on the village.

Boufflers recognised now that unless he could make a supreme effort the day was lost. Eugene was driving back the French left; Marlborough had pierced the centre; their right was uncovered. He was considering whether by a bold movement it might not be possible to restore the battle, when he received information that General Withers was already compromising his line of retreat. It was then 3 o'clock. To delay longer was madness. Boufflers therefore formed his men into three masses and began a general retreat.

This took place in good order, and the French Army reached, without much annoyance, the camp which had been prepared for it between Quesnoy and Valenciennes, twelve miles from the field of battle. The Allies were too exhausted to pursue, they rested where they had fought, their generals contenting themselves with despatching twelve squadrons to observe and report the enemy's movements.

Such was the famous Battle of Malplaquet, the bloodiest known till then in modern history. The loss of the victors was greater than that of the vanquished. That of the former amounted to from eighteen thousand to twenty thousand men, the French admitted a loss of seven thousand, but German writers raise it to fifteen thousand. Probably it did not exceed eleven thousand. Villars was so satisfied with the gallantry of his soldiers that he declared he could have "imagined he was leading the famed legions of Rome." If the conquered soldiers were of that stamp, too much praise cannot be rendered to the conquerors. A French officer wrote after the battle:

Till Malplaquet, the Allies had encountered no opposition worthy of the name. Now they can truly say that nothing can stop them.

And, in truth, when, the morning after the battle, the two leaders visited those parts of the field where the contest had been most severe, when they saw the corpses of twelve hundred men of the battalion of the Dutch Guard lying stiff and cold in front of the entrenchments they had failed to storm, and the ditch behind them so full of bodies that not a particle of earth was visible, they must have felt that to gain that victory they had sacrificed the very choicest of their troops, and that another such would leave them unable to profit by it.

The results of Malplaquet were in no way proportionate to its cost. The French Army retreated in good order, taking with it all its impedimenta, (*jusqu'à leure marmites*—even their pots) to a new position as strong as the former. There, under Berwick, who was sent to replace Villars, it watched the movements of the Allies. These resumed, indeed, the siege of Mons, and pressed the place so vigorously—Eugene commanding the besieging force and Marlborough the covering army—that on the 20th October it surrendered on honourable terms, its garrison being allowed to march out with all the honours of war.

But this was the solitary result of the victory. The losses sustained combined with the season of the year, aggravated by excessive rains, to prevent further operations, and the armies on both sides proceeded to take up winter quarters. If, then, Malplaquet was one of the bloodiest of battles, it was one of the least fruitful of consequences. Villars had fought it to save Mons. Though he had failed, he had inflicted upon the enemy a very sensible loss, and it has to be admitted that, viewing the campaign in its bearing upon a possible invasion of France, the French king had no great reason to be dissatisfied with it.

CHAPTER 12

The Campaigns of 1710-11

The campaign of 1709, in the other parts of Europe, had not been altogether very favourable to the Allies. In Spain, indeed, Starhemberg and Stanhope had more than held their own. In Italy the French had attempted nothing. Count Wirich Daun had indeed designed to invade France, and, uniting himself to the army which, under Count Mercy, had entered Franche Comté, to penetrate to and besiege Lyon. This design, however, had been completely frustrated by the French general, du Bourg, who had fallen upon Mercy and driven him, with the loss of half his army, across the Rhine. The future King of England, the Elector of Hanover, and who was designated by Eugene, in consequence of his lack of soldierly qualities, "the phantom of a prince," had attempted nothing to repair this disaster, but had persevered in the course of inactivity which had characterised his campaign of the previous year.

It seemed, then, at Vienna, necessary, if the King of France was to be crushed to the dust, to make the supreme effort in 1710 on lines similar to those on which Marlborough and Eugene had jointly operated in 1709. But many reasons induced the Allies, the Emperor alone excepted, to wish for peace on fair terms. The Dutch, especially, were tired of the war, they had gained all that they wanted, whilst the terrible losses at Malplaquet had filled the land with mourning. A strong and increasing party in England was denouncing the fruitless slaughter. The princes of the Empire, the King of Prussia especially, were unwilling to continue a war which would result mainly in the aggrandisement of the House of Habsburg.

On the other side, Louis XIV. was most anxious for peace. The convoys whom he sent to Gertruidenberg to treat for peace agreed to cede the entire Spanish dominions to the Emperor's brother, provided

Sicily and Sardinia were secured to his grandson, further, he offered that if his grandson were to refuse these terms within six months, he would contribute a fixed sum to aid in expelling him. It was the interest of Austria to accept terms so favourable. But the statesmen of Vienna were blinded by the victories which Eugene had gained for them. They insisted that the King of France should contribute his armies instead of a sum of money to expel his grandson, and when Louis refused, they had influence enough to cause the breaking off the negotiations.

Before that had happened, operations had begun. On the 18th April, Marlborough and Eugene had proceeded to Tournai to enter upon the campaign—practically the last they were to make together. They had resolved, as soon as their army should attain sufficient strength, to march on and besiege Douai. Douai lies nineteen miles south of Lille, on the River Scarpe, and is traversed by a canal. In 1710 it was covered on the side opposite the Scarpe by entrenched lines of considerable strength, occupied for the moment by forty battalions and twenty squadrons, commanded by the D'Artagnan who had fought at Malplaquet, who had for his conduct in that battle, where he had three horses shot under him, been nominated Marshal of France, and who had then taken the name of Montesquiou. The actual garrison, eight thousand strong, was commanded by General Albergotti.

On the evening of the 20th April the allied armies marched towards this place, and twenty-four hours later reached the plain of Lens—a plain famous for the victory gained by Condé over the Spaniards in 1648—and taking its name from the town of Lens, ten miles from Béthune.

The French Army, refreshed and strengthened since Malplaquet, was posted between those two towns. The sudden advance of the Allies completely disconcerted Montesquiou, who commanded it till Villars should arrive. He had but little time to reflect. He directed, then, his left wing to fall back on Béthune, whilst with the other he retreated on Vitry, behind the Scarpe. So hurried were his movements that his officers were forced to sacrifice all their baggage. From Vitry, Montesquiou, still deeming himself insecure, fell back on Cambrai, leaving the road to Douai open to the Allies. They pushed on, and on the 24th began the siege. On the 5th May they opened trenches. Three days later the siege-train arrived in camp.

Louis was most anxious to strike a blow to prevent the fall of Douai. He had received the wounded Villars with honour and distinction after Malplaquet, and had assigned him in his palace at Versailles the rooms of the Prince of Conti, where Villars received visits from the highest courtiers, and from Madame de Maintenon herself. Appealed to by Louis to save his frontier fortresses, Villars set out, at the end of April, for the army, his wounded knee clamped by iron plates. He reached Cambrai in May. On the twentieth his entire army was assembled there.

To relieve him, as much as possible, from the most arduous duties of command, Berwick and Montesquiou had been associated with him. On the 3rd of May he moved forward into the plain of Lens. Ranged before him, stretching from Vitry to Montigny, covered by entrenchments, was the allied army. Judging their position too strong to be attacked, Villars during four days employed all the arts of which he was a master to entice them from it, nor was it until he recognised that he had failed that he retreated. Eugene, it is said, was eager to pursue him, but the more cautious Marlborough held him back, saying that their first business was to take Douai. So closely did Eugene then press the siege of that place that on the 16th June, Albergotti sent a messenger to inform Villars that he could not hold out much longer.

Upon this Villars made a movement as though he would cross the Scarpe, but Marlborough marched at once to Bellone, and rendered the contemplated movement impossible without an action. This, Villars, under the circumstances, dared not risk. A defeat would have laid Paris open to a daring enemy. From this time, then, he gave up all hope of saving Douai, and directed all his measures to render the further progress of the Allies after the fall of that place impossible.

Douai surrendered the 29th June. In a political sense the capture of that place was a misfortune, for it enabled Eugene to carry with him the Allies in insisting upon terms of peace such as Louis XIV could not grant. He urged that France was so desolated and exhausted by war and famine that a continuation of hostilities would procure conditions even more favourable. It was his insistence, as representative of the House of Austria, which rendered the proceedings of the Congress of Gertruidenberg fruitless. In this he displayed a lamentable want of foresight and political wisdom. It may truly be said of him that, had he shown at the head of his army the same want of prescience which characterised him on the field of politics, he never would have gained a great reputation.

It was the less excusable, for he knew that, of all the allies, Austria—that is, the House of Habsburg, without the other princes of

Germany—was the only power interested in the continuance of the war, that England and Holland were weary of it, that a change of ministry in the former country would probably give effect to the national feeling in favour of peace, and especially, he ought to have calculated on the possibility of that happening which did happen—of the death of the Emperor and the succession of his brother. This was always looming in the future, and it was a possibility which would radically change all the conditions of the great European war. But, as has so often happened, the House of Habsburg was blind to its true interests, and Eugene partook largely of the blindness.

To resume. After Douai had fallen, the Allies resolved to besiege Arras. But Villars had not vainly employed his time. He now occupied an entrenched position covering that town and Cambrai, so strong that the Allies did not dare to attack him. As, however, to concentrate his army in that position Villars had exposed the entire country to the north-west and west as far as the sea, the Allies turned against Béthune, nineteen miles to the north-west from Arras. On the 16th July they sat before the place.

Béthune was a fortress of the third rank, but it was, in the opinion of Villars, worthy of an attempt to save it. On the 30th of July, then, he quitted his strong position between Cambrai and Arras, and, swinging his army round, took up a new position. He still covered Arras—now with his right—whilst he rested his left on Brétancourt, covering Hesdin, and thus barring the road into France from Béthune to the Allies. Here he threw up strong entrenchments.

He could not save Béthune. On the 28th August the commandant of that fortress made overtures for surrender. These were accepted, and the place was occupied by the Allies on the 31st. The two generals, then, unable to attack Arras, and unwilling from the strength of his position to assail Villars, marched towards Aire and St. Venant, and began simultaneously the siege of these two places, both to the north-west of Béthune, on the 6th September.

St. Venant surrendered the 2nd October, but Aire, a fortress of the second class, well situated for defence, from the fact that it was possible so to overflow the country around it as to render it liable to attack on one point only, held out till the 8th November. The *commandant* then notified his willingness to capitulate.

All this time Villars made no sign. He was content that his enemies should lose their men in sieges, whilst he kept his army in hand to cover France when they should have taken all the frontier fortresses.

And, certainly, never did a commander render more efficient service to his country. In the four sieges they had conducted, the Allies had lost thirty thousand men by sickness and the enemy's fire. They were further diminished in strength by from ten to fifteen thousand more, whom they had placed in garrisons in the conquered fortresses. Villars, on the other hand, had his army intact. Occupying unassailable positions, covering France, he had gained a year. And at that crisis, time was all in all to France.

From that point of view, it is impossible to dispute the conclusion that, though Marlborough and Eugene took four important fortresses, the advantage of the campaign of 1710 lay with Villars. He had done more than gain fortresses, he had gained for France the time necessary to strengthen the Peace Party in England and in Holland, to allow Nature to run her course with the Emperor, and that disunion to ferment which had been visible to the sharp-sighted French diplomatists at Gertruidenberg. He had not long to wait for his reward. On the 17th April, 1711, the Emperor Joseph died. That event changed fundamentally the conditions of the contest. Europe had aimed to prevent the Bourbons from monopolising the crowns of France and Spain. Would it fight now to secure those two crowns for one member of the House of Habsburg?

In another country, too, the time gained by Villars had been useful for France. In Spain, the English general, Stanhope, had been forced to surrender with his whole army at Brihuega (9th December) whilst Starhemberg, after having gained the battles of Almenara (27th July), of Saragossa (20th August), and proclaimed the Archduke King of Spain at Madrid (21st September), had been beaten at Villa Vicioza (10th December), and compelled to recross the Catalonian frontier.

The character of the new Emperor (Charles VI.) singularly aided the plans of Louis XIV. Charles had proceeded to Spain, an aspirant to the crown of that country, to give life by his presence to his cause. There he had imbibed a love for the Spanish character which had become a passion. Narrow, obstinate, precise, punctilious, a lover of forms and ceremonies, he imbibed an intense admiration for the national character of his adopted country. When the news reached him that by the death of his bother the double crown of Charles V. had fallen to him, he was with difficulty persuaded to quit Spain. Surrounded by Spanish councillors, who had imperilled their lives and fortunes to support him, he clung to a title which had more charms for him than the title of Emperor of Germany.

When at length he was persuaded to return, he returned a Habsburg indeed in obstinacy, a Spaniard in every other feature of character. For a long time, no statesman in his hereditary dominions dared even to whisper to him the advisability of the cession of an inch of the territories of Charles II. of Spain.

The death of the Emperor Joseph, then, made the Empire, as represented by the new Emperor, more than ever determined to continue the war. In England other sentiments prevailed. There the Whig Ministry had been replaced, August 1710, by a Tory Ministry, of which Harley and St. John were the prominent members. The object of this ministry was to preserve the balance of power in Europe. In their opinion Louis had been sufficiently humbled, and they had no desire to weaken France still further to the advantage of a prince who should wear the double crown of Germany and Spain. They were inclined, in cordial understanding with Holland, Portugal, Savoy, and Prussia, to treat with France on the basis of the recognition of the Protestant succession in England, of the severance of the French and Spanish Crowns, of the enlargement of the British colonies in America, and of a full satisfaction of the claims of the Allies. It was not to be expected that under such circumstances they would display much zeal in the war.

Under such circumstances the campaign of 1711 opened Eugene proceeded, as soon as possible after the death of the Emperor Joseph, to Mainz to assure the fidelity of the Arch-Chancellor to the cause of the new aspirant to the Empire, and thence to Bruchsal in the Grand Duchy of Baden (24th April) to assume there the command of the Reich's army. Recognising that little could be undertaken on that side, and that his presence was more necessary in the Netherlands, he made over the command of that army to the Duke of Würtemberg, he set out to proceed thither, and joined Marlborough at Anzin, two and a half miles south-west of Valenciennes.

It soon became evident to him that the death of the Emperor Joseph had gained another year for France. In the first place Charles had yet to be elected Emperor, and on this account, in order to prevent any disturbance at Frankfurt, the Imperial Army had been weakened. The disaster of Brihuega had caused likewise the despatch from the English Army of five battalions to Catalonia. On the other hand, Louis, perceiving the change in his favour which the death of the Emperor had wrought in Europe, and that the alliance against him was in process of dissolution, had ordered Villars on no account to risk a battle.

Villars did not risk a battle, but he did all in his power to annoy and cause damage to the enemy. With this view, he did not hesitate to weaken his army by detaching a strong corps under Max Emanuel of Bavaria to the Rhine. This action produced the effect which he had foreseen Eugene, dreading lest Max Emanuel should attack Frankfurt, or, worse still, should attempt to penetrate into Bavaria, broke away from Marlborough, and marched with all his available troops, twenty thousand strong, to the Upper Rhine (14th June). He marched by way of Düsseldorf to Mühlburg, becoming day by day more convinced that Charles was imperilling his election by prolonging his stay in Catalonia. It required, however, many earnest representations to induce that obstinate prince to quit the country which he loved: nor was it till the 20th September that he embarked to assume the dignities which were soon to devolve upon him. He landed at Vado the 12th October, the very day on which he was elected Emperor at Frankfurt.

Eugene remained throughout this time at Mühlburg, satisfied with having baffled any intention which Max Emanuel might have had either to disturb the election or to penetrate into Bavaria. When the country about Mühlburg had been exhausted he crossed the Rhine and encamped in the vicinity of Speyer. In his absence Marlborough had taken Bouchain, twelve miles south-east of Douai. But this was the solitary achievement of the campaign. Again, had Louis XIV. and Villars had the best of it. They had gained another year, and that a most important year; for at the close of it, Marlborough was recalled, and, the 1st January 1712, was deprived of all his employments.

To set against the loss of a year which witnessed the rapid cooling of the English, Dutch, and Prussian sympathies for the House of Habsburg, that House could boast of the pacification of Hungary, and the election of a new Emperor bent on carrying on the war to the utmost.

One of the first acts of the new Emperor was to despatch Eugene to England, to endeavour to change the pacific ideas of the English Ministry. Eugene reached London the 16th January. But the very instructions he carried with him foredoomed his mission to failure. He said to Harley:

> If there were any question on the part of England of ceasing to insist upon the claim of the Emperor to the throne of Spain and the Indies, I have no longer any business in this country.

He stayed in England two months, and returned to The Hague with the conviction that, for the assertion of his Spanish claims:

The Emperor had nothing to hope for from the English Ministry.

It became very soon as clear to Eugene that he had as little to hope for from the English Army. The successor to Marlborough in command of that army was the Duke of Ormond, a general of cavalry, who had never before commanded in chief. Before he left London, Ormond had been warned by St John to beware of the enterprising spirit of Eugene, and to agree to no military undertaking the success of which was not absolutely certain. He believed himself, moreover, to be clothed with the same powers which had been vested in Marlborough, and he made a representation to the effect to Eugene.

When the campaign of 1712 opened, the French Army, still commanded by Marshal Villars, occupied an entrenched position between Catelet, close to the source of the Scheldt, and Arras, barring the road to Paris. Eugene and Ormond, who had met at Tournai, joined the allied army at Anzin the 21st May. On the 23rd they passed it in review, and from the demeanour of his colleague on that occasion Eugene imbibed impressions so favourable that he proposed to him to attack the French marshal in his entrenched lines, and to undertake the siege of Le Quesnoy.

In pursuance of this idea Eugene, leaving Lord Albemarle with a division of Dutch troops to watch at Denain the road from the Scheldt to the Scarpe, by way of Souches, crossed the first-named river and took up a position at Haspres, eight miles south of Valenciennes. Thence, the following day, he despatched the two quartermasters-general, Cadogan and Dopff, escorted by a strong cavalry division, to examine the position of the enemy, and to ascertain whether it might not be possible to turn his right flank. They returned with the report that no particular difficulties offered to the prosecution of such a plan. The same day Eugene summoned Ormond and the deputies of the States-General to consult with him regarding the measures necessary to undertake such a plan.

He had been that day privately informed that Ormond would oppose any proposition for attack, but it was, he thought, necessary that he should learn the refusal to co-operate from the lips of that duke himself. At the conference, then, he began by pointing out how easily, and with what little risk, his plan of attack could be carried out. The enemy's position, he said, was so badly chosen, that they had it in their power to gain a victory more decisive than any yet achieved in the war. Should, for any reason, the deputies be averse to fighting, it was still possible to hold the enemy in check whilst Le Quesnoy or Landrecies, or both at the same time, should be invested.

The Dutch deputies, won over beforehand by Eugene, agreed at once to his proposition to attack the enemy. But Ormond sat for long silent. When at length he did speak, he declared that he had positive orders not to risk a battle; further, that it would be necessary even to refer to England as to whether he could co-operate in the proposed sieges. Eugene, prepared for such an answer, then asked the duke how it was, if such were his orders, that he had accompanied him without remonstrance into a position in close vicinity to the enemy's army, right between two hostile fortresses—a position tenable only for a short time, and the only justification for occupying which, lay in the fact that it was a good base for attack.

The duke must know, added Eugene, that it was impossible to remain there Villars had only to despatch his cavalry into the fortresses on their flanks to deprive them of the possibility of obtaining subsistence. If he would undertake nothing, he could not understand his presence there. Finally, he begged him, if England had already entered into an understanding with France, to let him know it. If she had not done so, her conduct, as interpreted by Ormond, was dangerous alike to herself and to Europe.

Ormond could not answer him. There was no doubt a secret understanding between the Ministers of Queen Anne and Louis XIV. Four days before the conference I have described, Villars had received an intimation from his sovereign that the English troops would join in no attack upon his army. Villars, then, under the pretext of negotiating for the exchange of the Marquis d'Alègre, then a prisoner in England, wrote to Ormond to inquire whether the orders he had received to be passive applied only to the English troops, or to all the troops in the pay of England. Ormond had not been sufficiently instructed by his government to be able to give a decided answer.

But, as far as the English troops were concerned, the order had gone forth, and the issue of it, at such a moment, rendered Eugene's position very dangerous. In front of him was a powerful enemy, on his flank a doubtful friend. He had no assurance that this "friend" might not, by a turn of the English Cabinet, become an open enemy. Under these circumstances he displayed a moral courage which astonished even his enemies. Believing that the position he occupied was well fitted for striking from it an offensive blow, he refused, with a view of deceiving Villars as to the intention of the English commander, Ormond's request to change the position he had assigned to him, then suddenly invested Le Quesnoy, placing his army in so advantageous a position behind the Sellé, that whilst one wing besieged that place, the other, looking towards Cambrai and the enemy, covered its operations. At the same time, he despatched a cavalry brigade, twelve hundred strong, across the Somme and the Oise, to spread terror in the interior of France.

Whilst the siege of Le Quesnoy, begun the 8th June, was progressing, Eugene was engaged in, amongst other weighty matters, assuring himself of the continued co-operation of the troops of the North German States, especially of Prussia. The latter were still commanded by Leopold of Anhalt-Dessau, who had fought so valiantly at Blenheim. The replies of Leopold, as well as the replies of the commanders of the Danish, the Saxon, and the Hessian contingents, were favourable to his wishes. But, regarding the English and the Hanoverians, there was very soon to be no doubt whatever. On the 17th June, Queen Anne laid before her Parliament the conditions of the treaty she had arranged with France. On the 23rd Ormond informed Eugene, by a messenger, that he had been ordered by his Court to withdraw, with the English troops and the troops in British pay, to Dunkirk, there to await the signing of the conditions of peace.

In vain did Eugene and the deputies of the States-General, at a personal interview, dwell upon the disgrace the English commander incurred in thus abandoning his allies in the presence of an enemy. Ormond insisted that he felt the shame of the conduct imposed upon him cannot be doubted, for, although he had given orders to the troops under his control to march on the 26th, he still lingered in his position. He was still there when, on the 4th July, Le Quesnoy surrendered, its garrison becoming prisoners of war. Not even then did he move. Not till the 16th, when Eugene took up a new position, did Ormond, taking with him twelve thousand men, separate for ever from the Imperial Army. That night, when he announced to his troops the conclusion of an armistice with France, the announcement was received in silence and sadness.

Nor, during his march, did he meet with any sympathy. The Dutch *commandants* of Bouchain, of Tournai, and of Douai shut their gates in his face, and refused all access to their towns. Even the King of France, enraged at finding he had not succeeded in withdrawing all the contingents in the pay of England, declared his promise to deliver to him

Dunkirk to be no longer binding. Scorned, then, by his former associates, scouted by Louis, Ormond had then to seek, with the troops who distrusted him, a refuge under the walls of Ghent and Brussels.

Not discouraged by the departure of Ormond, Eugene persisted in continuing the offensive. The very day of the departure of the English, he despatched Leopold of Anhalt-Dessau to invest Landrecies, whilst he made his headquarters at Querimaing to cover the siege Villars, however, was able to take more active measures than had been possible when the Allies were in full force. Strengthening his army by withdrawing from the frontier towns not immediately threatened the great bulk of their garrisons, he crossed the Scheldt near Cambrai on the 18th, and approached Eugene's position. That position was of some extent, for whilst his right wing maintained communication with Marchiennes, the town containing his magazines and depots, and Denain, the left stretched along the banks of the Sellé, which covered it, as far as the Sambre, on the further bank of which river stood Landrecies.

There can be no doubt but that, in the face of an active, skilful enemy such as Villars, the position of Eugene was too extended. No one knew this better than himself, and he had strongly urged upon the deputies of the States-General the advisability of transporting the magazines to Le Quesnoy, where they would be in his very midst. The parsimony of the States-General, the unwillingness to incur the expense of transport beyond Marchiennes, had caused the rejection of this proposal. Under other circumstances Eugene would have insisted; but the political situation was so delicate, the alliance with Holland was liable from any cause to be snapped, that Eugene dared not insist. He was forced to content himself with forming an entrenched camp at Denain, and in uniting that camp to Marchiennes by a double line of field fortifications. At Marchiennes he placed four thousand troops, in the entrenched camp at Denain, eleven thousand, the whole under the command of the first Lord Albemarle, who, naturalised as an Englishman by William III, was for the time, in the service of Holland, his native country.

Marchiennes is twelve miles from Denain, and Denain is fifteen miles distant from Landrecies. On the 20th July, Villars, accompanied by Montesquiou and other officers, reconnoitred Eugene's position between Denain and Landrecies, behind the Sellé, and the lines greatly advanced, before Landrecies. He recognised at once that on these points there was no hope of a successful attack. But at the further end of the long line the chances seemed much more hopeful. Montes-

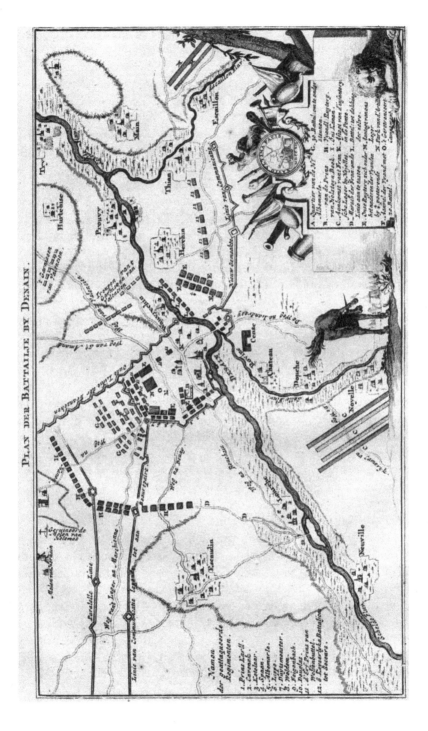

PLAN DER BATTAILJE BY DENAIN.

quiou, whom we have known as the Count of Artagnan, discovered, between Lourches and Denain, a weak point, lightly guarded, in the enemy s double line of entrenchments, and he had suggested to Villars that at this point it might be possible to pierce the enemy's centre. Villars in an instant recognised the value of the discovery. There was no bound to the results which might ensue from its successful application. It opened out the prospect of enormous advantages, the least of which would be the raising of the siege of Landrecies. Villars at once, then, made preparations to carry it into effect.

His first aim was to throw Eugene off his guard, so to manoeuvre as to induce the belief that he was bent solely and entirely on relieving Landrecies. Could he but induce Eugene to believe this, that commander would naturally concentrate his force in and about that fortress. Then would be the time to make a dash on the centre at Denain. Should he pierce the enemy's centre, then the magazines at Marchiennes would be at his mercy, and the siege of Landrecies would be raised. Such was his plan—a plan inspired by genius, but requiring for its execution delicacy of handling, secrecy, quickness of action, the eye of a great commander—in a word all those qualities so rarely bestowed upon one man, but which were possessed in rich abundance by Claude Louis Hector, Duke of Villars.

Confiding his plan to no one except to Montesquiou, who, I have said, had discovered the one weak point in the double line of entrenchment which rendered it possible of execution—not even to the general whom he valued next after Montesquiou, the valiant Albergotti—Villars, on the 22nd July, marched with his whole army towards Landrecies, industriously spreading the rumour that he was resolved, at all costs, to relieve that fortress. That this rumour might seem to embody the exact truth, he despatched General Coigny, with thirty squadrons, across the Sambre.

Having thus given vitality to the idea he wished to propagate, he ordered Count Broglie to march with forty squadrons, the night of the 23rd, along the Sellé, to watch all the fords and crossing-places of that river, and to take particular care that not a single human being should cross to the right bank of that river to give information to Eugene. At the same time, he despatched the Marquis de Vieux Pont, with thirty battalions, to throw a bridge over the Scheldt at Neuville, between Bouchain and Douai. Close upon Vieux Pont followed Albergotti, with twenty battalions, and then the rest of the army in five columns.

Eugene, meanwhile, had, up to the 23rd, watched the enemy's

BATTLE OF DENAIN

movements with an ever-increasing interest. There can be no doubt—indeed, Eugene in his despatch to the Emperor admits—that he was completely deceived as to the intentions of the French marshal. How he was rudely awakened I shall have presently to describe.

The daring plan of Villars was carried out during that night and the next morning, without let or hindrance of any kind. In the early hours of the 24th, Vieux Pont threw three bridges over the Scheldt, close to Neuville. Just before they were completed, de Broglie joined him with his forty squadrons, and, shortly after, Villars, with the rest of the army. To cross and carry the weak and weakly-defended entrenchment between Lourches and Denain, followed very rapidly. Villars then formed his army in order of battle and marched on Denain.

There, as I have said, stood Lord Albemarle, with eleven thousand Dutch troops. His cavalry had just quitted his camp for foraging purposes, when General Bothmar, who had that day the outpost duty, announced to him the approach of the French Army in great force. Instantly Albemarle sent to call in his cavalry, and made a preconcerted signal to the garrisons of Bouchain, Marchiennes and St. Amand. He then made the best dispositions possible under the circumstances. He placed seven squadrons under General Croix in front of the right face of his entrenchment looking towards Valenciennes to watch the garrison of that fortress which had taken post on some heights some distance from it. With his remaining sixteen squadrons he at first endeavoured to occupy the entrenched line communicating with Marchiennes, but no sooner did he become aware of the overwhelming strength of the enemy than he called them back as quickly as possible, with them and with ten battalions he lined the entrenchment upon which Villars was marching.

But the march of the French marshal had not been so secretly conducted to escape the observation of Eugene. At 7 o'clock in the morning the news reached him. Giving immediate orders to his army to march with all expedition, he waited till they were well on the way, then set out himself at a gallop in advance. He reached the position at Denain about 10 o'clock.

The enemy was then in sight. At a glance Eugene recognised that the troops under Albemarle did not nearly suffice to man the entrenchment. He drew then behind the lines the cavalry which had been posted on the right front, and drew to himself six battalions which were guarding the lines at a point beyond Denain in the direction of Marchiennes. He then galloped back to hurry on his main army, ordering Albemarle to defend himself to the last.

Shortly after he had left, Villars, his infantry in front, his cavalry in the rear, and the guns at intervals in the front line, approached the entrenchment. His men were within fifty paces of it when a heavy artillery fire opened upon them. Unshaken and undaunted they pressed on the faster. The outer defences, never very formidable, did not stop them. The soldiers of Holland, whether they were cowed by the enormous superiority of numbers and despaired from the outset of making a successful resistance, or from other causes, displayed nothing of the courage which had distinguished them at Malplaquet. There, whole regiments fell, the faces of the men to the foe, just outside the entrenchment they were endeavouring to storm.

Here, the men of the same nation offered a very feeble defence behind a banner which if not strong was defensible, and which was attacked solely by infantry. The French soldiers pushed aside the loosely piled stones, forced their way into the entrenchment, and, then, charging the Hollanders, forced them in a few minutes to take refuge in flight. Vainly did the gallant Albemarle and the officers under him try to rally them, fruitlessly did he endeavour to throw at least some battalions into the houses of Denain, to delay the progress of the enemy. In the attempt he was surrounded and taken prisoner. The same fate was experienced by three other generals, von Sickingen, von Zobel, and von Dalberg. Generals Dohna and Cornelis were even more unfortunate, they were drowned in the Scheldt.

The calamity I have recorded, great as it was, might yet have been repairable, had it stood alone. Better for Eugene that all the defenders of the lines of Denain should have been slaughtered, than they should have pursued the unreasoning course they actually adopted. Panic-stricken, careless of consequences, they made a hurried rush for the bridge of boats which had been constructed across the Scheldt at Denain, and over which Eugene was about to march his main army. So great was the rush, so overpowering were the numbers, that the bridge broke under their weight, and the passage was rendered for a very valuable time, impossible. At length, however, Eugene rallied to himself the entire cavalry which had been in the entrenched camp, and by degrees the fugitives came to take refuge under his wing.

But it was too late then to attempt to restore the fortunes of the day, or to prevent Villars from reaping the fullest success from his daring stroke. For that eminent soldier, a soldier worthy to take rank with the most distinguished of his profession, of any clime and of any age, proceeded to take the fullest advantage of his success. He had won the Battle of Denain the 24th July. On the 26th, he took St. Amand, then Mortagne, and three days later Marchiennes, containing all the magazines, stores, and provisions of the Imperial Army. The capture of this place carried with it the relief of Landrecies, for it made it impossible for Eugene to continue the siege.

The capture of these places produced a greater morale effect on the result of the war than, in a military sense, the slap at Denain. Already did the members of the States-General see in imagination the conquered barrier reconquered, and the French who had captured Marchiennes and, St. Amand before the gates of Ghent and Brussels. In vain did Eugene represent that Denain was but an accident easy to repair, if he were allowed a free hand. The terrified deputies insisted, as a condition of the employment of the Dutch troops, that he should renounce all offensive operations, and confine himself to a defence of the Dutch frontier.

Compelled, against his dearest convictions, to bend to the will of his allies, Eugene began his march towards the frontier. His astonishment can scarcely be conceived when, a few days later, the same deputies who had insisted upon his making the movement, came to him to intimate that they had changed their minds, and begged him to resume the offensive. But it was then too late. Eugene had lost the garrisons in the places which Villars had taken. Not only, then, did the latter, who had constantly received reinforcements, have under his command an army larger by twenty thousand men than that of his rival, but they were men of one nation. Eugene's army, on the other hand, was composed of contingents from many principalities, the rulers of some of which were already treating with the enemy. In war, opportunity is all in all, and Eugene saw that the opportunity had been lost. He was constrained now to assume an attitude purely defensive.

Villars, after taking Marchiennes and its rich booty, had marched against Douai, and had opened trenches against that fortress the 14th August. It was a great point with Eugene to save Douai. For that purpose, he posted his army at Chateaulieu and spent some days in reconnoitring Villars' position. At last he devised a plan which held out the most brilliant prospect of success; a plan which, if carried out with care and caution, involved but little risk. By his agreement with the States-General he could not execute it without the consent of the Dutch Deputies. These, however, pronounced it too hazardous, and

Eugene was forced to renounce it.

His patience, however, under this trial, and similar trials—and only the commander of an army can tell how bitter they are—was inexhaustible. When he saw that the deputies rejected every plan, and would allow him to do nothing to save Douai, he proposed to strike a counterblow at the enemy by marching against Maubeuge, on the Sambre, garrisoned by only three or four weak battalions. It was an operation comparatively easy, as the siege-train was at Le Quesnoy, and communications with the Netherlands could be maintained by the way of Mons. There was plenty of time, too, to entrench the army of observation, for Douai would still keep the enemy occupied. The capture of the place, moreover, would make Eugene master of the country between the Sambre and the Meuse—the districts whence Villars drew his forage.

So clear were the advantages of such an operation, so absolutely free from difficulties was it, that not even the deputies of the States-General could find a single argument to bear against it. But representing, for the most part, the party in Holland which was bent on peace, they determined that no enterprise should be undertaken which should imperil the progress of negotiations to that end; and, in this respect, also, they, in spite of the anger of Eugene, had their way.

The consequences were such as the Imperial commander had foretold to them. On the 8th September Douai surrendered to the French. Villars then turned his arms against Le Quesnoy, hemmed in that fortress on the 14th, covering the siege operations with his army ranged along the Deule.

To hinder this operation, Eugene, on the 11th, marched to the edge of the wood of Sart, close to the scene of the famous battle gained over the same adversary exactly three years before, and once more urged upon the deputies the advisability of attacking the enemy. He urged:

> They had nothing to lose, everything to gain; for whereas a victory would replace them in the advantageous position they had occupied at the beginning of the campaign, a defeat could not make the conditions of peace more disadvantageous than those which England had accepted.

But he might have spoken to the winds. The deputies replied in so many words:

> Count Tilly has declared the proposal to be bristling with im-

possibilities.

To his intense mortification, then, Eugene was compelled to abandon the conquests of previous campaigns and to content himself with covering Mons, Lille, Tournai, and the strong places behind them.

Undisturbed, then, by his enemy, Villars forced Le Quesnoy to surrender (5th October). He then turned to Bouchain—the last conquest of Marlborough—and took it after a short resistance. The solitary and small compensation to Eugene for these losses was the capture of the fort of Knocks, between Dixmuiden and Dunkirk, which the Prince of Holstein captured with a portion of the garrison of Lille.

Such, was the close of this campaign of 1712, full of glory for Marshal Villars, full of disappointment for Prince Eugene. In contrasting, in his brilliant history of the Peninsular War, the military characteristics of Napoleon and the Duke of Wellington, the late Sir William Napier wrote thus of the difficulties which beset the latter:

> Something besides the difference of genius must be allowed for the difference of situation: Napoleon was never, even in his first campaign of Italy, so harassed by the French as Wellington was by the English, Spanish, and Portuguese Governments.

If, writing of the campaign of 1712, we substitute the name of Eugene for that of Wellington, and the Dutch and petty German Governments for the Spanish and Portuguese, we shall recognise that the remark applies exactly to the Imperial commander. We see how, at the beginning of the campaign, he was thwarted on every occasion by Ormond, how, after the slap he received at Denain, by the Dutch. The generals of the Prussian king—a king as anxious for peace as was Holland, and never desirous to fight for the aggrandisement of the Habsburg—required very delicate management, and towards the end of the campaign they, too, carried their ill-will to the very verge of insubordination—in one instance, indeed, they passed that line.

That, at Denain, Villars achieved the greatest triumph a general can aspire to—that of outmanoeuvring a skilful adversary—cannot be denied. Yet even on this occasion Eugene was not absolutely master of his movements. It was the refusal of the States-General to send the magazines beyond Marchiennes which necessitated the long and weak line stretching from that place to Landrecies. It was, again, the weak defence, followed by the panic of the Dutch troops under Albemarle, which deprived him of the chance of snatching from the brow of Villars his half-won laurels. Under the circumstances of the composition of the two armies it would have disgraced no general, not the greatest who ever lived, to be beaten by Villars. Villars commanded troops all drawn from one nation, the army of Eugene was composed of men of many principalities, each with its own commander reporting to his own sovereign. Having regard to that fact, to the other above referred to of the thwartings he met with on every occasion from his allies, we can only wonder that he made the head he did against the marshal whose faultless campaign of 1712 has ever been the admiration of military students.

CHAPTER 13

The Campaign of 1718, and the Peace of Baden

On March 14th, 1713, England, France, Holland, Portugal, Savoy, and Prussia signed the Peace of Utrecht. The terms upon which the Emperor of Germany might be admitted to that Treaty were formulated, and he was granted till the 1st of June to declare his adherence to the same. But the Emperor Charles VI, never very wise, and still under the influence of his Spanish councillors, did not want peace. He preferred to wage war alone. He withdrew, then, at once, his ambassador from the Congress, and prepared to continue the war—on the Rhine.

The Emperor could not even control the contingents of the princes of the Empire. The Duke of Mecklenburg withdrew his to take part in the war then raging in the north between Poland and Denmark on the one side and Sweden on the other. Some princes, especially the Prince of Holstein, demanded, with the same object, the return of their troops. Others, to be presently referred to, displayed a remarkable disinclination to contribute either in men or in money to the prolongation of the war. The troops of the Empire who remained obedient to the summons of the Emperor had made in the previous year, under the Prince Alexander of Würtemberg, a campaign which, owing to their indiscipline and want of training, had culminated in an unsuccessful attack on the lines of Weisseinberg. The total number of these troops, even when joined by the few who had served under Eugene in the north of France the year preceding, did not exceed fifty thousand.

This army Eugene joined on the night of the 23rd May at Mühlburg, twenty-eight miles to the south-east of the fortress of Landau. To that fortress, before Eugene's arrival, Alexander of Würtemberg had been sent with instructions to defend it to the last. Eugene, then, as soon as he had received the money necessary for him to enter upon a campaign, examined the lines known as the lines of Ettlingen, occupied by a portion of his army. These lines stretched from Ettlingen to the Rhine, and thence southwards, parallel to that river, covering the Grand Duchy of Baden. Eugene found the defences in many places destroyed and the lines far too weakly occupied for their extent. He therefore despatched thither the cavalry general, Vaubonne, an officer of proved distinction, with the strictest orders to set to work immediately to repair and strengthen the lines in the places where repair was necessary. Whilst actively engaged in this work Vaubonne would, by the complete occupation of the lines, guard the Upper Rhine from the point opposite Ettlingen to the frontiers of Switzerland. At the same time Eugene, with a corps composed of North German troops, would watch the Middle Rhine.

But the difficulties in his path were all but insuperable. The German princes, the Emperor alone excepted, were tired of a war carried on solely in the interests of the House of Habsburg, and many of them found a pleasure in hampering Eugene. Thus, the Landgrave of Hesse-Cassel demurred to the placing of his troops under Eugene's orders, and would not allow them to move further than the Middle Rhine, the Prince of Saxe-Coburg Gotha would not permit his contingent to cross the Neckar, the ruler of the Palatinate contributed only four weak squadrons and one battalion to the army, the Prussian regiments remained immovable in the districts of Cologne. Many of the smaller princes made no demonstration whatever, and, to crown his difficulties, the funds which had been promised, and which were absolutely necessary, were conspicuous by their absence!

The general who thus, with but few troops and no money, had to defend a long frontier and to protect the territory beyond the Rhine of which Landau was the capital, was opposed by the most illustrious Marshal of France, wielding all the resources of that country. Far from suffering the difficulties which hampered every movement of Eugene, Villars disposed of two well-provided army corps, one under Marshal Bezons, a soldier of great experience, marching on Trèves, the other led by Lieutenant-General d'Asfeld, the second of four famous brothers, himself not the least illustrious, (see note following) which, by the direction of Villars, had crossed the Rhine and taken a position at Sellingen, below Rastatt. Here, on the 4th of June, Villars joined him, and at once ordered an advance towards Rastatt as though he intended to attack the Ettlingen lines.

The eldest of these brothers, Alexis Bidal, served in the French Army under the Duke of Luxemburg and Marshal de Créqui. Remarkable for his cool courage, he was killed on the field of battle at Aix-la-Chapelle in 1689. The second, Benoit Bidal, ten years younger than Alexis, joined him with the army, obtained the command of a regiment of cavalry, and distinguished himself at the battles of Fleurus, Steenkirk, and Neerwinden, and at the sieges of Mons, Namur, and Charleioi. He commanded the French cavalry at the battles of Chiari and Luzzara. The brilliant part which he bore in the campaign of 1713 will be seen from the text. The third brother, James Vincent Bidal, was a famous theologian, whose Jansenist opinions made him obnoxious to the ruling powers of France. The fourth, Claude Francis Bidal, was a very famous soldier, who, for his services in the Low Countries and in Spain, rose to be Marshal of France. The King of Spain bestowed upon him the Golden Fleece and the rank of Marquis "for himself, with descent to his relations, direct or collateral." We shall meet him in command of an army when we come to recount the last campaign of Prince Eugene.

★★★★★★

To parry this movement Eugene drew to those lines the troops posted at Philipsburg. That was exactly what Villars hoped he would do. He received the information that the Imperialist movement was in progress on the same night. Immediately he turned back in the direction of Lauterburg and despatched General de Broglie with seventeen battalions and twenty-two squadrons across the Rhine against Philipsburg. He followed the next day himself with forty battalions. That night de Broglie seized Halland, a village just opposite Philipsburg, and occupied it in such a manner as to render the passage of the Philipsburg bridge impossible to the Imperialists. That same day Villars reached Speyer and took a position on the rivulet of that name, thus severing the Imperialists' communications between the Rhine and the fortress of Landau.

This accomplished, Villars ordered Marshal Bezons with the first army corps, consisting of fifty-nine battalions and fifty squadrons, to lay siege to that fortress. To secure himself against attack, he posted General Du Bourg with a division at Fort Louis, General Alègre with a corps, mostly cavalry, at Worms. De Broglie formed an entrenched camp opposite Philipsburg, while, to cover the siege, Villars stretched out his army of observation from the Lauter to a point be-low Mannheim.

To complete the severance of the Imperialists from the fortress Villars then despatched Albergotti with a division to attack the bridge-head covering the flying bridge over the Rhine at Mannheim, occu-pied by four hundred and sixty men. The bridge-head was so strong that Albergotti was forced to open trenches against it. After a siege of ten days, however, the garrison evacuated the bridge and fell back into Mannheim (28th June).

The position of Eugene, meanwhile, was the most unpleasant it was possible to conceive. Opposed to a skilful and active enemy, he had still but the shell of an army. But few of the contingents of the German princes had yet reached him. In vain did he despatch the most urgent representations to the Emperor, to the *Diet* then sitting at Ratisbon, to the princes themselves. It was not, however, until he had promised them large payments in money that he succeeded in rousing the princes from their apathy.

Then it was too late. Bezons had opened trenches against Landau the 24th June. Though the place was gallantly defended by Prince Charles Alexander, and though in many sorties that prince succeeded in causing severe losses to the French, the siege nevertheless made steady progress. Eugene was long compelled to witness this without being able to attempt anything for the relief of the place. His position, in one respect, resembled that of his adversary during the two preced-ing years. Then, Villars commanded the army which was the last hope of France. A defeat, then, would have exposed Paris to the certainty of an attack. Similarly, now, Eugene commanded the only army of the German Empire, and, as he wrote to the Emperor:

If a misfortune should happen this side of the Rhine, the entire Empire would be exposed to imminent danger.

He was forced, then, to wait and hold himself in readiness to baffle the movements of the enemy after they should have taken Landau, the capture of which he could not prevent.

Under these circumstances it became a great object with him to prolong as much as possible the defence of Landau. The superior numbers of, and the strong position taken up by, the enemy rendered all idea of an attack upon them hopeless. A victory would only have forced them back on a second line of defence, whilst, as I have said, a defeat would have exposed the Empire to the direst consequences.

He could, then, do nothing but attempt to advise Prince Alexander of Würtemberg as to the line he should adopt under various circumstances. But by this time Landau was so hemmed in that even this consolation was denied him. By the 18th August its defences were so shattered that Villars made preparations to storm it. The garrison was not in a position to repulse such an assault as the French marshal could direct, for gunpowder and serviceable muskets were alike wanting. Hopeless, then, of success. Prince Alexander offered, on the 19th, to capitulate. Villars was strong enough to dictate his own terms, and to insist upon the garrison becoming prisoners of war. He took possession of the fortress on the 20th.

Great, in the highest sense of the term, as a warrior, Villars had no sooner taken Landau than he summoned his best generals to a council at Speyer to hear their opinions on the plan he would lay before them to force the Emperor to terms. A general with a small grasp might have contented himself with a war of sieges, and for this purpose Rheinfels, Ebenburg, Trarbach, Mainz itself, offered temptations sufficient to seduce a less daring nature. But Villars possessed to a very great extent the profundity of military genius which in later years made Napoleon the wonder of the world, and inspired him with a desire to neglect minor advantages in order to strike a blow direct at the heart. His design on this occasion was to force the lines of Ettlingen, to penetrate then by way of Freiburg to the valley of the Danube, and to threaten Vienna.

It is scarcely to be doubted that had Eugene been in the position of Villars he would have acted as Villars proposed to act. This at least is certain, that, as soon as Landau fell, he despatched fifteen battalions under his best infantry general, General d'Arnau, to General Vaubonne, to aid him in the defence of the lines, warning him at the same time that there existed strong probabilities that he would be attacked. He had no certain knowledge of the intentions of Villars, and he felt bound to ward off a possible attack on the Rhine fortresses. He, therefore, with the rest of his army, watched the river between Hüningen and Mainz.

After many feints Villars, leaving one strong corps to guard the Kinzig, another to protect the lines of Lauterburg, crossed the Rhine at Strassburg (18th September), marched straight on Freiburg, and then turning against the part of the Ettlingen lines known as the Rosskopf, broke through them with overwhelming force. With forty battalions he then attacked the redoubt which bore the number 13. This position was well defended, and had there been a competent general at hand to supervise the general plan of defence the attack might have been repulsed. But Vaubonne, fearing a succession of feints, had given orders that the garrison of each redoubt should confine itself to the defence of its own post.

The consequence was that Villars was able to gain a position within the lines which cut the Imperialist Army in two. That part of it which was nearest to Freiburg, consisting of eleven battalions, took refuge then in that town, whilst the remainder, under d'Arnau, fell back on the main body which, under Vaubonne, guarded the part of the lines the defence of which he had deemed all-important. But Villars, by his unexpected attack and its success, had turned that position Vaubonne, then, fearing to be cut off from Villingen and Rottweil, and possibly to be forced to surrender, hastened to evacuate his position and fall back on Villingen. But, once on the move, he deemed even Villingen an unsafe halting-place, and continued his retreat to Rottweil, where he entrenched himself in a strong position.

Eugene could not understand this sudden abandonment by his subordinate of a position which, at the very worst, could have been held sufficiently long to enable him to march with his whole army to its support, and he, therefore, ordered Vaubonne to retake it. Vaubonne remonstrated, but before his remonstrance could reach his commander-in-chief, Eugene had countermanded the order and directed Vaubonne to remain at Rottweil. He had, in fact, recognised that the mischief was done, and that it became him now to thwart the magnificent conception of his enemy—the capture of Freiburg and the penetrating thence into the valley of the Danube.

The hills about Freiburg had been the scene, in the lifetime of the preceding generation, of many desperate contests between the same nations. There the fiery Condé and the prudent Turenne had during three days fought with an enemy worthy even to contend against them, the pertinacious and skilful Mercy. In the year of which I am writing the city was strongly occupied and the garrison was commanded by Baron von Harsch, an Alsatian who had been a great traveller and seen much service, who had improved his great natural gifts, and who was credited with possessing a resolution equal to the greatest emergencies. Harsch had received orders from Eugene to defend Freiburg to the last stone.

Villars, we have seen, had broken through the enemy's lines on the Rosskopf, a hill about eleven hundred feet high, in the vicinity of

Freiburg, on the 20th September. By the 26th he had completed the circumvallation of the town; on the 30th he opened trenches. Harsch displayed great skill and courage. The 15th October he made a sortie, which cost the besiegers two thousand men. But Villars was resolute, and by the 30th of that month he had made such an impression on the forts as to be ready to risk the chances of storming. First, however, he offered terms to Harsch. Harsch, true to his character and to his orders, replied that he would defend the place to the last stone. He agreed, however, to send an officer to Eugene, representing the situation of the defences and of the garrison.

Meanwhile Harsch had to witness a sight which would have melted the heart of a man less stern and resolute. He had been compelled to withdraw his garrison to the forts. The town lay exposed to the French. In it, to save his supplies, he had left his sick and wounded, and the officers' wives, five thousand in all, commending them to the mercy of the French. Villars caused them all to be confined in the convent of the Capucines, sending, at the same time, a message to Harsch requiring him to provide their food. When Harsch refused, Villars ordered that a number of wounded and sick men (Germans), who had received no food for some days, should be exposed under the walls of the lower fort, to die of hunger before the eyes of the garrison. It was touching to see how the men of the garrison shared with these the scanty provisions which were their own portion!

Meanwhile, the officer sent by Harsch reached Eugene at Mühlberg, where, not strong enough to attempt the relief of Freiburg, he was watching the course of events. He heard the officer's report, then, unwilling to decide without the agreement of the prince whom the loss of the forts would most affect, the Duke of Würtemberg, he hastened to Ludwigsburg, near Stuttgart, to consult with that high personage. After consultation with the prince, Eugene despatched the following reply to Harsch:

> If he considered himself strong enough, and had supplies enough to maintain the forts against the enemy during the winter months, he was to maintain them, but if he were not sufficiently strong, or if the supplies could not hold out, then he was authorised to enter into a capitulation, by the terms of which the seventeen battalions which he commanded might march out with all the honours of war. In that case he was to join the force at Rottweil.

This power to choose one of two alternatives did not please gallant Harsch. He had supplies but for four weeks, yet—he wrote to Eugene—he would not surrender the forts or treat for their surrender without a positive order from his superior. Before Eugene received this letter, he had written again to Harsch directing him to make terms if he should only have six weeks' supplies. Thus, commanded to act, Harsch entered into negotiations with Villars. By the terms of these he surrendered the forts on the 17th November, and, the next day, marched with his seventeen battalions to join Vaubonne at Rottweil. The defence had lasted long enough to render it impossible for Villars to carry out, that year, his designs against the valley of the Danube.

Notwithstanding the issue of this campaign, the Emperor Charles VI, obstinate and dull-minded, would still have continued the war. Events, however, were too strong for him, and he was finally forced to confer upon Prince Eugene powers to negotiate at Rastatt for peace with his opponent on the battlefield, Marshal Villars.

Already the obstinacy and dullness of the Emperor had borne their fruit. It had been in the power of the Emperor, at any time between 1704 and 1711, to insist upon, and from the latter year to March 1713 to negotiate with a certainty of success for, the transfer of Bavaria in exchange for the Netherlands. But a condition which would have made the Habsburgs supreme in Southern Germany was now no longer to be hoped for. Louis XIV. had no desire to pluck a thorn from the side of the traditional enemy of France. Eugene, indeed, made the proposition. Villars first evaded, finally rejected it. The exchange might, perhaps, still have been possible had it been pressed with the necessary vigour from Vienna.

But Charles was still under the influence of his Spanish surroundings, and his contracted mind was unable to deal with more than one subject at once. The opportunity then was lost. The peace negotiated at Rastatt, signed there the 6th March, and confirmed on the 8th September at Baden in Switzerland, restored to Max Emanuel his rights and dignities in Bavaria. On the other hand, it gave back to the Emperor, Kehl, Alt-Breisach, and Freiburg, and ceded to him the Spanish Netherlands, Naples, Sardinia, as well as the fortresses and harbours on the coasts of Tuscany. The advantages were high-sounding, but specious.

CHAPTER 14

The Campaigns of 1718 against the Turks

The hopes of Eugene that he might now enjoy some well-merited repose did not long continue. Appointed Governor-General of the Netherlands, he had not proceeded to take up his post when the *Sultan*, Ahmed III.—the same whose army, directed by the *grand vizier*, Baltaji Muhammad, had spared Peter the Great in 1711—declared war, 1715, against the Venetians, and despatched an army to the Morea. To obtain the neutrality of the Empire, Ahmed had sent an ambassador to Vienna full of peaceful professions. The Emperor felt, however, that the conquest of Venice by the Osmánli would only serve to strengthen the hereditary enemy of his House, and, to put a stop to the further progress of the Turkish arms, he concluded, the 13th April, 1716, a defensive alliance with the Republic, and ordered his army to be put upon a war footing.

Nineteen days later Eugene wrote to the *grand vizier* a letter in which he required that the relations of the Porte with Venice should be replaced in the position they occupied by the terms of the Peace of Carlowitz. The Porte replied, in a document written by the *grand vizier*, Damad Ali Pasha, that the stipulations of the Peace of Carlowitz contained no provision for the rendering by the Empire of assistance to Venice; and that the Power which should make war on such a pretence must be regarded as the peace-breaker. Damad Ah Pasha followed up this declaration by the formation of a powerful army, the destination of which was to be Belgrade.

To meet this demonstration Count Pálffy received orders to assemble the Imperial Army at Peterwardein and Futak—a castle eight miles from Peterwardein, on the left bank of the river. The force so collected

218

amounted, by the end of June, to sixty-five thousand men, of which one-third was cavalry. Eugene assumed command at Futak the 9th July. War had not even then been declared. The day after his arrival at Futak, moreover, Eugene received a letter from the *grand vizier*, in which, in terms very complimentary to himself, Damad Ah protested that the Porte did not wish for war, and vehemently denounced the general who should break the peace as one whom posterity would curse.

At the same time, he continued his preparations, and towards the end of July had collected an army of two hundred thousand men in the vicinity of Belgrade. On the 26th and 27th he crossed the Save and took post at the village of Panowce, on the Danube, about fifteen miles south of Salankament. Marching thence two days later, he reached Salankament the 1st August, and the following day pushed on to Carlowitz. There, on a height not far from the chapel of Mariafried, he pitched his camp. The position was very favourable for defence, and the *grand vizier* strengthened it by utilising his wagons as a kind of outer fortification.

To reconnoitre this position, Eugene despatched Pálffy, with a detachment of fourteen hundred cavalry and four hundred infantry, supported by two regiments of *cuirassiers*. Pálffy had the strictest orders on no account to be enticed into an engagement, but he had not proceeded three parts of the way, and had just been joined by the two *cuirassier* regiments referred to, when he spied twenty thousand Turkish horsemen galloping at full speed towards him.

The position of Pálffy was critical. The ground was unfavourable for defence, he would not fall back without fighting, and he could not hope to fight successfully against such enormous odds. The last, however, seemed to him the only chance to escape destruction, and he prepared to meet the danger with the coolness which had characterised him throughout his brilliant career. Forming his troops as best he could, he received and repulsed the Osmánli charge. Again, and again, and again, during a period of more than four hours, was the charge renewed—always with the same result. Then, seeing reinforcements approaching the enemy, Pálffy fell back. He conducted his retreat with the same coolness, the same calm courage, the same success, which had characterised his long defence, and with the remnant of his little force reached Peterwardein the same night.

His loss had been severe. He had had two horses shot under him, two general officers wounded, one, Count Siegfried Brenner, after greatly distinguishing himself, taken prisoner, through the falling of his horse in the midst of the enemy, and four hundred men killed. The Osmánli, who had followed Pálffy to within sight of Peterwardein, took promptly a position within sight of that fortress and began to entrench themselves. Although the works they constructed were in the fullest sense of the term "irregular," thrown up inartistically, without any fixed plan of affording mutual defence, yet the depth of the ditches which covered them made them formidable. The ramparts behind, covered with different coloured flags, gave them a picturesqueness often wanting in war.

Whilst the Turks were thus engaged, Eugene had crossed over from Futak, and concentrated his army in Peterwardein, in the same entrenchments in which, two-and-twenty years before, the Osmánli had blockaded Count Caprara. There he resolved to remain, his army well in hand, watching his opportunity.

The opportunity was not long in coming. The main body of the Turkish Army had followed its vanguard to the entrenched position within sight of Peterwardein, and, pushing forward within cannon-shot, had opened upon him a heavy artillery fire. Confident in the superiority of his numbers, the *grand vizier* then despatched a summons to Eugene to surrender. The summons reached Eugene just as he was completing his preparations to attack his enemy. It need scarcely be added that it was not replied to.

The resolution to attack was Eugene's own, arrived at contrary to the opinion, even to the earnest solicitations, of some of his best generals. Looking to the enormous superiority of the Osmánli these would have had him leave a strong and well-provided garrison in Peterwardein, and, crossing the river, wait the time when the Turkish Army should have been exhausted by vain efforts against the fortress. But Eugene argued that such a course would probably cause the war to drag on, the campaign would be uneventful, his troops, by long inaction, would be discouraged, he would prefer to strike a blow which should be decisive. It is true he was largely outnumbered, but Pálffy's combat had proved the relative value of the troops of the two nations, and he believed that, in this instance, quality more than counterbalanced quantity.

On the 4th August his preparations for attack were completed, and he gave orders for the movement on the following morning. The baggage was to be left behind, the soldiers were to carry only what was necessary for fighting, each infantry soldier carrying fifty, each cavalry soldier twenty-one rounds each grenadier—for, in those days, grenadiers were a distinct class, answering by their occupation to their name—four hand grenades, the left wing, which was still on the left bank, was to cross by two bridges of boats during the night, so as to be ready to take part in the attack, which was ordered for daybreak.

The entrenchments thrown up by Caprara in 1695, and occupied now by Eugene, consisted of a double line, the main front of the first of which looked upon the open country, whilst the flanks rested, the one on the Danube, the other on the fortifications of Peterwardein. The second line was parallel to and supported the first. Whilst the entrenchment, the approaches to which were steep, lay, as it were, under, and was protected by, the guns mounted on the fortifications, these served as a *point d'appui* in case of defeat. It is scarcely possible to imagine a position better adapted to strike from it an effective blow.

Eugene took the fullest advantage of the lay of the ground. He disposed all his infantry, with the exception of eleven battalions, behind the outermost entrenchment, in three lines, the first of which was commanded, on its right, by Count Max Starhemberg, on its left by General Regal; the second, similarly, by Prince Bevern and Count Harrach, the third, by Baron von Lôffelholz. Of the battalions excluded from these alignments, five were placed to guard the inner entrenchment, six, led by Prince Alexander of Würtemberg, were posted outside the entrenchment on the flank of its left front.

Behind these last, but still more to the left, and thus, in a sense, forming the left wing of the entire army, was ranged the cavalry, commanded by Count Pálffy, and formed in five columns, led respectively by Counts Mercy, Martigny, Nádasdy, the Barons von Falkenstein and Battée. A sixth division, formed of four regiments, and commanded by the Baron von Ebérgenyi, was posted on the extreme right of the army. More were not required there, as the ground was unfavourable for cavalry movements. The position thus occupied was covered on the left by a morass, on the right by steep declivities.

The troops were already marching to take up their allotted positions, when nature intervened in a manner which threatened to render nugatory the well-thought-out schemes of man. A terrible storm, in its force not inferior to a hurricane, tore from their cables several floating-mills on the Danube, and dashed them with so great a force against the two bridges of boats, that many of the boats composing these were driven from their position. The injury thus produced caused a delay of two hours in the passage of the troops. It gave the same time to the Osmánli to perfect their dispositions for defence.

That these were aware of the coming attack was at once clear to the Imperialists. The Turks had begun moving before daybreak, and the morning light showed hill and valley covered with countless numbers. Their cavalry took post opposite the Imperial cavalry, the greater part of the *Janissaries* took post behind the foremost ditch, supported by a second line of the same famous soldiers. Another considerable body of troops formed the Osmánli left. It will be seen, however, that these never came into action.

As the bells sounded 7 o'clock, Eugene ordered Alexander of Würtemberg to attack. This prince, the reader will recollect, was posted with six battalions of infantry outside the Imperial entrenchment on the flank of its left front. Advancing boldly, the prince charged the Turkish battery opposite to him, and carried it with but little opposition. The cavalry posted nearly behind him then dashed to the front and put to flight the Osmánli horsemen. It seemed to Prince Alexander, for the moment, as though an easy victory were in prospect.

But it was not so. Almost immediately after the prince had begun the attack on the left, the first and second lines of infantry issued from the entrenchment and marched against the Turkish centre. But the ground they had to traverse was interspersed with many small posts, and the necessity to storm these not only delayed the advance, but broke the line in many places. It thus happened that when the vicinity of the enemy was reached, the Imperial troops were blown and flurried, and their line was anything but perfect.

They pressed on, nevertheless, with their accustomed valour, and succeeded for the moment in forcing the enemy's position. Only, however, for a moment. The *Janissaries*, who had noted their foes' disarray, quickly re-formed, and, charging with the determination which characterised them, drove back the Imperialists headlong, not only to their first line of entrenchment, but across it to the second. They were in the act of storming this also, when they were assailed in flank by the Imperial cavalry and forced to relinquish their hold.

The repulse of their centre seemed, then, to counterbalance the success of the Imperial left. But in that quarter the success was becoming every moment more and more pronounced. In vain had the Spáhis endeavoured, by constant charges, to stem the advance of the horsemen of Pálffy and the veteran infantry of Prince Alexander. When repeated failures had discouraged and shattered them, then in a splendid charge the *cuirassiers* and hussars of Austria and of Hungary swept them from the field. Nought remained then to check the onward progress of Prince Alexander. He pressed on until he had obtained the position, evacuated by the Spáhis, on the right flank of the Turkish centre.

From a commanding position Eugene had watched the progress of the fight, had seen how the first line of the centre had been driven back, how his left had achieved a success which might be made decisive. The repulse of the centre he prepared to redeem by moving to the front the third line commanded by Baron Löffelholz. Then, strengthening Alexander of Würtemberg with all the infantry he could spare, he directed him to wheel to his right and take the exposed Turkish centre in flank, whilst with his retired centre he should renew the attack in front.

His instructions were carried out with the exactness which characterises an ordinary field-day of well-trained soldiers. The *Janissaries*, assailed simultaneously in front and in flank, fell back to their entrenchments. Vainly did they look for the Spáhis to effect a diversion. These, pursued still by the Imperialist cavalry, were either in flight or striking a last blow for their wagon-fortress. Hopeless, then, of assistance, the *Janissaries* relaxed their efforts. Fruitlessly did their officers point to the line of entrenchment still sufficient to protect them, in vain did the *grand vizier*, who had stood by the sacred standard watching the fight, rush forward to animate them by his words, by his gestures, even by blows with the flat of his scimitar, and, these failing, by his noble example. Despair—the despair of real soldiers who know that the key of their position was in the hands of their enemy—had possession of their souls. They allowed Damad Ali Pasha to dash alone into the ranks of the enemy, and to fall under an Austrian bullet. The spirit to fight had oozed out of them, little recked they then of the *certaminis gaudia*, demoralised, they cared only to quit the field alive!

Thus, it happened that the forward movement rendered possible by the splendid success of Alexander of Würtemberg and the cavalry on the left became absolutely decisive. The Osmánli, without a further struggle, abandoned the field. Before mid-day the Turkish camp, with its tents, its treasures, its rich booty, its cannons, one hundred and seventy-two in number, its wagons, was in the hands of the victors. The passions of these were lashed to fury when they beheld the bodies of Count Brenner and of other soldiers taken prisoners in the cavalry fight of the 2nd August. These prisoners had been killed but a few minutes before, and the body of Brenner gave evidence of cruelties to which the living man had been subjected.

BATTLE OF

PETERWARDEN

The victory was as decisive as it was great. It was not gained, however, without loss. It cost the Imperial Army just over three thousand men, amongst the killed, of whom were two field-marshal-lieutenants, one major-general, five colonels, and one adjutant-general amongst the dangerously wounded, one field-marshal-lieutenant, two major-generals, and four colonels. The loss of the Osmánli was calculated to be six thousand, amongst whom, as stated, was the *grand vizier*. (According to Hammer, the *grand vizier* was severely wounded and died two days after the battle.)

For his victory, Eugene received many congratulations from all parts of Europe. The Emperor expressed himself in the most grateful terms, Pope Clement XI. sent him a consecrated hat and sword, but perhaps what he valued most of all was a letter from his old adversary, Marshal Villars.

To take full advantage of his victory, Eugene despatched Count Pálffy with a strong cavalry corps to hem in the important town of Temesvar, the capture of which he deemed necessary before he should undertake the siege of Belgrade. On the 14th August, Eugene followed with the main army, and after a difficult march of twelve days, in the course of which he passed by Zenta, the scene of his first victory, and crossed the Theiss, he encamped on the 26th before the town.

Of the siege of this place it is necessary only to record that Eugene opened trenches the 1st September. The commander of it, however, Muhammad Aga, who had eight thousand men at his disposal, defended it with so much skill and courage that Eugene dreaded lest it might hold out till a relieving army, which was being organised at Belgrade, should arrive to succour it. On the 22nd he learned that such an army was approaching along the Temes.

The next day the camp of Count Pálffy was attacked by a corps twenty thousand strong. The attack, three times renewed, was however beaten back with loss. Pushing on the siege vigorously, Eugene determined then to storm. On the first October this was successfully accomplished by Alexander of Würtemberg with thirty battalions, four companies of grenadiers, accompanied by two thousand workmen. The loss, however, was heavy, amounting to fifteen hundred killed and double that number wounded. The fortress surrendered sixteen days later.

The fall of a fortress, which had lain under the yoke of the Osmánli a hundred and sixty-four years, caused the greatest enthusiasm at Vienna. It meant, everyone recognised, the restoration of Imperial rule in the entire Banát. Leaving Count Mercy to complete the programme, which consisted in the administration of the reconquered lands and the rounding off of their borders by the reduction of Pancsova, Ujpalanka, and, if possible, Orsova, Eugene returned to Vienna.

During his absence, Mercy took Pancsova and Ujpalanka, but the attitude of the Osmánli at Orsova was so resolute, and their numbers were so large, that he deferred the attack to a more convenient season. In Transylvania and on the borders of Moldavia fighting continued throughout the winter, not always to the advantage of the Imperialists.

At Constantinople, endeavours were made during this winter period to bring about a solid peace. The new *grand vizier*, Khálil Pasha, supported by the representatives of England and Holland, urged, as a preliminary, the propriety of agreeing to an armistice. Various solid reasons prevented the Emperor from agreeing to such a proposal. He had, at great expense, provided the necessary requirements for two campaigns, one of which only had been made. The success obtained in the first promised a success still more signal in that which was impending. Confiding in the judgment of Eugene, who had declared that the Porte had not been sufficiently humiliated, and that a peace then would lead to a renewal of the war at the moment when the Empire should be embarrassed, the Emperor rejected the Turkish proposals, and re-victualing and rearming his fortresses in Hungary, and summoning to his support the contingents of the minor German princes, displayed his resolution to act with vigour and energy.

The defeat by a Turkish force of an Imperial detachment, under Baron von Petrasch, on its return to Peterwardein after having thrown supplies into Pancsova, at the end of April 1717, served to hasten the departure of Eugene from Vienna. On the 14th May, two days after the birth of the illustrious Maria Theresa, he quitted that capital, and a week later joined the army at Fatak. The next few days he spent in reconnoitring the enemy's position, then, determined to strike a blow at Belgrade, he ordered the concentration of his army—though as yet all his troops had not arrived—at Pancsova, a town on the Temes, close to the junction of that river with the Danube, and to cross thence the latter river into Turkish territory.

He preferred that route to the more direct route across the Save for the following reasons first, because the way to the Danube, was easier and more practicable, secondly, because the stream of the Save, though not so broad, was more rapid and, therefore, more difficult for small vessels, whilst its banks were higher, more defensible, and generally more fortified, third, because near Pancsova the Danube lent itself to the passage of an army, in that its bed formed at that point three islands, each of which, strongly occupied, could be utilised as covering points to the army crossing.

Thoroughly impressed with the soundness of his plan, Eugene broke up from Peterwardein the 9th June, reached Pancsova the 14th, and effected the passage of the Danube, without the smallest opposition, the 15th and 16th. The army, now on Turkish ground, consisted of sixty-one battalions and a hundred and seventy-six squadrons. Despatching to Vienna fresh proposals of peace which reached him there through the English Minister at Constantinople, Eugene pushed on, and on the 18th reconnoitred Belgrade. The very same day he began the construction of lines to be occupied by a portion of his army which should cover the siege operations. These lines were to completely hem in the city. Marked out so as to rest the left on the Save, the right on the Danube, they commanded the bridges across both rivers. His fleet Eugene ranged along the banks, on both sides of the bridge over the Danube, so as to make it possible for him to assist his crews should they be attacked by the Turkish vessels, and for those crews to prevent the entrance of reinforcements into the city.

Belgrade comprised at that time three distinct portions the castle, the city, and the suburbs. The city lay on the point where the Save flows into the Danube, and was washed by the waters of both, beyond this, stretching towards the land, and extending from one river to the other, were the suburbs, between the town and the suburbs, was a hill steep towards the city, easy of access from the suburbs, on the summit of this was the castle. The declivity towards the city needed no defence, but the slopes towards the suburbs were strongly fortified.

The garrison of Belgrade consisted of thirty thousand men. Amongst them were the *élite* of the *Janissaries*. The commander of the garrison, Mustapha Pasha, possessed a reputation second to none in the Ottoman Empire. He deserved it.

But it was not only the garrison that Eugene had to reckon with. Whilst he was constructing his lines Khálil Pasha was marching from Adrianople with an army which, according to the rumour which reached Belgrade, was the most numerous ever collected. To ward off the attack of such an army Eugene, whilst continuing his operations against the city, fortified the exterior of his lines. He made the ramparts all round the line of circumvallation so high, the ditches so broad and deep, he strengthened them with so many bastions, that the whole resembled a fortress. Even the openings necessary to allow the easy ingress and egress of the troops he caused to be well protected by ravelins. (These famous lines, were allowed to remain intact. They were used to good purpose by the illustrious Loudon when he besieged and captured Belgrade in 1789—Malleson's *Loudon*.) At the same time, he directed a detachment, left at Peterwardein, to march against and occupy Semlin, whilst, to secure his own position, he directed the occupation by five battalions of the bridge-head on the left bank of the Danube.

Semlin had been occupied by eight battalions and two regiments of cavalry. To strengthen it further against attack, two of the largest Austrian ships of war, the *St Stephen* and *St. Francis*, had been brought to anchor under its walls. But the Osmánli, anxious to regain the place, collected all the vessels at their disposal, and supporting them by strong divisions of *Janissaries* and *Spáhis*, directed on the 5th July a resolute attack on the two ships named, which were much larger and better appointed than any of their own, determined, if the attack were successful, to penetrate within the town. It failed, however, but the contest had been so severe that Eugene despatched a third large vessel, the *St. Eugene*, and four *levantines*, to strengthen the post.

Meanwhile Khálil Pasha was advancing, gathering strength as he marched along. At first it seemed as though by threatening Transylvania the *grand vizier* was trying to entice Eugene from Belgrade, but, noting that the Imperial leader was fixed and would not move, Khálil Pasha directed his course rapidly towards Belgrade.

Before he could arrive, an event had happened which had caused great damage to the besiegers. Eugene, in anticipation of the arrival of the Turkish host, had resolved to complete the circumvallation of Belgrade, and for this purpose had despatched Count Mercy to drive the enemy from a small island which is formed by the junction of the Dunawitza with the Danube opposite the city. Various circumstances had prevented the carrying out of this plan, and on the 13th July, it was still unfulfilled.

On the evening of that day there suddenly set in one of those terrible cyclones which are witnessed only in their greatest force in the East. In less than an hour the damage worked by this tempest was enormous. The bridges of boats over the Save and the Danube were severely damaged, numberless vessels laden with stores and ammunition were sunk, houses and tents were blown down. Disorder, the consequence of such destruction, prevailed everywhere.

It was under these circumstances that Mustapha Pasha made a very earnest effort to finish the work which the storm had begun. At the head of ten thousand men he crossed the Save, and attempted, with loud shouts, to storm the Imperial entrenchments. He had almost succeeded, but the daring and persistent defence made by a small detachment of Hessians, sixty in number, gave time to Count O'Dwyer—who commanded the post nearest to it—to bring up two companies of grenadiers. Eventually this attack was repulsed.

A second sortie, made a few nights later by the *Janissaries* on the unfinished works of Eugene's camp, was more nearly successful. A dispute between two Imperial generals, Count Marsigli and Count Rudolph Heister, as to the manner in which the attack should be met, was still progressing when the *Janissaries* came upon them. The Imperialist soldiers, left without orders, were thrown into disorder. Vainly did the two leaders try, too late, to atone by their gallantry for their folly. Attempting to stem the fierce onslaught, they were cut down. The men then fled, the triumph of the *Janissaries* seemed assured. Suddenly, however, Lieutenant-Colonel Freiherr von Miglio dashed to the front at the head of two hundred and fifty men of the *Cuirassiers* of Hesse-Darmstadt. The *Janissaries* could not withstand the shock. Under cover of that splendid charge the Imperialists re-formed and drove back their daring foes.

Two days later the works were completed, and the bombardment began in real earnest. It destroyed the town, but affected not the spirit of the defenders. These counted on Khálil Pasha, and on the 30th July, they had the gratification of beholding from the battlements of the castle the *Spáhis* who formed the vanguard of his army. The next day their eyes were gladdened by the appearance, within long cannon shot of the fortress, of numberless green and yellow tents, betokening the arrival of the infantry. Similarly, the opening of an artillery-fire on the Imperialist camp proved that the guns likewise had come up. It was evident that Eugene would have to deal with the massed army of Khálil Pasha before he could take Belgrade.

During the twelve days that followed the Turks threw up battery after battery, each more advanced than the other, against the entrenched camp of the Christians, for, as I have already pointed out, the Imperialists, though besieging Belgrade, had fortified their camp so as to make it a very fortress. Day by day the situation of Eugene became thus more critical. In front of him was the unsubdued fortress, its garrison commanded by a man who knew not fear, the brave

Mustapha Pasha, in his rear, and hemming him in, cutting off from him all means of supply from the surrounding country, was an army estimated roughly to be two hundred thousand strong, and led by a *grand vizier* whose one hope in life was to restore the waning prestige of the Osmánli. In the face of such an enemy it was not even possible to abandon his work, for their numbers would have rendered impossible the passage of either the Save or the Danube.

Of the two possibilities before him—to await in his camp the assault of the Turks, or to anticipate them and attack their camp—the second had the greater charm for a warrior like Eugene. Watchfully to wait might, indeed, opposed as he was to a people who, though as brave as any in the world, are careless, especially during the night, procure him the opportunity he longed for, but, on the other hand, his provisions might fail, the sickness already prevailing might increase, his losses from the ever-increasing artillery-fire might disable him, and the opportunity might not offer. None of these difficulties stood in the way of an immediate attack. The project was bold, but the case was one of those, more common in life than is generally supposed, in which boldness was prudence. Eugene, reviewing his situation in his own mind, resolved, then, to attack. Firm in this resolution, he summoned his generals, 15th August, and communicated to them his plan and his reasons. Not a single objection was raised. The attack was then ordered for the following morning.

Eugene had one enemy, the reader knows, in front of him, and another behind him, in front the fortress, behind the army of Khálil Pasha. To watch the first, he disposed seven, regiments of cavalry, eight battalions and four grenadier companies of infantry. To guard his own camp, he told off four battalions and a number of dragoons for whom there were no horses. The entire remainder of his force he disposed for the attack on the enemy. In the centre he placed his infantry, under the command of the well-tried Prince Alexander of Würtemberg, on the right and left the cavalry, under the general command of Count John Pálffy, having under him, on the right, Generals Ebergényi and Mercy, on the left, Montecucculi and Martigny. A reserve of fifteen battalions was posted on the outer edge of the lines of circumvallation, under Count Seckendorff, who had instructions to lead his men to that part of the battlefield where his presence might be most necessary.

Before midnight of the 15th August the several divisions of the army set out, in the deepest silence, to occupy the positions which Eugene had carefully marked out for each. Emerging from the lines of circumvallation by the openings which, I have shown, Eugene had been careful to provide, they entered the broad plain immediately beyond it and there formed up. At 1 o'clock a m. on the 16th the formation of the front line was completed. The night was bright and clear, and it was dreaded lest a Turkish sentry, more watchful than his fellows, might notice the movement and give the alarm. This, however, did not happen, and towards 3 o'clock there rose a mist so thick that it was impossible for the men to see ten paces in front of them. Covered by this mist the line advanced.

The Imperialists had not proceeded far, however, when they discovered that, however useful the mist might be to conceal them from the enemy, it rendered their own advance on a given line impossible. Despite of every possible precaution, the cavalry of the first line of the right wing lost their way, and Pálffy, who was leading it, found himself suddenly in some new trenches, at which the Osmánli were working. Both parties were surprised, but the Turks, taking in the position on the moment, seized their arms, and, whilst despatching a messenger to the leader of their own cavalry for aid, opened a heavy musketry fire on the assailants. This gave the alarm throughout the camp, and in a few minutes the entire Turkish Army was under arms and in battle array. The still heavy mist, however, prevented, on both sides, except on the Imperial right, any decisive action.

On the right the Imperialists had, so to describe its stumbled into action—action of the severest character. For the famous *Spáhis* had reached the spot, and the combat between the horsemen of the West and of the East was furious and, for long, doubtful. At length, at a critical moment, there came up, on the flank of the Osmánli, Mercy, with the second line of the right wing. Their arrival gave a momentary advantage to the Imperialists. The Turks were driven back. Soon, however, they re-formed and opposed a firm front to Pálffy. Scarcely had they done so, however, when the right of the front line of the Imperialist infantry, led by Maximilian Starhemberg, emerged from the mist and charged their front. They could withstand no longer, but yielded the position and batteries to the enemy.

Despite the continuance of the mist, and of the fact that it seemed every moment to increase in density, action had by this time commenced all along the line. Slowly and cautiously the Imperialist's centre had advanced till it found itself confronted by the hostile trenches. A sudden rush placed these very quickly in the hands of the aggressors.

The contest, however, like all contests in the dark, was, to a great extent, of a haphazard nature, depending a great deal on the favours of the goddess Fortuna. Those favours, however, are generally rightly confined to the bestowal of opportunities. To those unable to spell that word they are granted in vain.

Thus, it happened that, in the darkness, a formidable division of Osmánli, pressing forward and meeting no opposition, found itself suddenly on the right flank of the Imperial centre, whilst that centre was hotly engaged in the trenches. The Imperialist right was so completely severed from its centre that from it no danger was to be apprehended. One hour of leadership such as that of Bajazid Ilderim, of either of the Amuraths, or of Muhammad II, and the Christian host had been annihilated. But the actual leader belonged to the numerous class of men who wait to receive their impulses from stronger natures. He hesitated—and was lost. For whilst he was still doubting, the mist cleared away, and disclosed to Eugene the danger which his army had incurred, and from which it was not yet free.

Like Napoleon in 1796, like Massena throughout his glorious military career, like Frederic, like Loudon, like Condé, like Clive, Eugene was never so great as when called upon suddenly to confront a pressing danger. Realising on the instant all the possibilities available to the Turkish division, and seeing that with the mists the doubts of the Turkish leader were disappearing, and that he was preparing for the attack which, if not baffled, must be fatal, he galloped at full speed to his second line of infantry, commanded by the Prince of Bevern, and, wheeling it to the right, dashed at the advancing foe.

But by that time the blood of the Osmánli was up. They had recognised the advantage of their position, and were by no means inclined to yield it. The battle raged here, long, and with terrible fury. It was evident that victory would be to the side which could first bring up its cavalry. The vision of Eugene was quicker, and truer, and more decisive than that of his enemy. From the outset he had provided for that great necessity. Whilst, then, the battle between the hostile infantry was still doubtful, an opportune cavalry charge on the flank of the Osmánli compelled these to fall back. The Imperialists followed, renewed touch with their right, and, having dispelled this great danger, resumed the forward movement.

It now became evident that whilst several Turkish batteries had been stormed in the darkness of the mist, one, the principal and central, remained intact. Behind and about this were concentrated in thick masses the formidable *Janissaries*. To storm this little fortress

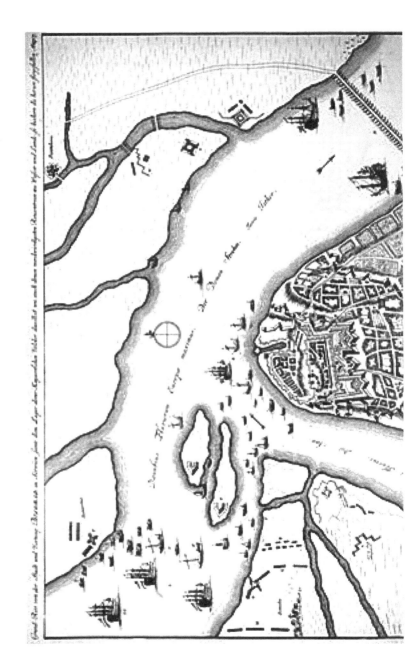

PLATTE GROND der Stadt en Vesting BELGRADO, benevens het Leger der Keyserie, daar voor leggende, alsook de merkwaardige ontmoetinge te Water en te Land tot ie toe voorgevallen. Anno 1717.

became now the object of Eugene. With this view he drew together ten grenadier companies and four battalions, and, covering their flanks with two regiments of cavalry, ordered them to the storm. With flying colours and to national music, in serried array, the soldiers of the House of Austria pressed forward, not attempting to return the murderous file poured upon them from the battery. Arrived within charging distance, they lowered their bayonets and charged. Not even the *Janissaries* could resist the solid *phalanx*. In a few minutes the battery was carried.

About the same time the last post held by the enemy on his left was stormed, and he hastened to quit his entrenched camp. It was past 9 o'clock Eugene, always provident, feared lest the sight of the booty might distract his men, still in the presence of an army rather repulsed than beaten from the more serious work before them. He led them, then, from the heights they had gained, in pursuit of the Osmánli. It was only when his horsemen were well amongst them, rendering rallying impossible, that he selected detachments from the troops of all the nationalities serving under him to take possession of the booty in trust for the whole army. It was enormous.

The victory was complete. Before the day closed the Osmánli were fleeing, broken into detachments, towards the country whence they had come. They had lost twenty thousand men in killed and wounded, about two hundred cannon, fifty-one standards, nine horse-tails. Nor were the losses of the victors slight. Fifteen hundred men lay dead on the field, and three thousand five hundred were severely wounded.

The effect of the victory was immediately apparent. The day following, Mustapha Pasha despatched two officers to the victor to treat for the surrender of Belgrade. The negotiations were soon concluded. On the 18th August, Mustapha and his brave companions obtained permission to march out with all the honours of war. On the 22nd the Imperialists took possession of the fortress with its six handled guns, its flotilla on the Danube, its still enormous quantity of munitions of war.

Belgrade did not fall one moment too soon. The very day after its occupation news of a threatening character from many sides reached the prince. A corps, fifteen thousand strong, had penetrated by way of Moldavia into Transylvania, and thence into Upper Hungary. The Hungarian commander on the spot, Count Karolyi, who should have checked their progress, had fallen back in dismay behind the Theiss. This pusillanimous action exposed Grosswardein and the dominating castle of Huszt to attack. Already the enemy were devastating the country with fire and sword alike to check their further progress and to cut off their retreat. Eugene despatched General Viard with two regiments of cavalry into Transylvania; Mercy, with twelve battalions and eight cavalry regiments to the Banat, Count Martigny with four regiments of cavalry by way of Pancsova, and Arad to Upper Hungary. But before these troops could reach their destinations the enemy had fallen back and succeeded in reaching Turkey.

It would appear that many of the Austrian and Hungarian generals who served in the war were of little use unless when serving under the immediate eye of their commander. Thus, Counts John Draskowich and Charles Königsegg, who had been sent to take Novi, were not only repulsed before that place, but, marching carelessly in their retreat, were surprised and defeated by the Osmánli. But for the timely aid of the Imperial commander on the Croatian border, not only would they have been destroyed, but incalculable injury would have resulted.

Meanwhile at the headquarters on both sides more peaceful counsels were prevailing. The defeated *grand vizier*, Khálil Pasha, had been removed, and the son-in-law of the *Sultan*, Muhammad Pasha, a wise and peace-loving statesman, had replaced him. Mustapha Pasha, too, the gallant soldier who had so well defended Belgrade, had written to Eugene (5th September) to inform the prince that if he wanted peace he could have it, and that he would do all in his power to facilitate negotiations.

Eugene referred the matter to the Emperor Charles VI, ever more a Spaniard than an Austrian, was burning to conclude the war with Turkey in order that he might baffle the Italian policy of the Spanish Bourbon. He, therefore, at once despatched full powers to Eugene. The result, after many negotiations, was the assembly of a congress at Passarowitz. There, on the 21st July, 1718, was signed between the Porte, the Emperor, and the Republic of Venice, the Peace which bears the name of the town. By its conditions the Porte was finally excluded from Hungary, the Emperor obtaining the cession of Temesvar and the Banat, Belgrade, part of Bosnia, Servia, and Wallachia. Venice surrendered the Morea to Turkey, and Austria ceded to the same Power certain commercial rights tending in the direction of freedom of trade between the two countries.

On the conclusion of the treaty Eugene quitted Belgrade, 28th July, proceeded up the Danube to Orsova, and thence by land by way of Mehadia and Lugos to Temesvar. Thence he journeyed to Vienna.

There he received the congratulations of the Emperor and the acclamations of the people. An urgent invitation from Frederic William I of Prussia to visit Berlin reached him shortly after his return, but the duties which were immediately forced upon him compelled him unwillingly to decline it.

SIEGE OF BELGRADE

CHAPTER 15

Sixteen Years of Peace

For the sixteen years that followed the Treaty of Passarowitz Eugene enjoyed the fruits of Peace with Honour. In political circles, indeed, his influence, never very weighty, suffered at first a marked declension. Charles VI still clung to his Spanish councillors, with whom Eugene had no sympathy, and it was due to the proclivities in this direction of the Emperor that the peace which extended over Europe did not include the cessation of hostilities with Spain. These continued, mainly in Italy, till the year 1720. Not only did Eugene take no part in these, but he was never even consulted as to the manner in which they should be conducted. His enemies prevailed so far at one time that his dismissal from the Court was a question for consideration,

Prominent amongst those enemies were, besides the Spanish Councillors, Count Althan, the Emperor's favourite till his death in 1722, Count Guido Starhemberg, who had been his contemporary in war, but who had long been jealous of his fame. The most bitter of all, however, was his cousin, Victor Amadeus of Savoy. This prince, distant himself from Vienna, confided his subtle plans against Eugene to the Abbot Prospero Tedeschi, a Florentine, and to the Imperial Chamberlain, the Count von Nimptsch, a brother-in-law of Count Althan. Bent upon the dismissal of Eugene, and on his banishment from the Court he had served so truly, these conspirators insinuated to the Emperor, the passion of whose life was the seeming to his own daughter the succession to the Hereditary States and the Kingdoms of Hungary and Bohemia, that Eugene was working to secure the inheritance for one of the daughters of the late Emperor Joseph I, towards whom he had felt a warm personal attachment.

The suspicions of Charles having been aroused, a watch was placed over the movements of Eugene, and Nimptsch, who was charged to exercise a secret supervision over his movements, took care to make frequent reports to the Emperor, each more and more implicating the intended victim. It was due to an accident that the plot was betrayed. The valet of Count Nimptsch was a devoted admirer of Eugene. Rendered curious by his master's conduct, by his constant change of garments for the purpose of espionage, by his repeated secret interviews with Tedeschi, by his rising at all hours of the night, and by his reception of men of strange mien, and dreading lest a conspiracy should be on foot, he made straight one day to Eugene and revealed to him the matters which caused him so much perplexity.

Eugene directed him to obtain fuller information as to the actual doings of Nimptsch. In a few days the secret papers of the count, containing full details of the plot, were in the hands of the prince. Securing first the safety of the valet, who might otherwise have been sacrificed, by despatching him to Switzerland, Eugene summoned his friends, placed the papers before them, and stated his intention, subject to their opinion, to lay them at once before the Emperor. Their opinion coinciding with his own, he proceeded at once to Charles to demand satisfaction against his enemies. Should this be denied him, he added, he would resign all the posts he held into the hands of his Master, and would appeal to Europe to repair the injury which had been done him.

Charles must have felt more than humiliated as he listened to the words of the man to whom more than to any living being he owed his empire. It was due, he must have felt, to his narrow views and jealous nature that the plot had proceeded so far. For the moment he embraced Eugene and expressed a hope that they would remain the friends they had ever been.

The prince, dissatisfied with mere words, insisted that a formal inquiry should take place. A commission composed of three of the highest noblemen in the country—the President of the Imperial Council, the Count von Windischgrätz, the Court Chancellor, the Count von Stürgth, and the Imperial Councillor, von Blümegen—was constituted.

The result of their inquiry brought the guilt home to Tedeschi and Nimptsch. The punishments assigned to each are worthy of being recorded. Tedeschi, convicted of having slandered the Court of Vienna and attributed to its statesmen words they had never used, was sentenced to be placed for two hours in the pillory, in the open market-place, to receive thirty stripes on his bare back from a rod wielded by the public executioner, and then to be banished the Imperial States. Nimptsch, on the other hand, was degraded from all his employments, imprisoned for two years, and banished for ever from Vienna and from all places where the Imperial Court might be. These sentences were carried out.

The death of Althan in 1722 removed the last hindrance to the perfect reconciliation between the Emperor and Eugene. The death of the head of the Spanish party, the Bishop of Valencia, three years later, brought them still nearer together, and from that date Eugene may be said to have held the first place in the Emperor's esteem.

But Eugene never thrust himself into politics. He preferred the social and literary enjoyments which were abundantly at his command in Vienna. He was extremely fond of reading. When in London, in 1712, he had purchased a number of rare and curious editions, and to these, whenever opportunity offered, he added. Until the Peace of Passarowitz he had little leisure to devote to their perusal, but from that time leading shared, with the embellishing of his palace, and the society of his friends and of the fair sex, all the time at his disposal. Amongst his intimate associates in his earlier days had been the illustrious Leibnitz. After his death, in 1716, the friendship which had always existed between the prince and the distinguished poet, J B Rousseau, greatly increased.

The admiration of the French poet for the Imperial general was extreme. In an ode in which he portrayed him, he describes Eugene as the pattern for all heroes, as a man who had perfected greatness, not from the vain love of glory, but in the service of truth and virtue. Higher than his victories on the battlefield Rousseau rated the power of the prince to win the hearts of men. Great in everything which deserved admiration, he was greater still in the inexhaustible kindness and in the unpretentiousness of demeanour which recalled the simple manners of earlier ages. His glorious example would descend to posterity as a model.

Amongst other famous men in whose friendship Eugene rejoiced were J B Mariette, the learned son of a learned father, the historian, Pietro Giannone, the Cardinal Alessandro Albam, a lover of art in the highest sense, the Abbot Silvio Valenti Gonzago, one of the best instructed men of his time; and the statesman—the enemy of the Jesuits and firm upholder of the rights of the Church—Domenico Passionei, afterwards Cardinal, renowned for his collection of books and precious manuscripts.

By the kindness of these and other learned men constantly employed for him in The Hague, in Brussels, in London, in Milan, in Bologna, in Rome, Eugene collected a library, which, as a private library, was unsurpassed, certainly in the States of the Empire.

The rooms in which his books were disposed were adorned with portraits and engravings, as rare and as precious as his books. He possessed one palace in the Himmelspforte-Gasse, another, previously referred to, known as the Belvedere, attached to which was a large garden containing rare plants, and places reserved for beautiful birds and wild animals. Amongst the last might be seen a lion, some tigers, and two bison, a present from King Frederic William of Prussia. He possessed besides, considerable properties in Hungary.

After the conclusion of the Treaty of Baden, Eugene had been appointed Governor-General of the Netherlands. Unable, however, by reason first of the war with the Turks, and subsequently of the onerous duties devolving upon him as President of the Council of War, to reside in Vienna, he had nominated the Marquis de Prié to be his deputy there. After some years of painful experience of the difficulty of governing from a distance through a nobleman with whom he was not always in sympathy, Eugene, in 1725, resigned his office. It would be too long to state here the intrigues which forced this conclusion upon him as the one best calculated to promote the interests of the Empire. He confined his energies thenceforth to the care for the army.

His efforts in this direction were ill seconded by the Emperor. Charles VI had but one son, and that son had died shortly after his birth. Hopeless of further male offspring, and the last representative himself, in the male line, of the House of Habsburg, Charles from that time directed his main efforts to secure the agreement of the several Powers of Europe to an instalment, known in history as the Pragmatic Sanction, which should guarantee the inheritance to his daughter, Maria Theresa. It was in vain that Eugene assured him that the only guarantee worth having was an army of two hundred thousand men and a full treasury.

Charles systematically neglected his army, and his treasury was invariably empty. Eugene was the more pressing because he was well aware that on the death of the Emperor the Elector of Bavaria would lay claim to the Empire, and that his claims would be supported by a majority of the *Diet*. In many other particulars the policy of the Emperor, especially in his dealings with Spain, seemed to him insensate, and it was only by means of a very earnest opposition that he succeeded in diverting his master from marrying Maria Theresa to the son of the King of Spain, afterwards Charles III.

Prince Eugene was never married. He was fond of the sex, but though very capable of loving, love exercised over him only a passing influence, and never enslaved him.

CHAPTER 16

The Last Campaigns—and Death

On the 1st February, 1733, an event occurred which plunged Europe once more into war. On that date Augustus II, King of Poland, died. The Cabinets of Europe had been disputing as to his successor. His death precipitated a quarrel for which, of the Continental Powers, France only was prepared.

The candidate for the throne of Poland supported by France was Stanislaus Leszczynski, father-in-law of Louis XV. The Emperor, on the contrary, upheld the pretensions of the Elector of Saxony, son of the deceased prince. Stanislaus himself was disinclined to enter upon a struggle from which he anticipated no permanent success. The very journey to Warsaw bristled with difficulties. Russia was opposed to his intentions, and a Russian fleet was cruising in the Baltic. Austria and Prussia barred to him the land route. Pushed on by the Court of Versailles, he finally, however, agreed to accept the position, and, giving out that he was about to sail with a French fleet from Brest, quitted France secretly by the land route, and, travelling only by night, succeeded in reaching Warsaw the night of the 8th of September.

On the 11th of the same month he was proclaimed King of Poland. His reign, however, was but brief. The Elector of Saxony entered Poland, supported by a Russian Army. Stanislaus, abandoned by the bulk of the Polish Army, fled to Dantzig. All Poland submitted then to the Elector, who was crowned at Cracow, the 17th January, 1734. The 27th June following Stanislaus escaped, in the disguise of a peasant, from Dantzig, besieged by a combined Russian and Saxon Army. Fortune had decided against him.

But France was not in a humour to submit to this rebuff. The illustrious Villars, notwithstanding his eighty years, was placed, with the title of Marshal-General, at the head of the army, and despatched

SIEGE OF DANZIG 1734

to Italy. A second army, led by the Duke of Berwick, marched to the Rhine. Once again were the flames of war kindled. The Emperor had no army ready to meet the contingency, and he could find no allies. Holland had made a treaty of neutrality with France, England declined to act without Holland, Prussia displayed a marked unwillingness to fight. Money, likewise, was, as usual, scarce. Before suitable defensive preparations could be made, Villars had opened the campaign in Italy, and had taken Novara, Tortona, Pizzighettone and Milan. All that the Emperor could attempt was the defence of the Rhine, and to assure that defence he nominated Eugene commander-in-chief of the Imperial Army in Germany.

Eugene proceeded to Ettlingen, but before he could collect a sufficiency of troops to constitute an army, Berwick was in the field. In the first week of April that capable leader had marched with his army, a hundred thousand strong and formed into three columns, against the German fortresses. At the head of the first of these columns, fifty thousand strong, Berwick had taken part at Heiligenstein, opposite Philipsburg: the second, thirty thousand strong, he had dispatched, under the Duke of Noailles, to Kaiserslautern. Count Belleisle had led the third, twenty thousand strong, into the country about Trier, and had begun the siege of Trarbach.

Noticing the passiveness of the Imperialists, and attributing it to the true cause, Berwick resolved to mass his troops and drive Eugene from the lines of Ettlingen. Calling Noailles and his army corps to himself, and leaving Marquis d'Asfeld with thirty battalions at Speyer, Berwick divided his force into two columns, and crossed the Rhine at Kehl and Fort Louis. His plan was to attack the lines at their two extremities, whilst d'Asfeld, with a portion of his troops, should cross the Rhine at Rheingönheim and occupy the valley of the Neckar.

Eugene, meanwhile, leaving a small body of troops in the lines, had, with fifteen thousand men taken at Waghäusel a position whence he would be able to prevent any serious attack on Philipsburg. But no sooner did he obtain information of Berwick's passage of the Rhine than, divining his object, he marched towards the lines to strengthen the defenders. Riding in front of his men, he entered the lines on the 4th May. The information which reached him then was of a character to startle. Whilst on the one hand he learned that Berwick was marching in overwhelming force to attack the lines, he received a despatch on the other telling him that d'Asfeld had crossed the Rhine, and was moving towards the Neckar valley.

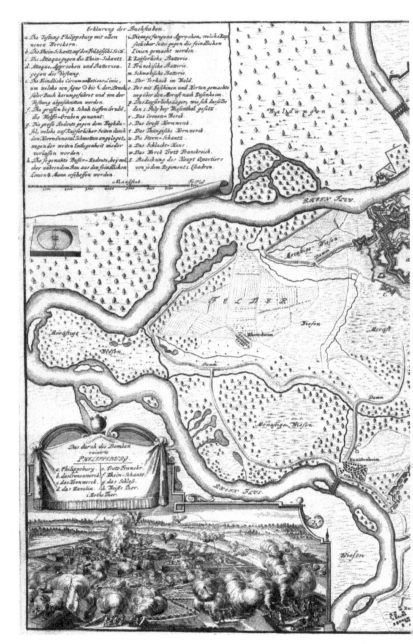

SIEGE OF

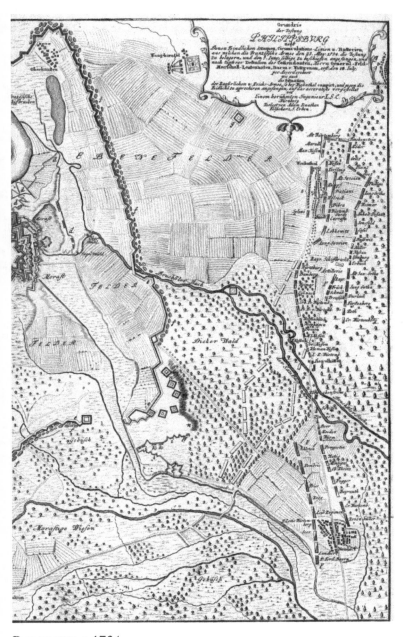

PHILIPPSBURG 1734

There was no time for hesitation little even for consideration. To stay where he was, was to expose himself to a simultaneous attack on front and rear. Instantly he resolved to evacuate the lines. Despatching, then, a message to the troops he had preceded to halt, he marched with those who had occupied the lines on Bruchsal. There he collected his entire force the next morning. It did not exceed twenty thousand men in number.

But Bruchsal was no safe halting-place. The same day information reached Eugene that Berwick, not halting in the evacuated lines, was marching against him with a force three times as strong as his own, whilst d'Asfeld was threatening his communications. He fell back, then, still further on Heilbronn (9th May). From this place he wrote to the Emperor, the same date, stating that it depended entirely on the movements of the enemy whether he should be compelled to retire still further, that he was in the position of one man fighting five, but that the Emperor might be assured that all that it was possible to do should be done.

The enemy did not immediately press him, and, whilst still at Heilbronn, Eugene had the satisfaction of hearing that the Hessian contingent had turned at Mainz. He sent pressing orders to Prince George, who commanded it, to hurry on to join him, and wrote at the same time urgent letters to the generals leading the Prussian, Hanoverian, Danish, and Upper Rhenish troops to march forward with all speed.

Berwick was in many respects a great commander. Distinguished amongst the generals of his epoch by an extreme prudence, he was yet capable of extreme daring. But, on this occasion, fortunately for Eugene, the prudence carried the day against the daring. It is difficult to assign any other reason for the month's leisure which Berwick gave to his adversary after he had, on the 4th May, forced him to evacuate the lines of Ettlingen, and on the 5th to retreat from Bruchsal.

The memoirs of the marshal, written by himself, throw no light upon this subject. Berwick followed on the heels of Eugene as far as Bruchsal, and, halting there, was joined on the 11th by d'Asfeld. He was still halting there, his troops devastating the country, on the 13th, when he despatched d'Asfeld to invest Philipsburg, but the French troops appeared before that fortress only on the 23rd May, and opened trenches only on the 3rd June. Of the nearly four weeks' grace thus given to Eugene, who had at one time but twenty thousand men to oppose the French marshal's one hundred thousand, there can be no satisfactory explanation.

Eugene was very sensible of his adversary's forbearance. He wrote to the Emperor from Heilbronn, the 20th May:

> I confess, that, despite all my preparations, I do not know how I should have warded off the enemy's attack if he had done what he ought to have done. As little do I understand why, during the last twelve days, he has remained inactive, contenting himself with ravaging the country. He has given me time to refresh my tired troops, to send away my heavy baggage, to draw troops to myself, so that in a few days I shall have thirty thousand available fighting men.

The relief to Eugene was still greater when he learned, the 22nd May, that Berwick, instead of following him, was about to besiege Philipsburg, for Philipsburg was a strong fortress, was well garrisoned, and the *commandant*, the Freiherr von Wutgenau, had a good reputation.

The French Army drew their lines of circumvallation before Philipsburg the 23rd May. Within the next few days the investment was complete from Waghäusel and Oberhausen to the banks of the Rhine. Belleisle directed the attack from the left bank of that river, where was a bridge fortified by a strong bridge-head, whilst Berwick, at Weisloch, covered the siege. On the 2nd June Belleisle delivered two attacks on the bridge-head in both he was repulsed, but Wutgenau, who had lost four hundred men, withdrew the defenders within the fortress.

From that moment the duel between the besiegers and the besieged assumed a very resolute character. Berwick, though he commanded the covering army, really directed the siege. It was his wont, early every morning, to repair to the trenches to examine the work done during the night, and to discuss with the chief engineer the plans for the night that was to follow. On the 12th June he had entered the trenches as usual, and had stopped for a moment on the banquette below the crest of the sap, which was commanded alike by the French and German batteries, and where a sentinel had been placed to prevent the men from stopping, and especially from mounting on the *banquette*. Whilst he was taking his observations from this point the guns from the opposing batteries continued to fire, and a ball from one of those, it was never known from which side, carried off the marshal's head. "I was always right in saying that Berwick was more fortunate than I," exclaimed Villars when the news reached them Berwick was succeeded in the chief command by d'Asfeld.

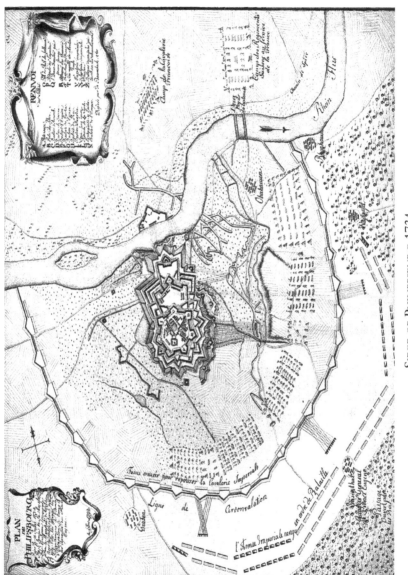

SIEGE OF PHILIPPSBURG 1734

Eugene, meanwhile, had remained quiet at Heilbronn, drawing to himself reinforcements. He was joined there on the 5th June by the Hanoverians, sixteen thousand strong. The Prussians arrived the day following. He still, however, had to wait for money. At last this arrived, and, on the 19th, Eugene, crossing the Neckar by two bridges, reached Adelshofen the 21st. There he received a few lines from Wutgenau expressing his need of immediate aid. Eugene pushed on, then, and reached Bruchsal the 26th, only three hours distant from the French lines of circumvallation. Halting his troops here, he rode forward to reconnoitre the enemy's position.

The result of his examination, and of a further intimation from Wutgenau, that the French might at any moment attempt to storm the place, caused Eugene to move, the 1st July, to Wiesenthal, about twenty minutes' march from the enemy's position. He drew up his army in array on the Rhine plain opposite that position, his left resting on Neudorf, his right on Waghäusel.

Should he fight? Would he, in a similar position, have fought when he was in the prime of dazzling youth? Age and responsibility affect the hardiness of even the most resolute of men. The Napoleon of 1796 would have employed his last reserves at the Battle of the Moskowa to render the victory complete and decisive. The Napoleon of 1812 would not, and lost his throne in consequence. The Frederic II of 1756-63 would have attacked the Emperor Joseph in his position in the Bohemian mountains in 1768, but the Frederic II of 1768, despite the murmurs of his generals, would not. On this occasion, too, the Eugene of Turin, of Blenheim, of Malplaquet, would have attacked, but the Eugene of 1734, aimed at the allotted period of man's life, would not. Was it that, having grown old, he feared to compromise by defeat so many years of glory—a defeat which might have been fatal to his country? That was the reason which weighed with Frederic, possibly, to an extent unknown to himself, with Eugene also.

But it has to be admitted that he found the enemy's position much stronger than he had anticipated. Two of his generals, Seckendorff and Schmettau, were, indeed, anxious that he should risk an attack. But Eugene had to recollect that even then he was not so numerous as the enemy, and that he commanded an army, brought together with the greatest difficulty, which constituted the last hope of the Empire. His troops, too, were for the most part new to war, and the attitude of Bavaria, whose Elector's wife was disinherited by the Pragmatic Sanction, was, at the best, doubtful. (She was a daughter of Joseph I, elder brother of Charles VI.) Should he be defeated, Bavaria would certainly either join with France or strike a blow on her own account. Eugene confined himself therefore to an attempt, by flooding the enemy's trenches, to render their position untenable, but, before his labours in this respect could be completed, Philipsburg fell (18th July, 1734).

Eleven days before that event there arrived in the Imperial camp a personage who was destined to become one of the greatest of generals, in one sense, indeed, to revolutionise the art of war as it was then understood. This was no other than Prince Frederic of Prussia, afterwards King Frederic II, the first despoiler of the House of Austria. Frederic brought with him a letter from his father to Eugene, commending him to his care, and stating that the prince was burning with anxiety to serve under the greatest captain of the age.

The king himself followed a few days later. He had been suffering from gout, and on his return, after a few days' visit, was again so severely attacked that he was supposed to be dying. Eugene, meanwhile, had done his utmost to win the young prince, who remained with him, for the Imperial House, but whatever effect his exhortations may have had at the time, they would appear to have been evanescent. Frederic William continued to live for nearly six years, and Frederic, who may have been impressionable in 1731, when he was only twenty-two, had become cynical and hard in 1740, when he was in his twenty-ninth year.

After the fall of Philipsburg, Eugene remained halted in his camp to watch the further movements of the enemy, but when, at the end of six days, they made no sign, he fell back on his earlier camp at Bruchsal, to be ready to take advantage of any false movement on their part. A few days later, d'Asfeld, leaving twenty-five battalions and twenty squadrons in the lines of Philipsburg under the Duke of Noailles, recrossed the Rhine with the rest of his army and marched towards Oppenheim, with the intention, apparently, of threatening Mainz. The moment Eugene discovered this intention he set out in the direction of that fortress, and reached the market town of Trebur on the 8th of August. Thence, his left resting on the Rhine and his right extended close to the banks of the Main, he despatched a provision of two thousand horses to the *commandant* of Mainz, who was in need of them.

His skilful movement so baffled d'Asfeld that he fell back in the direction of Worms. Eugene made a corresponding movement with the full intention of attacking him should opportunity offer. On the

19th he reached Heidelberg, and there made a halt, uncertain still whether the French marshal had designs on Alt Breisach or on the Neckar valley.

The campaign here ended, both sides remaining inactive, d'Asfeld not caring to expose himself, and Eugene waiting for an opportunity. In October the hostile armies went into winter quarters, and Eugene returned to Vienna.

Affairs had gone badly for the Imperial arms in Italy in 1734. After a series of mishaps Königsegg had been beaten at Gnastalla, and Sicily and Naples had been won by the enemy. Under these circumstances Eugene earnestly counselled peace, but, as in 1712, so now in 1735, the *Kaiser* was obstinate, and determined to continue the war.

In May, 1735, then, Eugene joined his army at Bruchsal. He found it in a state of indiscipline, caused mainly by the dissensions between the two generals next to him in command, Seckendorff and the Prince of Würtemberg. The Prussian and Danish generals would obey no orders, Prince George of Hesse had marched off his contingent in spite of an order to the contrary, desertions were frequent, unchecked, and unpunished.

Eugene had received from the Emperor the most stringent orders to attack. But though the numbers of the two armies were more nearly even than in the preceding year, the French Army was still the stronger. In view of this fact, and of the state of his own army, Eugene resolved to await at Bruchsal a decisive movement of the enemy, whilst, by a corps under Seckendorff he covered the Rhine from Mannheim to a point opposite Coblentz. He was anticipating the arrival of a corps of Russian troops, for Russia had, it will be recollected, sided with Austria in the original dispute.

The Russian corps arrived, only, indeed, almost immediately afterwards to retreat, for just at that time France made proposals for peace. (With this Russian Army marched Loudon, then a youth in the Russian service). Eugene earnestly counselled their acceptance. He pointed out that for the Empire the war was without an object, and that, if continued without allies, it could end only in disaster.

His advice was followed. On the 3rd of October preliminaries were signed at Vienna. By this treaty the Duchies of Bar and Lorraine were ceded to Stanislaus Leszczynski, the whilom pretended to the crown of Poland, to be ceded on his death to France. The cession actually took place thirty-one years later.

Eugene then returned to Vienna to resume his life of repose. But the sands of life had almost run. One evening in the spring of the following year (20th April, 1736) he was at the house of his most intimate friend, the Countess Batthyányi. He played piquet with her till nine o'clock, when, feeling gravely indisposed, he was compelled to cease to play. One of the guests, Count Tarouca, accompanied him to his house and consigned him to his chamberlain.

Urged by the latter to take the prescription recommended for such an attack by his medical adviser, Eugene replied that there was time enough in the morning, and went to bed. For him that morning never broke. His servants found him dead, with all the appearance of having passed away quietly and without pain. He had lived seventy-two years six months and three days.

What is his place among great commanders? A French writer, one not prone to judge him too favourably, (Pierre-Antoine-Jules Latona, in *Encyclopédie des Gens du monde*) has declared that Eugene, shaking off the burden of existing rules, confided in the inspirations of his genius, that his courage and capacity did the rest. He continues:

> He belongs, assuredly to the small number of generals who, in the seventeenth century, brought the art of war to its greatest perfection. Napoleon, whose opinion in this respect is not open to suspicion, places him in the same rank as Turenne and as Frederic, and regards as *chefs d'oeuvre* all the plans of his campaigns.

This I believe to be the truth. There were, indeed, in that age two men, rivals and opponents, who were the true precursors of Napoleon. Those men were Eugene and Villars. The wonderful campaign of Turin, related in the eighth chapter, in which Eugene, with a force smaller than either, made head against two hostile armies, and finally defeated both, was the real forerunner of the campaign of 1796. Villars, again, in his conception to decide the war by marching from Ratisbon on Vienna, a conception to which I have alluded in the sixth chapter, which he assuredly could have carried out, but which, imbibed at second-hand by Tallard and Marchin, naturally failed in their feebler grasp, gave utterance to a principle which Napoleon carried to its full completeness in 1805.

Eugene and Villars were, in fact, great strategists. Marlborough was a splendid tactician, admirable to carry through a well thought-out plan, quick at realising all the advantages of the plan when proposed. But it should never be forgotten that the inspiration for the campaign which was his greatest, the inspiration for the campaign of Blenheim, came from Eugene.

Eugene was a great tactician as well as a great strategist. He possessed the marvellous power, without which no man can be a general at all, the power of maintaining his coolness and self-possession, of keeping all his faculties about him, in times of tumult and danger. In battle he was worth thousands of ordinary men. His quick eye detected the true point of attack, the point of pressing danger, on the instant, and he possessed, with Napoleon and with Villars, the power of rousing the most complete enthusiasm of his men, of exciting them to stupendous exertions.

No criticism can be more false than that which has been made by island prejudice, to the effect that Eugene owes his fame to having been associated with Marlborough. A perusal of this book will dispel that error. There was no Marlborough by the side of Eugene when he made his famous campaign of Turin. Eugene, in fact, owed nothing to Marlborough. At Blenheim, at Oudenarde, at Malplaquet, the force at the disposal of Marlborough was to that of Eugene in the proportion of at least three to two, and yet, at those battles, Eugene contributed certainly a moiety to the success. But for his generous and timely despatch of cavalry, indeed, Blenheim might have been a defeat.

Yet, great as he was in conception, great in execution, there was one point in which Eugene and Marlborough alike fell short of the great Master of modern times. Comparing the battles of Wellington and Napoleon, the late William Napier wrote thus:

> In following up a victory the English general fell short of the French Emperor. The battle of Wellington was the stroke of a battering ram, down went the wall in ruins. The battle of Napoleon was the swell and dash of a mighty wave, before which the barrier yielded, and the roaring flood poured onwards, covering all.

The criticism applies equally to Eugene and Marlborough. Witness their long and useless halt after Blenheim, their failure to take full advantage of Malplaquet. Left to himself, Eugene seems less obnoxious to the reproach, for, certainly, he utilised his victory at Turin to recover Italy for the Emperor, and that he was thoroughly cognisant of the advantage of the principle is shown by the surprise caused to him by the failure of Berwick to take full advantage of his retreat at the head of twenty thousand men from the lines of Ettlingen, when Berwick had one hundred thousand.

Yet, he was a great general, a loyal true-hearted man, a pillar of the German Empire. Well might Charles VI exclaim, when he heard of his death:

The fortunes of the Empire have perished with Prince Eugene.

For a time, owing to the neglect by the obstinate monarch of the advice of the eminent soldier, the inheritance he bequeathed to his daughter did fall into imminent danger. That advice is valuable to all nations, not excepting our own. It has been given often, but it will bear repetition.

The only guarantee of peace worthy of the name is a powerful and well-equipped army and a full treasury.

Printed in August 2019
by Rotomail Italia S.p.A., Vignate (MI) - Italy